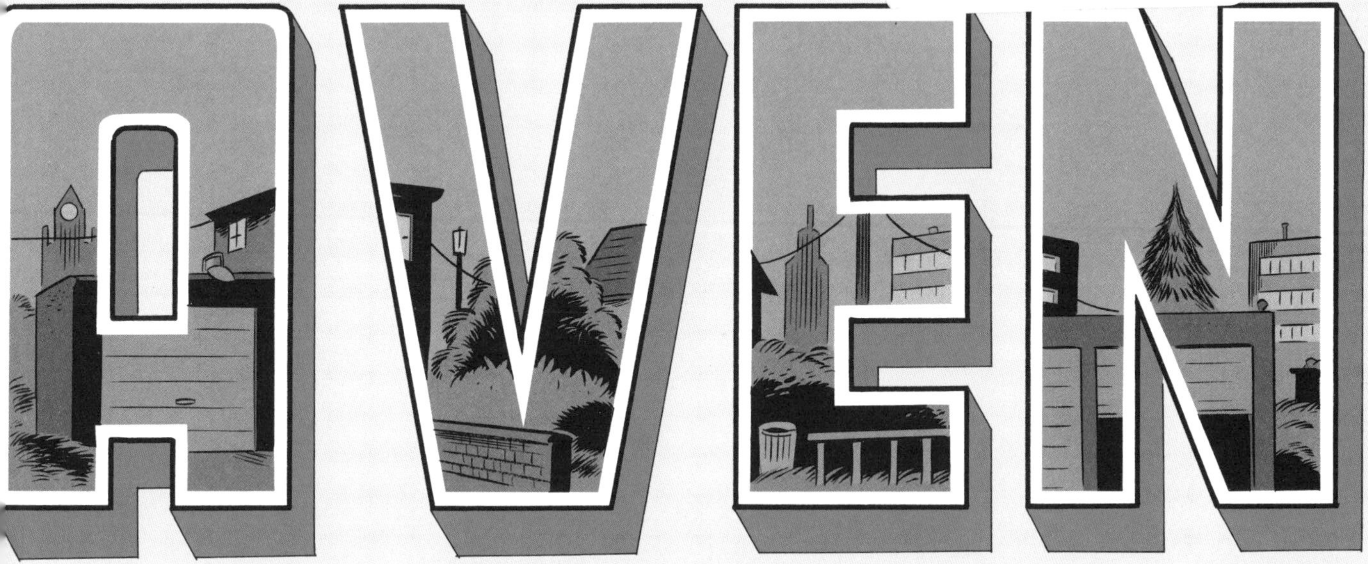
AVEN

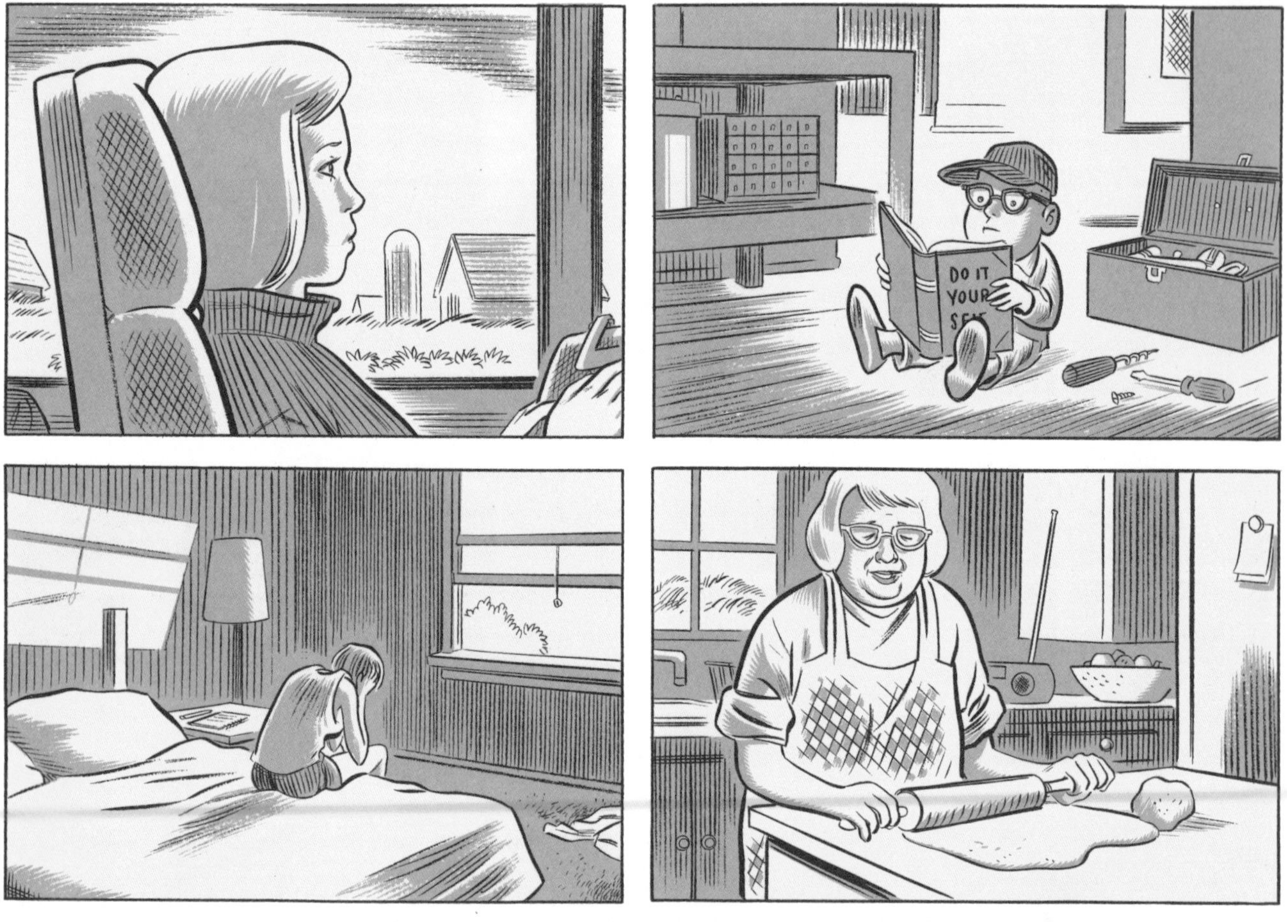
DO IT YOUR

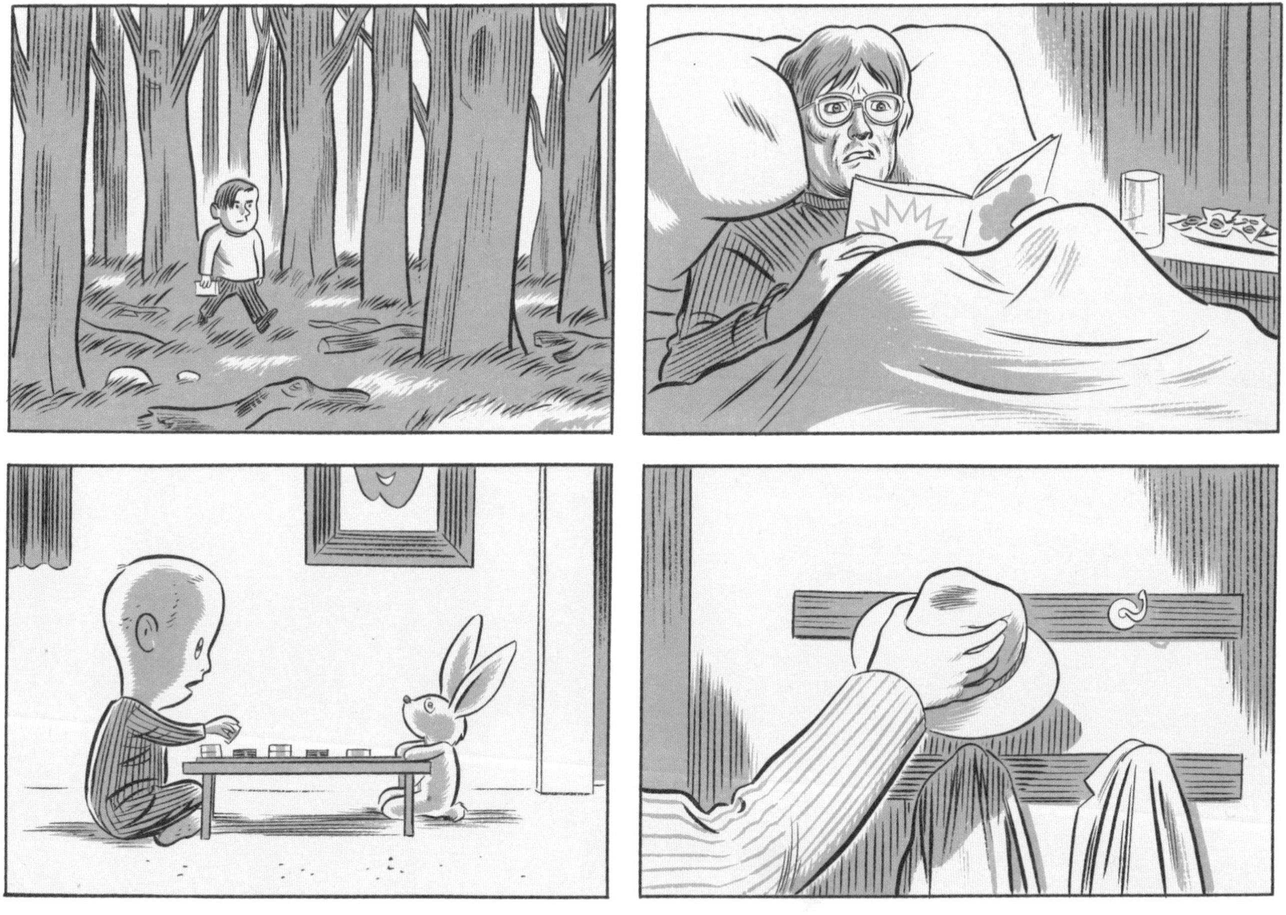

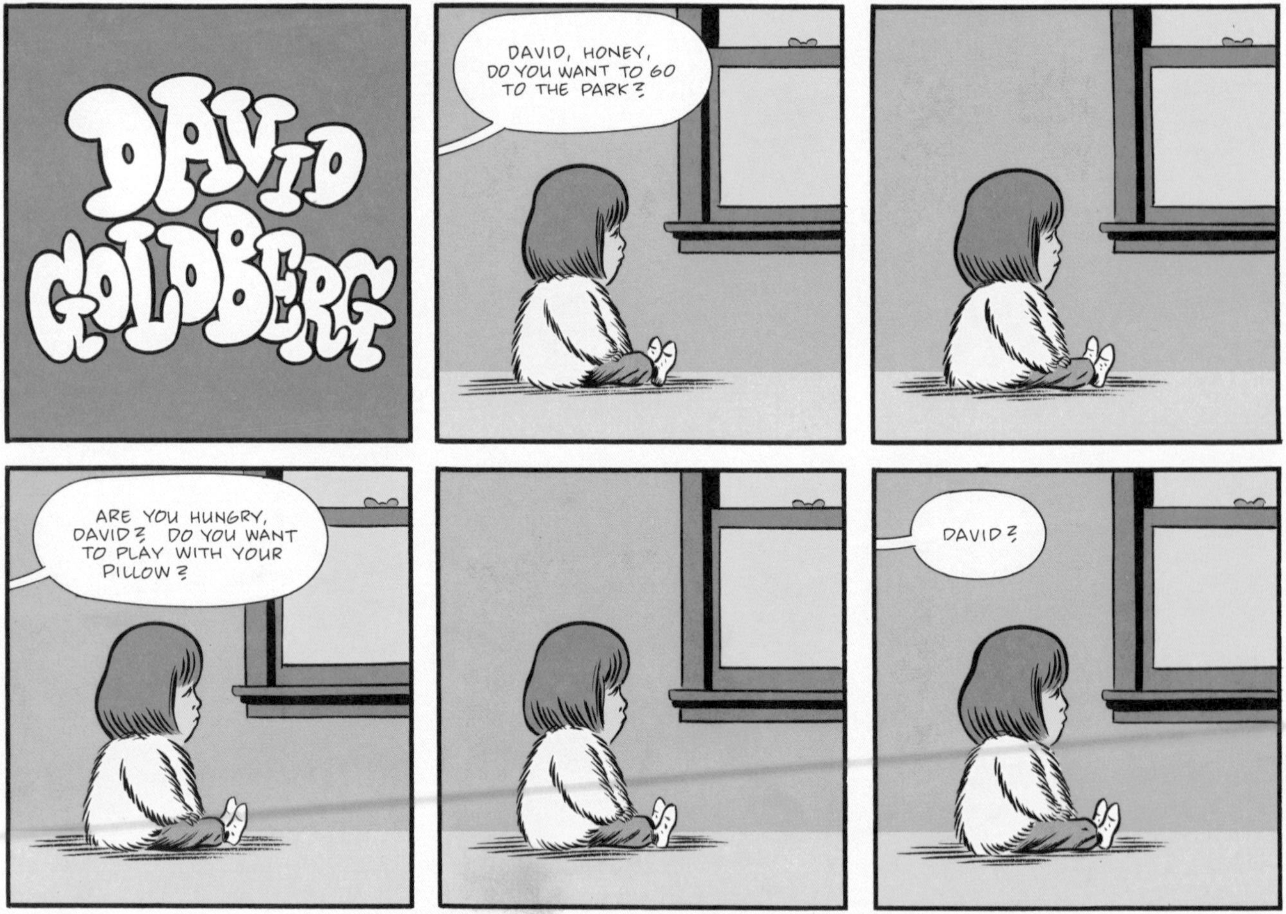
DAVID GOLDBERG
DAVID, HONEY, DO YOU WANT TO GO TO THE PARK?
ARE YOU HUNGRY, DAVID? DO YOU WANT TO PLAY WITH YOUR PILLOW?
DAVID?

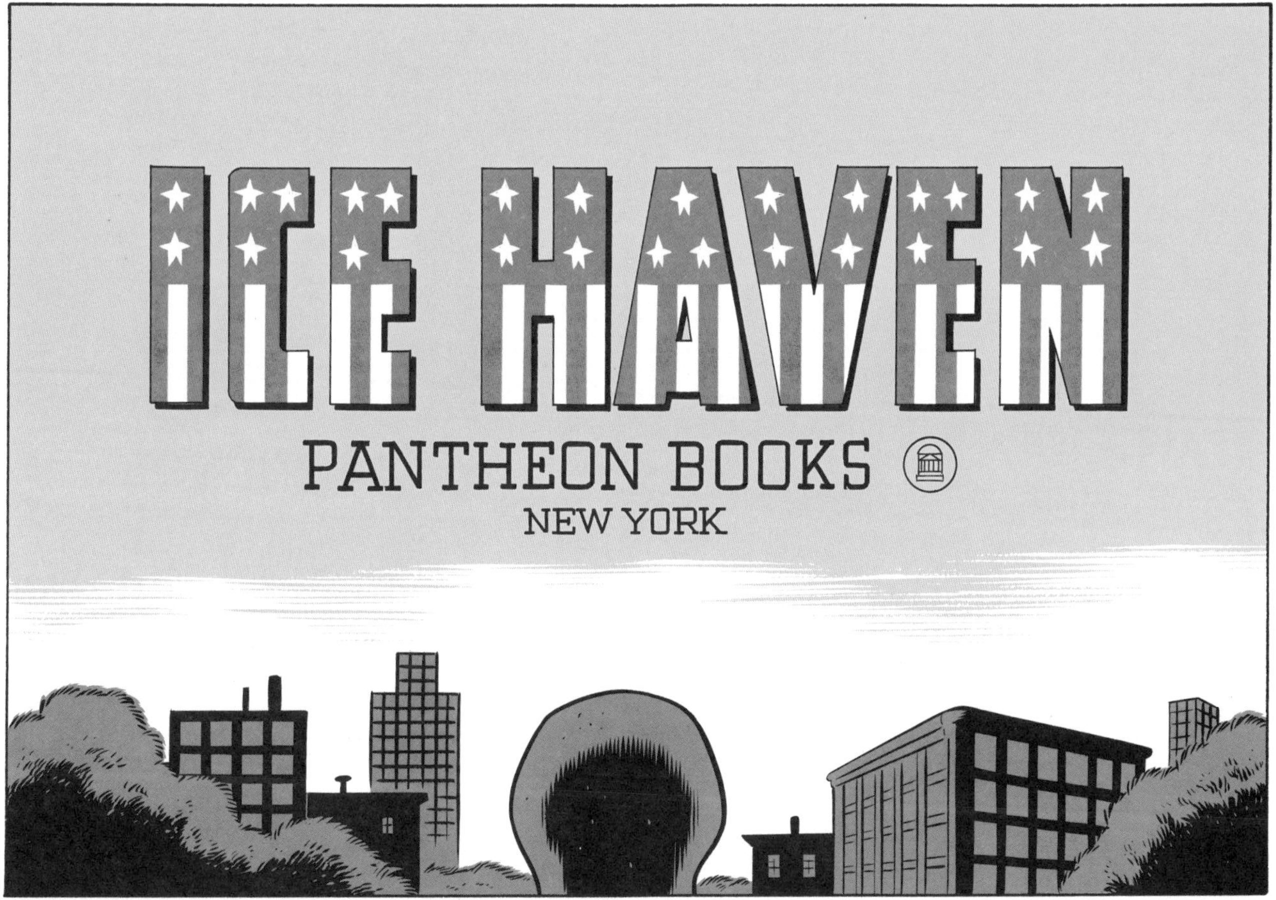
ICE HAVEN
PANTHEON BOOKS
NEW YORK

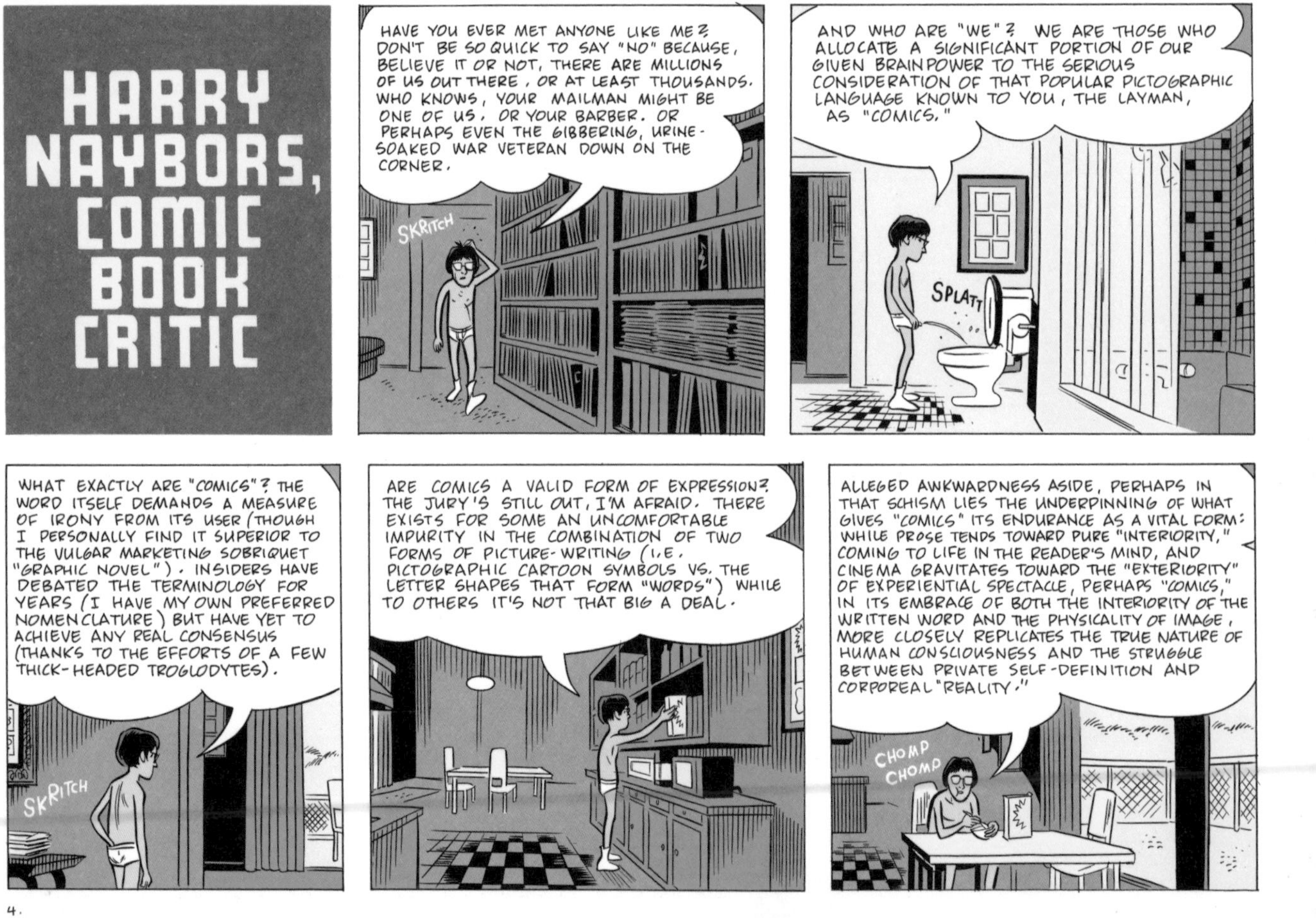
HARRY NAYBORS, COMIC BOOK CRITIC
HAVE YOU EVER MET ANYONE LIKE ME? DON'T BE SO QUICK TO SAY "NO" BECAUSE, BELIEVE IT OR NOT, THERE ARE MILLIONS OF US OUT THERE. OR AT LEAST THOUSANDS. WHO KNOWS, YOUR MAILMAN MIGHT BE ONE OF US. OR YOUR BARBER. OR PERHAPS EVEN THE GIBBERING, URINE-SOAKED WAR VETERAN DOWN ON THE CORNER.
SKRITCH
AND WHO ARE "WE"? WE ARE THOSE WHO ALLOCATE A SIGNIFICANT PORTION OF OUR GIVEN BRAINPOWER TO THE SERIOUS CONSIDERATION OF THAT POPULAR PICTOGRAPHIC LANGUAGE KNOWN TO YOU, THE LAYMAN, AS "COMICS."
SPLATT
WHAT EXACTLY ARE "COMICS"? THE WORD ITSELF DEMANDS A MEASURE OF IRONY FROM ITS USER (THOUGH I PERSONALLY FIND IT SUPERIOR TO THE VULGAR MARKETING SOBRIQUET "GRAPHIC NOVEL"). INSIDERS HAVE DEBATED THE TERMINOLOGY FOR YEARS (I HAVE MY OWN PREFERRED NOMENCLATURE) BUT HAVE YET TO ACHIEVE ANY REAL CONSENSUS (THANKS TO THE EFFORTS OF A FEW THICK-HEADED TROGLODYTES).
SKRITCH
ARE COMICS A VALID FORM OF EXPRESSION? THE JURY'S STILL OUT, I'M AFRAID. THERE EXISTS FOR SOME AN UNCOMFORTABLE IMPURITY IN THE COMBINATION OF TWO FORMS OF PICTURE-WRITING (I.E. PICTOGRAPHIC CARTOON SYMBOLS VS. THE LETTER SHAPES THAT FORM "WORDS") WHILE TO OTHERS IT'S NOT THAT BIG A DEAL.
ALLEGED AWKWARDNESS ASIDE, PERHAPS IN THAT SCHISM LIES THE UNDERPINNING OF WHAT GIVES "COMICS" ITS ENDURANCE AS A VITAL FORM: WHILE PROSE TENDS TOWARD PURE "INTERIORITY," COMING TO LIFE IN THE READER'S MIND, AND CINEMA GRAVITATES TOWARD THE "EXTERIORITY" OF EXPERIENTIAL SPECTACLE, PERHAPS "COMICS," IN ITS EMBRACE OF BOTH THE INTERIORITY OF THE WRITTEN WORD AND THE PHYSICALITY OF IMAGE, MORE CLOSELY REPLICATES THE TRUE NATURE OF HUMAN CONSCIOUSNESS AND THE STRUGGLE BETWEEN PRIVATE SELF-DEFINITION AND CORPOREAL "REALITY."
CHOMP CHOMP

A NARRAGLYPHIC PICTO-ASSEMBLAGE BY

DANIEL CLOWES

COPYRIGHT © 2001, 2005, BY DANIEL G. CLOWES · BOOK DESIGN BY THE AUTHOR.
TECHNICAL SUPERVISION AND PRODUCTION ASSISTANCE BY JOHN KURAMOTO.
ALL RIGHTS RESERVED UNDER INTERNATIONAL AND PAN-AMERICAN COPYRIGHT CONVENTIONS.
PUBLISHED IN THE UNITED STATES BY PANTHEON BOOKS, A DIVISION OF RANDOM HOUSE, INC.,
NEW YORK, AND SIMULTANEOUSLY IN CANADA BY RANDOM HOUSE OF CANADA LIMITED,
TORONTO. PANTHEON BOOKS AND COLOPHON ARE REGISTERED TRADEMARKS OF RANDOM
HOUSE, INC. WWW. PANTHEONBOOKS. COM. PRINTED IN SINGAPORE · FOR ERIKA.
FIRST EDITION · 9 8 7 6 5 4 3 2 1. SOME OF THE MATERIAL IN THIS BOOK ORIGINALLY
APPEARED IN *EIGHTBALL* #22· *EIGHTBALL* IS PUBLISHED BY FANTAGRAPHICS BOOKS.

Library of Congress Cataloging-in-Publication Data :
Clowes, Daniel ·
Ice Haven/Daniel Clowes.
p. cm.
ISBN 0-375-42332-X
1. Graphic Novels. I. Title.
PN6727. C565I33 2005 2004058732

AROUND ICE HAVEN

WITH RANDOM WILDER

"IT'S NOT AS COLD HERE AS IT SOUNDS."

THAT'S WHAT MEN OF MY FATHER'S GENERATION USED TO SAY TO ENCOURAGE RELUCTANT VISITORS, BACK WHEN TALK OF EXPANSION WAS IN THE AIR···

BUT OUR LOVELY NAME, INTENDED TO CONJURE A WONDROUS WINTERLAND, BROUGHT TO MIND ONLY GLOOM AND FROSTBITE.

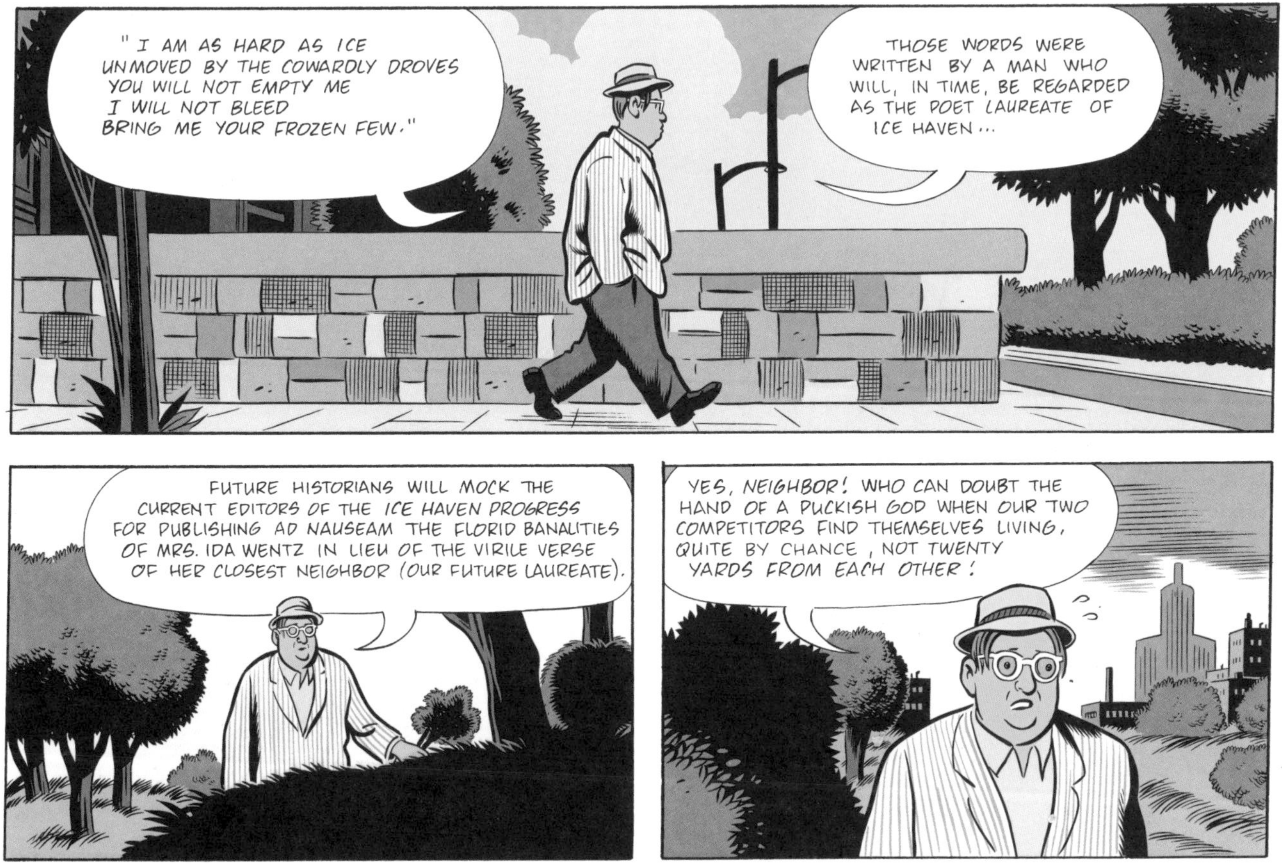
"I AM AS HARD AS ICE
UNMOVED BY THE COWARDLY DROVES
YOU WILL NOT EMPTY ME
I WILL NOT BLEED
BRING ME YOUR FROZEN FEW."
THOSE WORDS WERE WRITTEN BY A MAN WHO WILL, IN TIME, BE REGARDED AS THE POET LAUREATE OF ICE HAVEN...
FUTURE HISTORIANS WILL MOCK THE CURRENT EDITORS OF THE *ICE HAVEN PROGRESS* FOR PUBLISHING AD NAUSEAM THE FLORID BANALITIES OF MRS. IDA WENTZ IN LIEU OF THE VIRILE VERSE OF HER CLOSEST NEIGHBOR (OUR FUTURE LAUREATE).
YES, *NEIGHBOR*! WHO CAN DOUBT THE HAND OF A PUCKISH GOD WHEN OUR TWO COMPETITORS FIND THEMSELVES LIVING, QUITE BY CHANCE, NOT TWENTY YARDS FROM EACH OTHER!

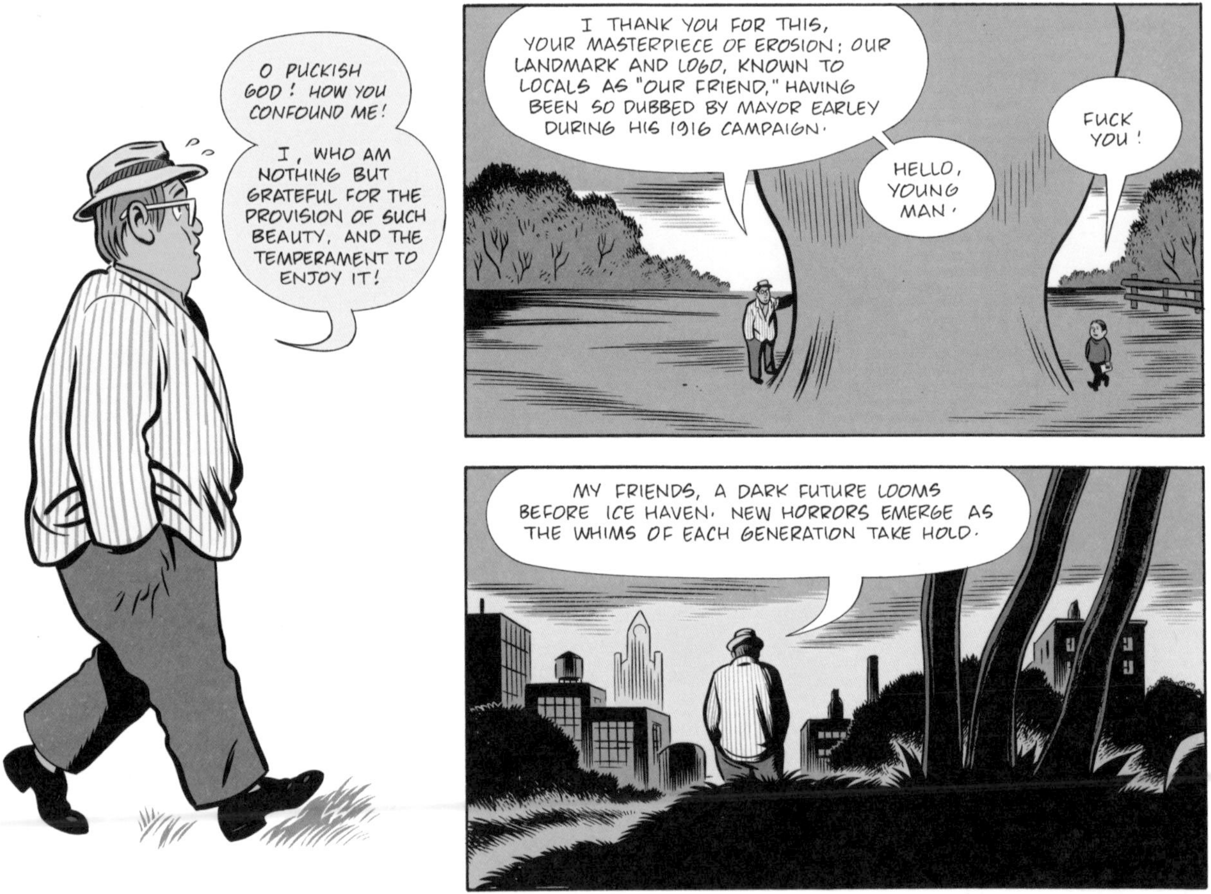
O PUCKISH GOD! HOW YOU CONFOUND ME!
I, WHO AM NOTHING BUT GRATEFUL FOR THE PROVISION OF SUCH BEAUTY, AND THE TEMPERAMENT TO ENJOY IT!
I THANK YOU FOR THIS, YOUR MASTERPIECE OF EROSION; OUR LANDMARK AND LOGO, KNOWN TO LOCALS AS "OUR FRIEND," HAVING BEEN SO DUBBED BY MAYOR EARLEY DURING HIS 1916 CAMPAIGN.
HELLO, YOUNG MAN.
FUCK YOU!
MY FRIENDS, A DARK FUTURE LOOMS BEFORE ICE HAVEN. NEW HORRORS EMERGE AS THE WHIMS OF EACH GENERATION TAKE HOLD.

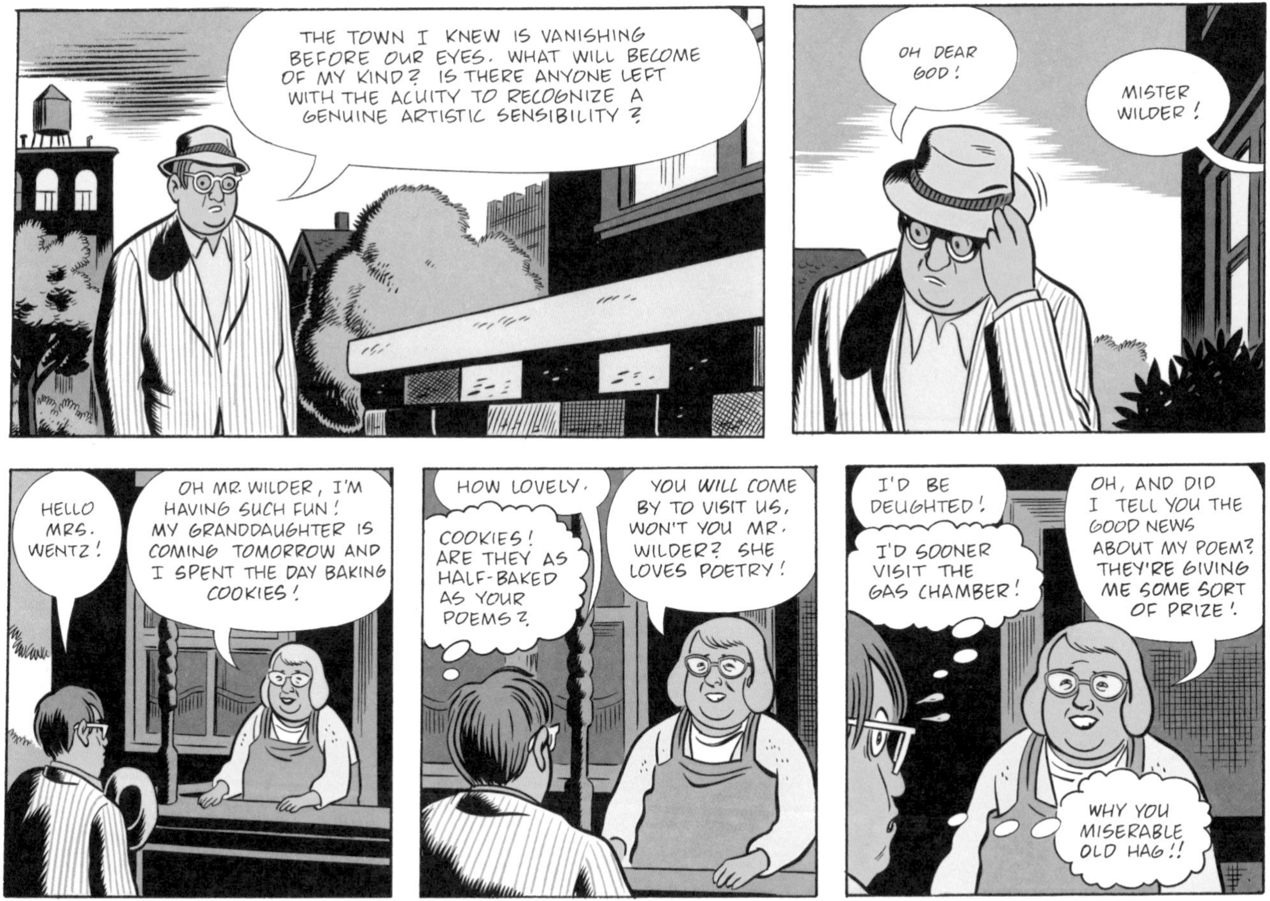
THE TOWN I KNEW IS VANISHING BEFORE OUR EYES. WHAT WILL BECOME OF MY KIND? IS THERE ANYONE LEFT WITH THE ACUITY TO RECOGNIZE A GENUINE ARTISTIC SENSIBILITY?
OH DEAR GOD!
MISTER WILDER!
HELLO MRS. WENTZ!
OH MR. WILDER, I'M HAVING SUCH FUN! MY GRANDDAUGHTER IS COMING TOMORROW AND I SPENT THE DAY BAKING COOKIES!
HOW LOVELY.
COOKIES! ARE THEY AS HALF-BAKED AS YOUR POEMS?
YOU WILL COME BY TO VISIT US, WON'T YOU MR. WILDER? SHE LOVES POETRY!
I'D BE DELIGHTED!
I'D SOONER VISIT THE GAS CHAMBER!
OH, AND DID I TELL YOU THE GOOD NEWS ABOUT MY POEM? THEY'RE GIVING ME SOME SORT OF PRIZE!
WHY YOU MISERABLE OLD HAG!!

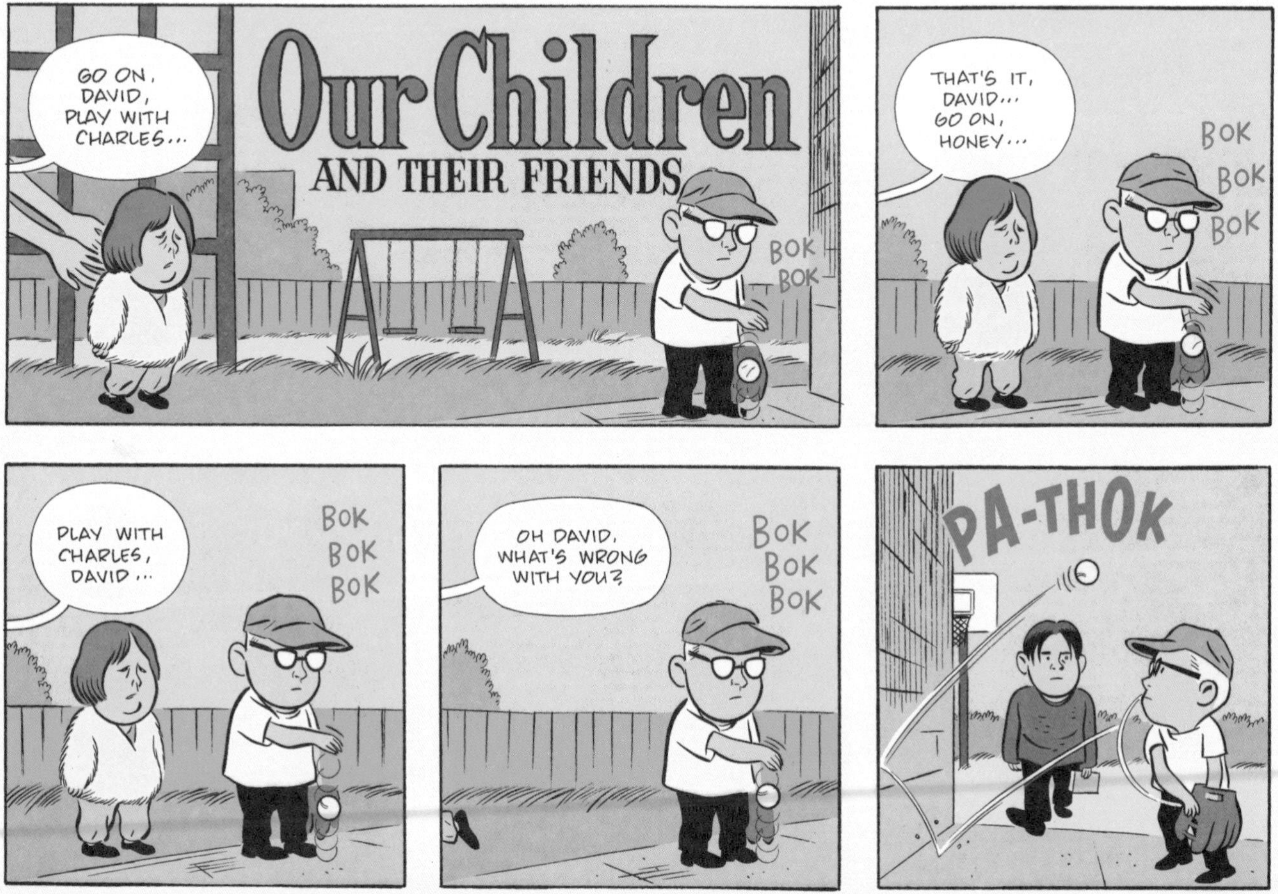
Our Children
AND THEIR FRIENDS
GO ON, DAVID, PLAY WITH CHARLES...
BOK BOK
THAT'S IT, DAVID... GO ON, HONEY...
BOK BOK BOK
PLAY WITH CHARLES, DAVID...
BOK BOK BOK
OH DAVID. WHAT'S WRONG WITH YOU?
BOK BOK BOK
PA-THOK

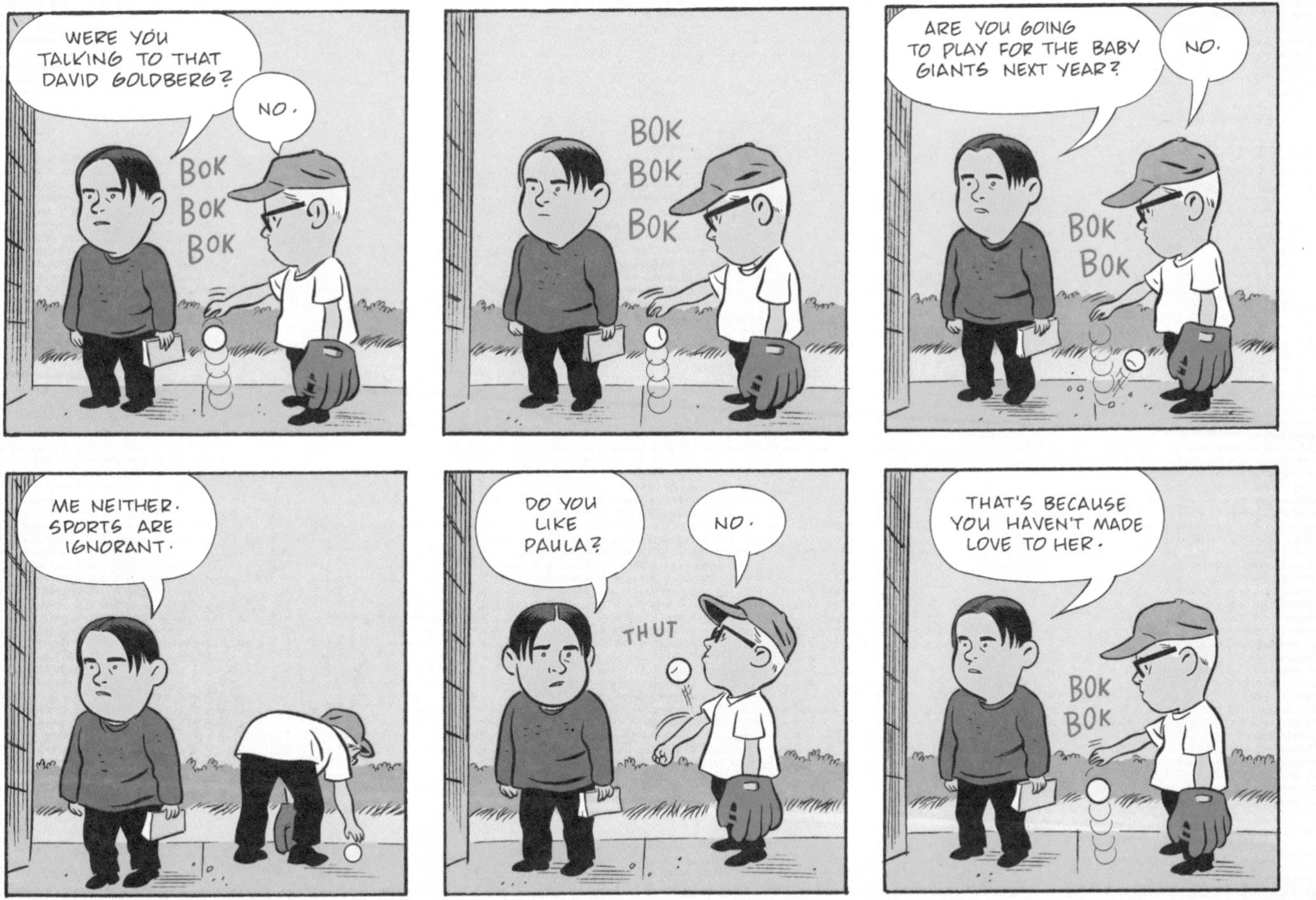
WERE YOU TALKING TO THAT DAVID GOLDBERG?
NO.
BOK BOK BOK
BOK BOK BOK
ARE YOU GOING TO PLAY FOR THE BABY GIANTS NEXT YEAR?
NO.
BOK BOK
ME NEITHER. SPORTS ARE IGNORANT.
DO YOU LIKE PAULA?
NO.
THUT
THAT'S BECAUSE YOU HAVEN'T MADE LOVE TO HER.
BOK BOK

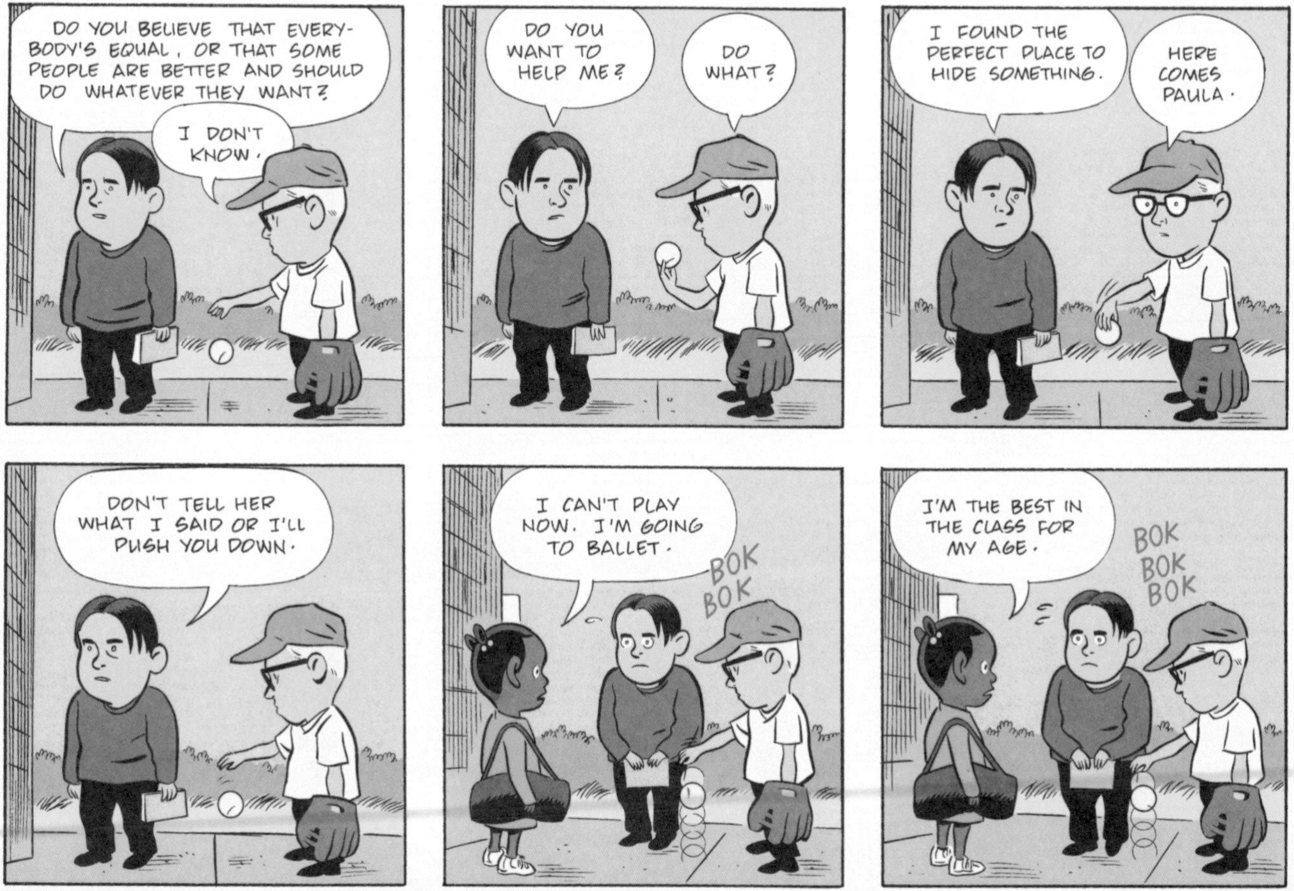
DO YOU BELIEVE THAT EVERYBODY'S EQUAL, OR THAT SOME PEOPLE ARE BETTER AND SHOULD DO WHATEVER THEY WANT?
I DON'T KNOW.
DO YOU WANT TO HELP ME?
DO WHAT?
I FOUND THE PERFECT PLACE TO HIDE SOMETHING.
HERE COMES PAULA.
DON'T TELL HER WHAT I SAID OR I'LL PUSH YOU DOWN.
I CAN'T PLAY NOW. I'M GOING TO BALLET.
BOK BOK
I'M THE BEST IN THE CLASS FOR MY AGE.
BOK BOK BOK

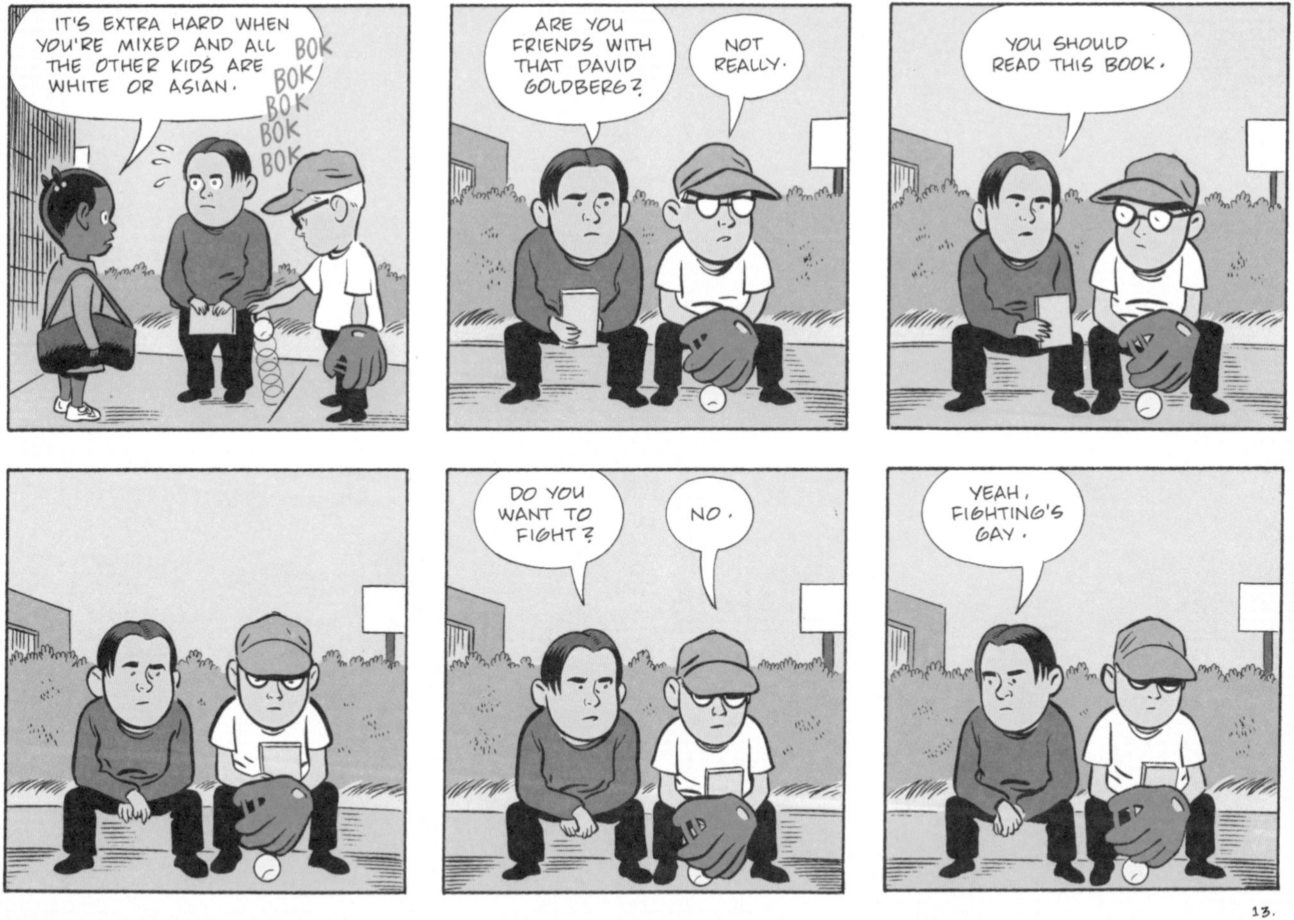
IT'S EXTRA HARD WHEN YOU'RE MIXED AND ALL THE OTHER KIDS ARE WHITE OR ASIAN.
BOK BOK BOK BOK BOK
ARE YOU FRIENDS WITH THAT DAVID GOLDBERG?
NOT REALLY.
YOU SHOULD READ THIS BOOK.
DO YOU WANT TO FIGHT?
NO.
YEAH, FIGHTING'S GAY.

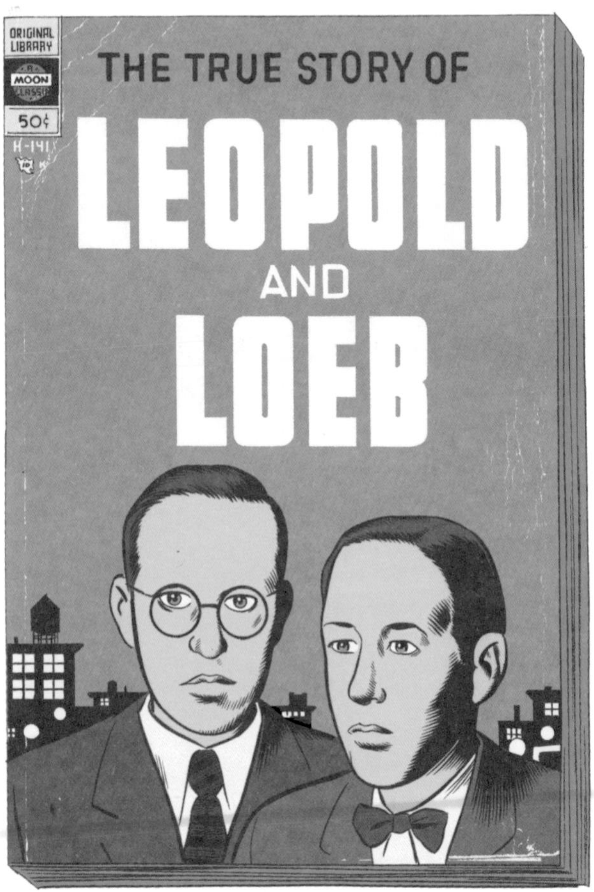
ORIGINAL LIBRARY
A MOON CLASSIC
50¢
H-141
THE TRUE STORY OF
LEOPOLD
AND
LOEB

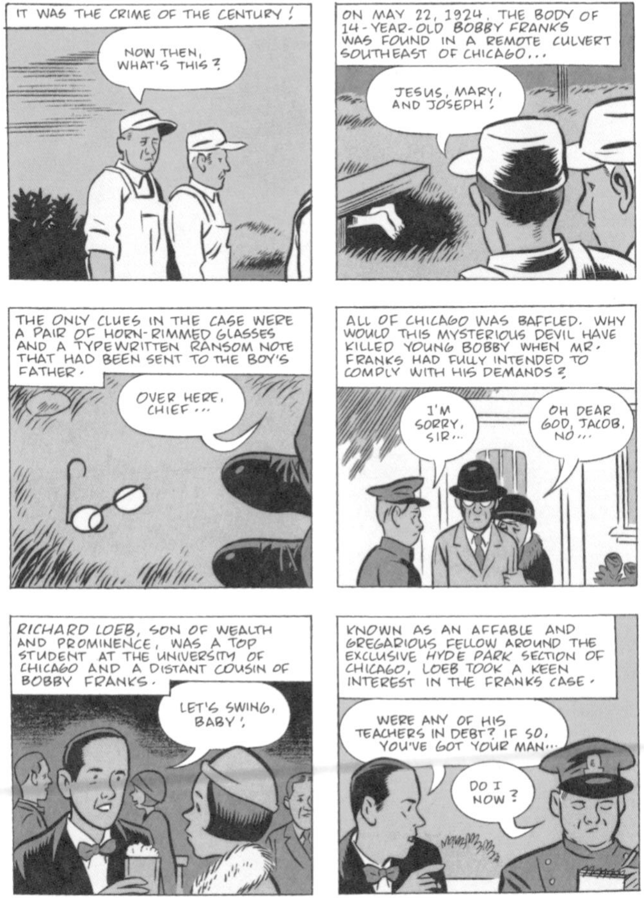
IT WAS THE CRIME OF THE CENTURY!
NOW THEN, WHAT'S THIS?
ON MAY 22, 1924, THE BODY OF 14-YEAR-OLD BOBBY FRANKS WAS FOUND IN A REMOTE CULVERT SOUTHEAST OF CHICAGO...
JESUS, MARY, AND JOSEPH!
THE ONLY CLUES IN THE CASE WERE A PAIR OF HORN-RIMMED GLASSES AND A TYPEWRITTEN RANSOM NOTE THAT HAD BEEN SENT TO THE BOY'S FATHER.
OVER HERE, CHIEF...
ALL OF CHICAGO WAS BAFFLED. WHY WOULD THIS MYSTERIOUS DEVIL HAVE KILLED YOUNG BOBBY WHEN MR. FRANKS HAD FULLY INTENDED TO COMPLY WITH HIS DEMANDS?
I'M SORRY, SIR...
OH DEAR GOD, JACOB, NO...
RICHARD LOEB, SON OF WEALTH AND PROMINENCE, WAS A TOP STUDENT AT THE UNIVERSITY OF CHICAGO AND A DISTANT COUSIN OF BOBBY FRANKS.
LET'S SWING, BABY!
KNOWN AS AN AFFABLE AND GREGARIOUS FELLOW AROUND THE EXCLUSIVE HYDE PARK SECTION OF CHICAGO, LOEB TOOK A KEEN INTEREST IN THE FRANKS CASE.
WERE ANY OF HIS TEACHERS IN DEBT? IF SO, YOU'VE GOT YOUR MAN...
DO I NOW?

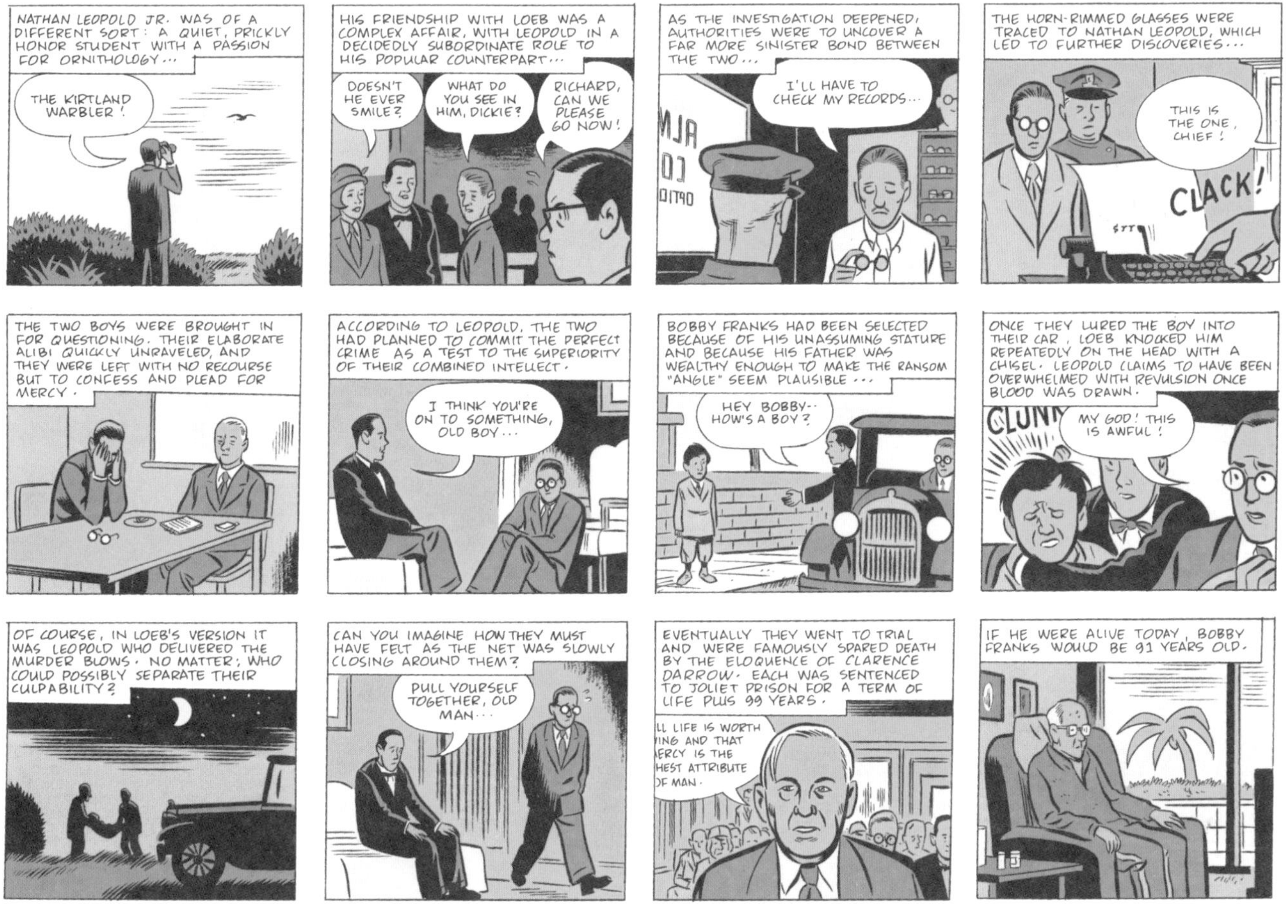
NATHAN LEOPOLD JR. WAS OF A DIFFERENT SORT: A QUIET, PRICKLY HONOR STUDENT WITH A PASSION FOR ORNITHOLOGY...
THE KIRTLAND WARBLER!
HIS FRIENDSHIP WITH LOEB WAS A COMPLEX AFFAIR, WITH LEOPOLD IN A DECIDEDLY SUBORDINATE ROLE TO HIS POPULAR COUNTERPART...
DOESN'T HE EVER SMILE?
WHAT DO YOU SEE IN HIM, DICKIE?
RICHARD, CAN WE PLEASE GO NOW!
AS THE INVESTIGATION DEEPENED, AUTHORITIES WERE TO UNCOVER A FAR MORE SINISTER BOND BETWEEN THE TWO...
I'LL HAVE TO CHECK MY RECORDS...
THE HORN-RIMMED GLASSES WERE TRACED TO NATHAN LEOPOLD, WHICH LED TO FURTHER DISCOVERIES...
THIS IS THE ONE, CHIEF!
CLACK!
THE TWO BOYS WERE BROUGHT IN FOR QUESTIONING. THEIR ELABORATE ALIBI QUICKLY UNRAVELED, AND THEY WERE LEFT WITH NO RECOURSE BUT TO CONFESS AND PLEAD FOR MERCY.
ACCORDING TO LEOPOLD, THE TWO HAD PLANNED TO COMMIT THE PERFECT CRIME AS A TEST TO THE SUPERIORITY OF THEIR COMBINED INTELLECT.
I THINK YOU'RE ON TO SOMETHING, OLD BOY...
BOBBY FRANKS HAD BEEN SELECTED BECAUSE OF HIS UNASSUMING STATURE AND BECAUSE HIS FATHER WAS WEALTHY ENOUGH TO MAKE THE RANSOM "ANGLE" SEEM PLAUSIBLE...
HEY BOBBY-- HOW'S A BOY?
ONCE THEY LURED THE BOY INTO THEIR CAR, LOEB KNOCKED HIM REPEATEDLY ON THE HEAD WITH A CHISEL. LEOPOLD CLAIMS TO HAVE BEEN OVERWHELMED WITH REVULSION ONCE BLOOD WAS DRAWN.
MY GOD! THIS IS AWFUL!
OF COURSE, IN LOEB'S VERSION IT WAS LEOPOLD WHO DELIVERED THE MURDER BLOWS. NO MATTER; WHO COULD POSSIBLY SEPARATE THEIR CULPABILITY?
CAN YOU IMAGINE HOW THEY MUST HAVE FELT AS THE NET WAS SLOWLY CLOSING AROUND THEM?
PULL YOURSELF TOGETHER, OLD MAN...
EVENTUALLY THEY WENT TO TRIAL AND WERE FAMOUSLY SPARED DEATH BY THE ELOQUENCE OF CLARENCE DARROW. EACH WAS SENTENCED TO JOLIET PRISON FOR A TERM OF LIFE PLUS 99 YEARS.
LL LIFE IS WORTH
ING AND THAT
ERCY IS THE
HEST ATTRIBUTE
OF MAN.
IF HE WERE ALIVE TODAY, BOBBY FRANKS WOULD BE 91 YEARS OLD.

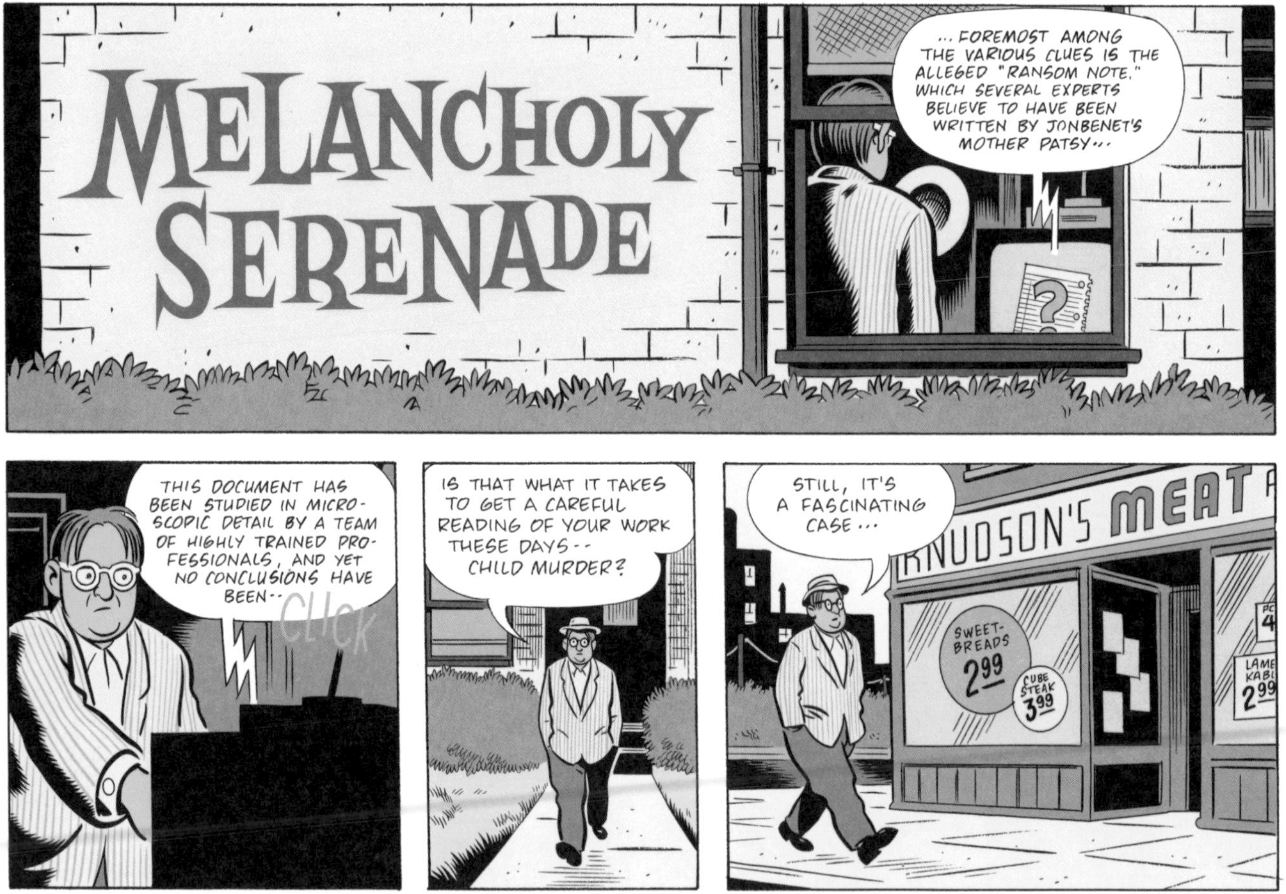
MELANCHOLY SERENADE
... FOREMOST AMONG THE VARIOUS CLUES IS THE ALLEGED "RANSOM NOTE," WHICH SEVERAL EXPERTS BELIEVE TO HAVE BEEN WRITTEN BY JONBENET'S MOTHER PATSY...
THIS DOCUMENT HAS BEEN STUDIED IN MICRO-SCOPIC DETAIL BY A TEAM OF HIGHLY TRAINED PRO-FESSIONALS, AND YET NO CONCLUSIONS HAVE BEEN--
CLICK
IS THAT WHAT IT TAKES TO GET A CAREFUL READING OF YOUR WORK THESE DAYS -- CHILD MURDER?
STILL, IT'S A FASCINATING CASE...
MEAT
SWEET-BREADS 2.99
CUBE STEAK 3.99

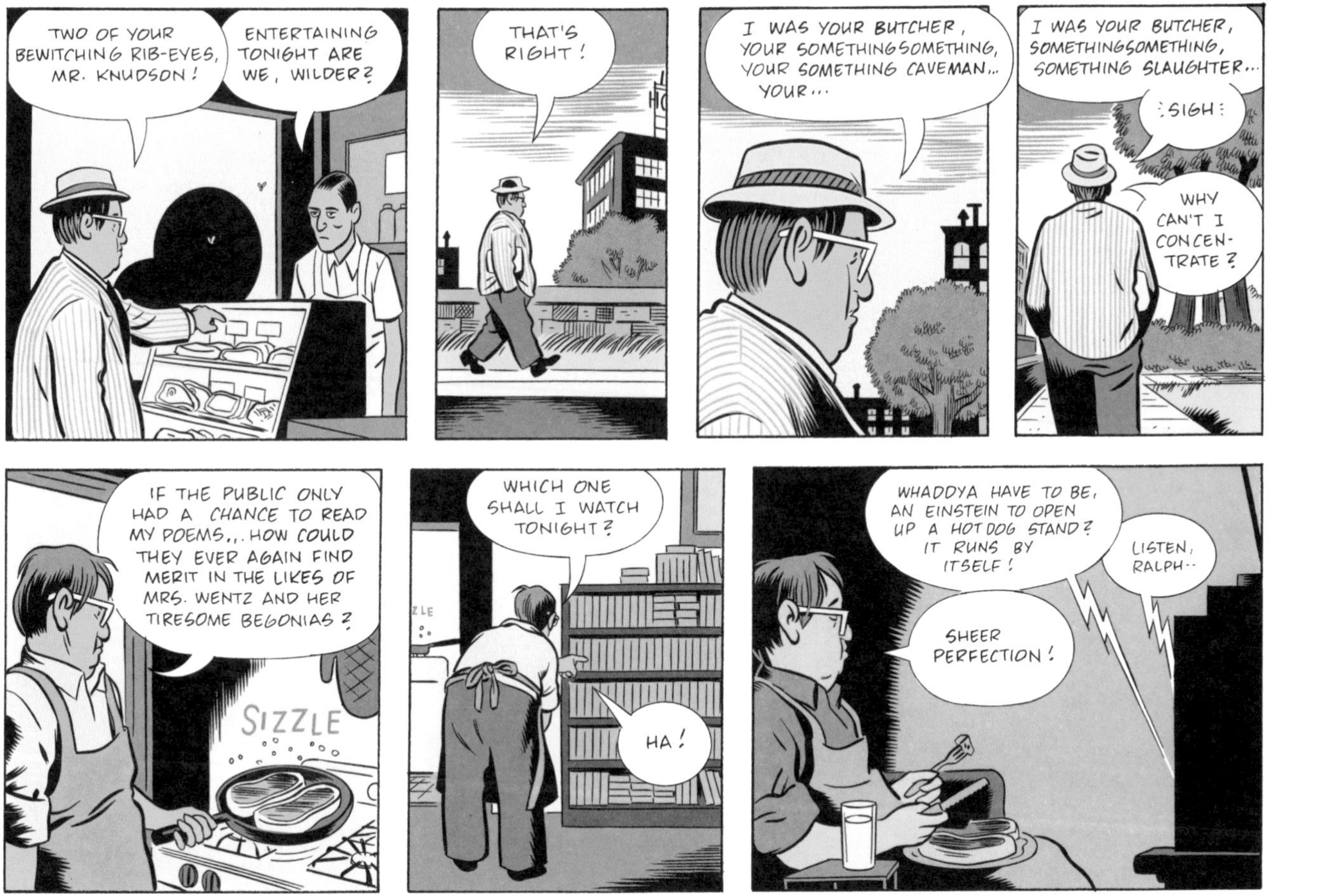
TWO OF YOUR BEWITCHING RIB-EYES, MR. KNUDSON!
ENTERTAINING TONIGHT ARE WE, WILDER?
THAT'S RIGHT!
I WAS YOUR BUTCHER, YOUR SOMETHINGSOMETHING, YOUR SOMETHING CAVEMAN... YOUR...
I WAS YOUR BUTCHER, SOMETHINGSOMETHING, SOMETHING SLAUGHTER...
SIGH
WHY CAN'T I CONCENTRATE?
IF THE PUBLIC ONLY HAD A CHANCE TO READ MY POEMS... HOW COULD THEY EVER AGAIN FIND MERIT IN THE LIKES OF MRS. WENTZ AND HER TIRESOME BEGONIAS?
SIZZLE
WHICH ONE SHALL I WATCH TONIGHT?
HA!
WHADDYA HAVE TO BE, AN EINSTEIN TO OPEN UP A HOT DOG STAND? IT RUNS BY ITSELF!
LISTEN, RALPH--
SHEER PERFECTION!

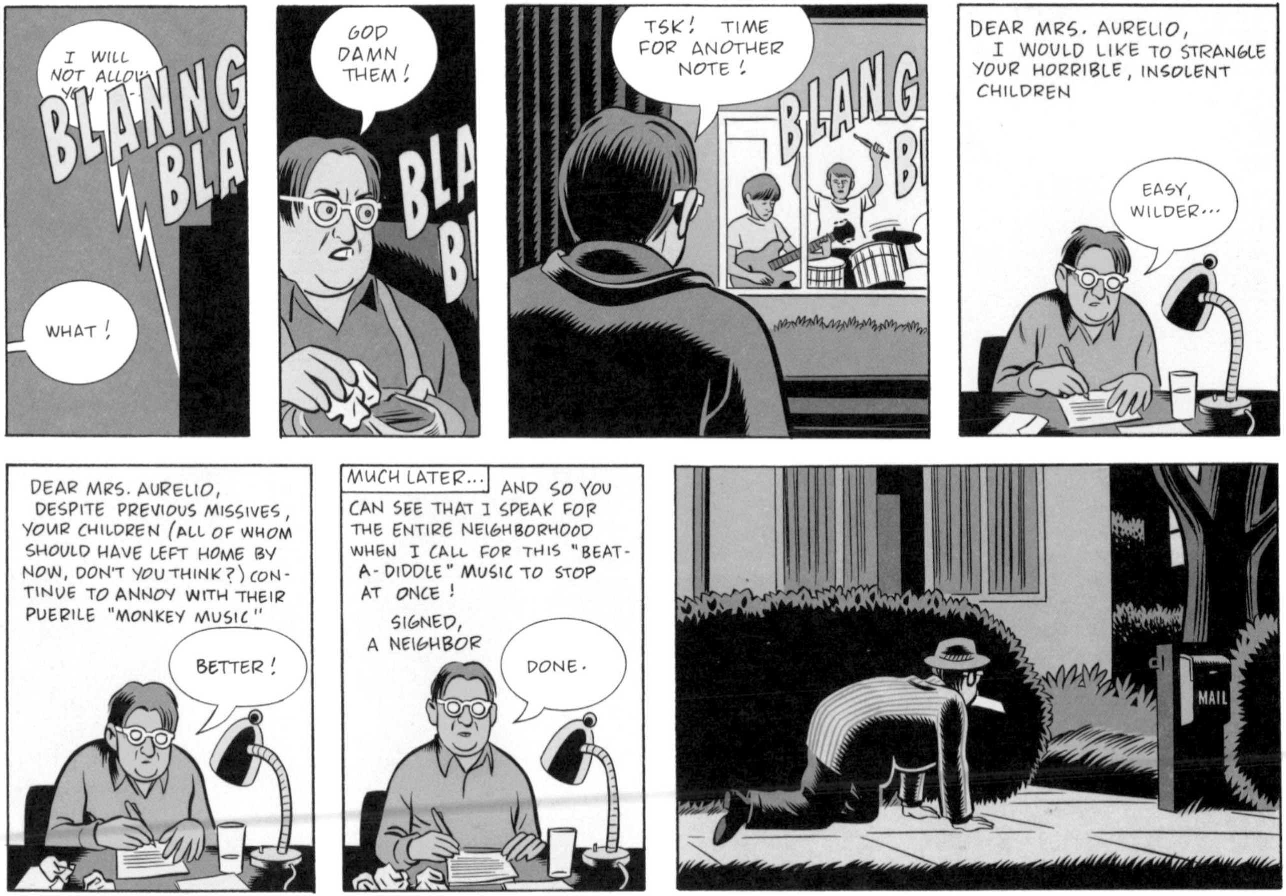
I WILL NOT ALLOW
BLANNG
WHAT!
GOD DAMN THEM!
TSK! TIME FOR ANOTHER NOTE!
BLANG
DEAR MRS. AURELIO,
I WOULD LIKE TO STRANGLE YOUR HORRIBLE, INSOLENT CHILDREN
EASY, WILDER...
DEAR MRS. AURELIO,
DESPITE PREVIOUS MISSIVES, YOUR CHILDREN (ALL OF WHOM SHOULD HAVE LEFT HOME BY NOW, DON'T YOU THINK?) CONTINUE TO ANNOY WITH THEIR PUERILE "MONKEY MUSIC"
BETTER!
MUCH LATER...
AND SO YOU CAN SEE THAT I SPEAK FOR THE ENTIRE NEIGHBORHOOD WHEN I CALL FOR THIS "BEAT-A-DIDDLE" MUSIC TO STOP AT ONCE!
SIGNED,
A NEIGHBOR
DONE.
MAIL

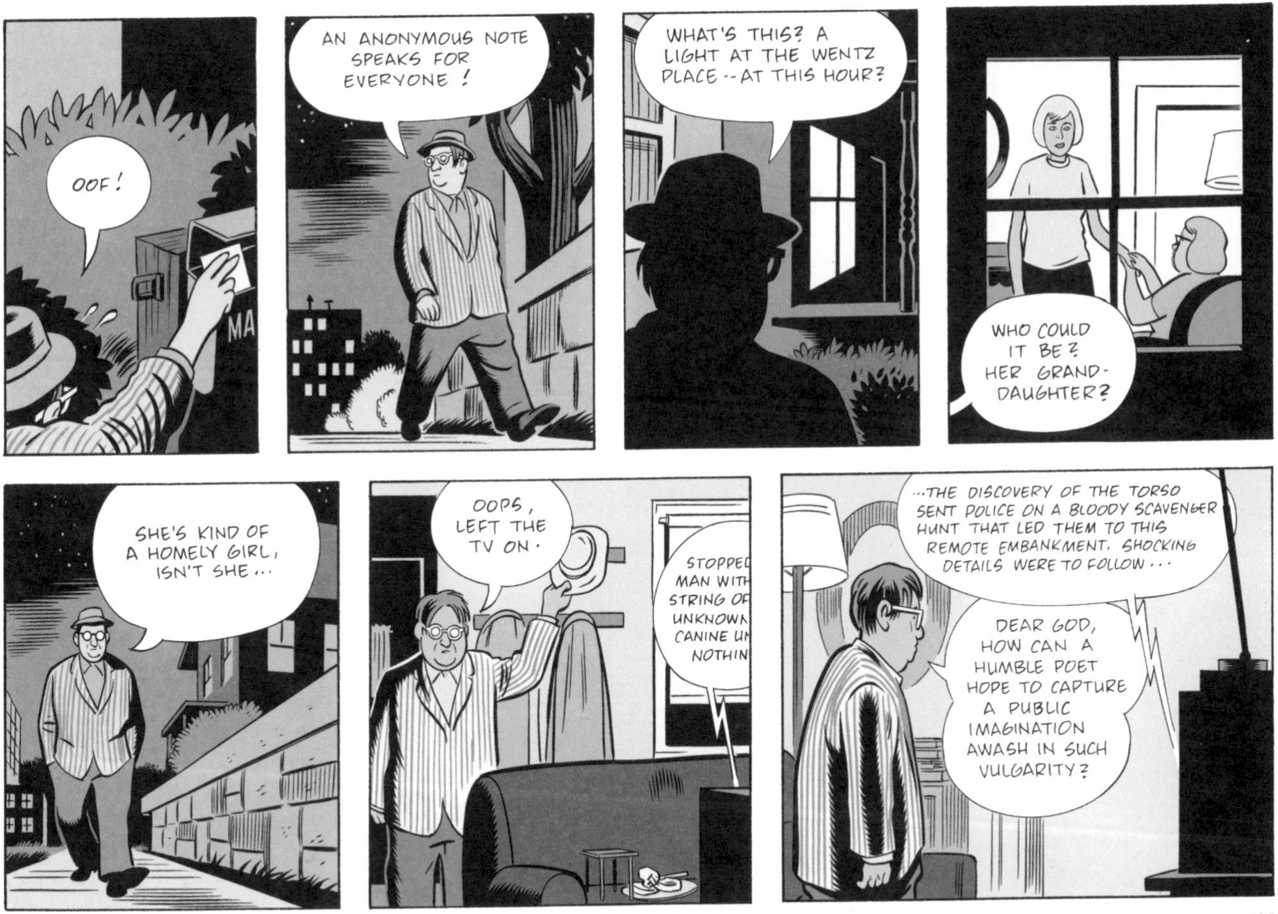
OOF!
AN ANONYMOUS NOTE SPEAKS FOR EVERYONE!
WHAT'S THIS? A LIGHT AT THE WENTZ PLACE -- AT THIS HOUR?
WHO COULD IT BE? HER GRAND-DAUGHTER?
SHE'S KIND OF A HOMELY GIRL, ISN'T SHE...
OOPS, LEFT THE TV ON.
STOPPED MAN WITH STRING OF UNKNOWN CANINE UN NOTHIN
...THE DISCOVERY OF THE TORSO SENT POLICE ON A BLOODY SCAVENGER HUNT THAT LED THEM TO THIS REMOTE EMBANKMENT. SHOCKING DETAILS WERE TO FOLLOW...
DEAR GOD, HOW CAN A HUMBLE POET HOPE TO CAPTURE A PUBLIC IMAGINATION AWASH IN SUCH VULGARITY?

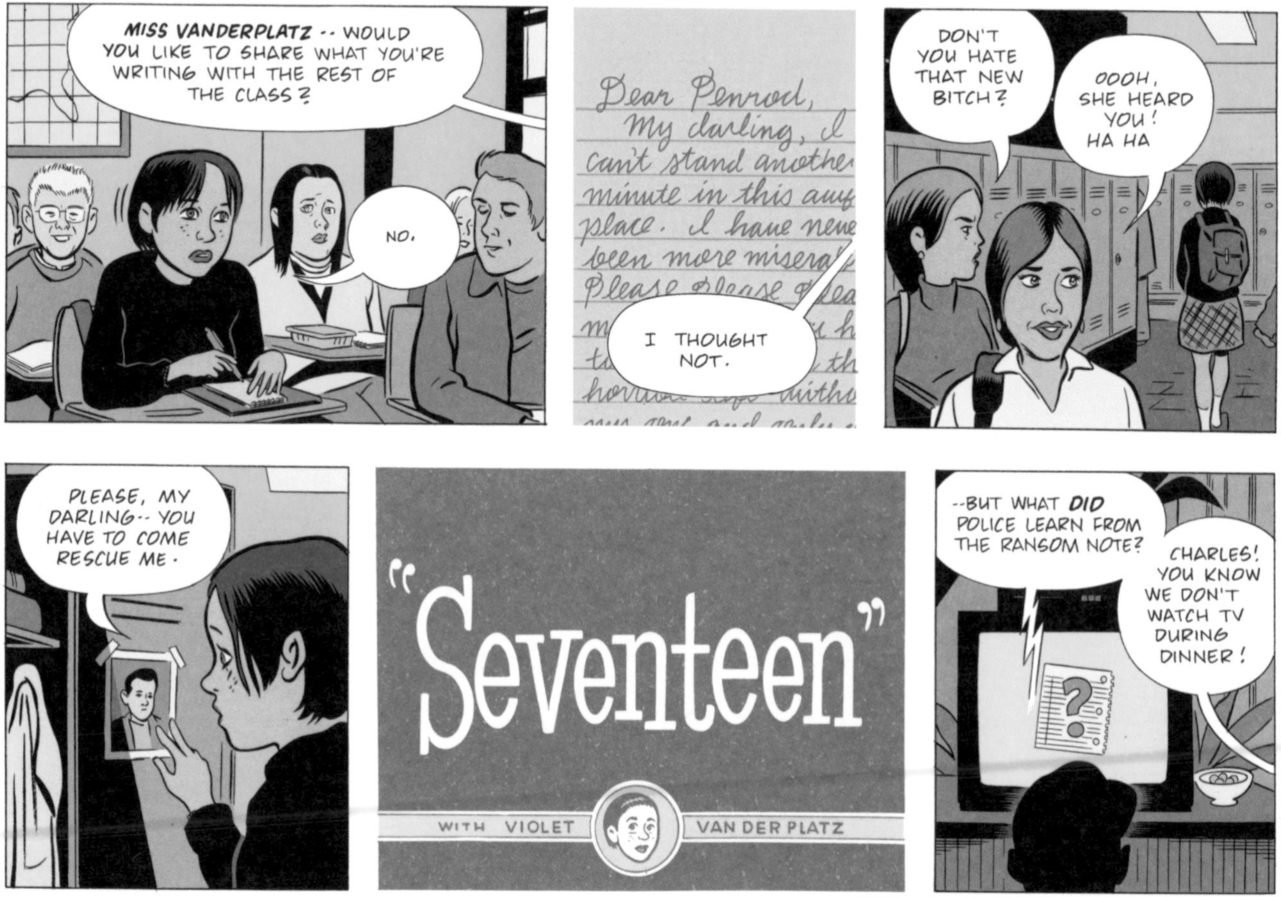
MISS VANDERPLATZ -- WOULD YOU LIKE TO SHARE WHAT YOU'RE WRITING WITH THE REST OF THE CLASS?
NO.
Dear Penrod,
My darling, I
minute in this
place. I have
been more
I THOUGHT NOT.
DON'T YOU HATE THAT NEW BITCH?
OOOH, SHE HEARD YOU! HA HA
PLEASE, MY DARLING -- YOU HAVE TO COME RESCUE ME.
"Seventeen"
WITH VIOLET VAN DER PLATZ
--BUT WHAT DID POLICE LEARN FROM THE RANSOM NOTE?
CHARLES! YOU KNOW WE DON'T WATCH TV DURING DINNER!

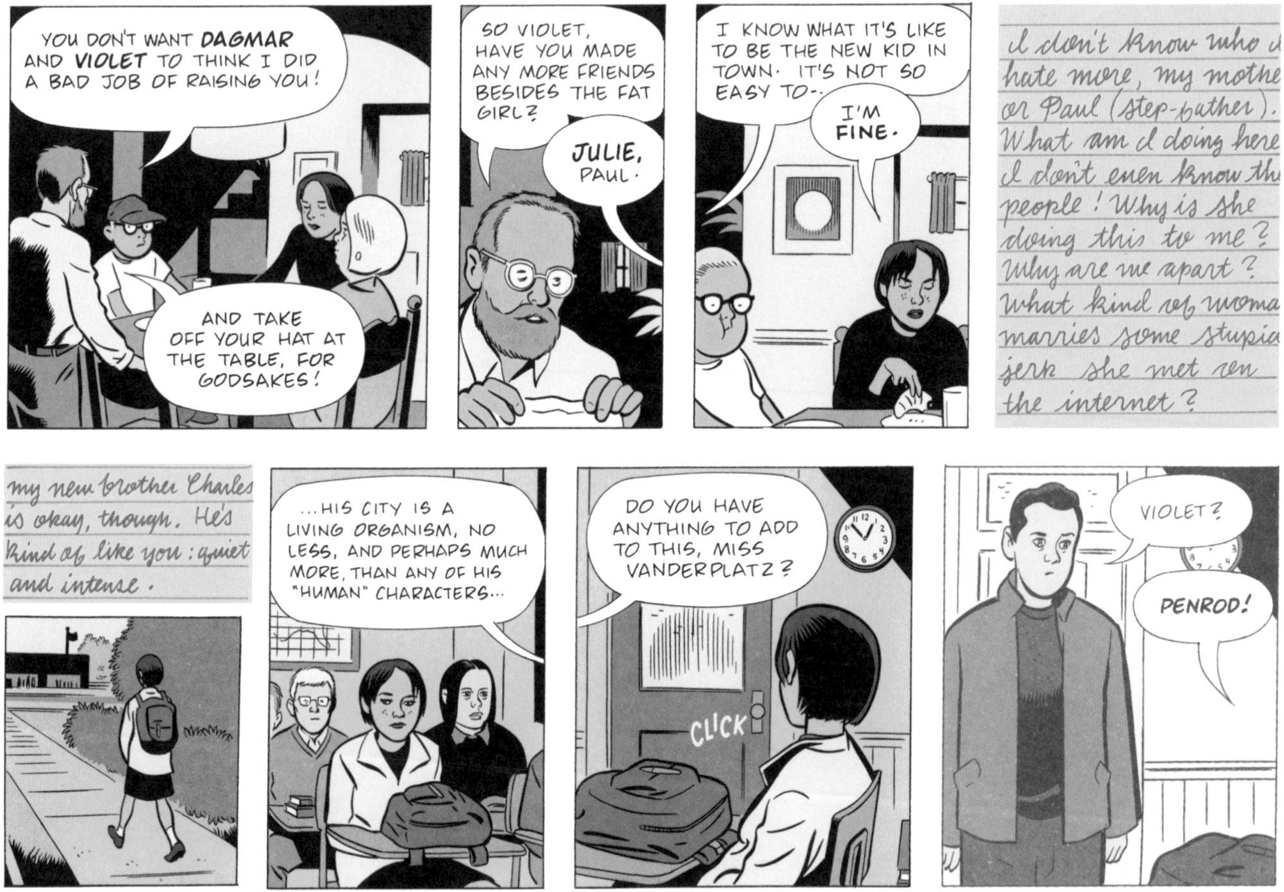
YOU DON'T WANT DAGMAR AND VIOLET TO THINK I DID A BAD JOB OF RAISING YOU!
AND TAKE OFF YOUR HAT AT THE TABLE, FOR GODSAKES!
SO VIOLET, HAVE YOU MADE ANY MORE FRIENDS BESIDES THE FAT GIRL?
JULIE, PAUL.
I KNOW WHAT IT'S LIKE TO BE THE NEW KID IN TOWN. IT'S NOT SO EASY TO--
I'M FINE.
I don't know who I hate more, my mothe or Paul (step-father). What am I doing here I don't even know the people! Why is she doing this to me? Why are we apart? What kind of woma marries some stupid jerk she met on the internet?
my new brother Charles is okay, though. He's kind of like you: quiet and intense.
...HIS CITY IS A LIVING ORGANISM, NO LESS, AND PERHAPS MUCH MORE, THAN ANY OF HIS "HUMAN" CHARACTERS...
DO YOU HAVE ANYTHING TO ADD TO THIS, MISS VANDERPLATZ?
CLICK
VIOLET?
PENROD!

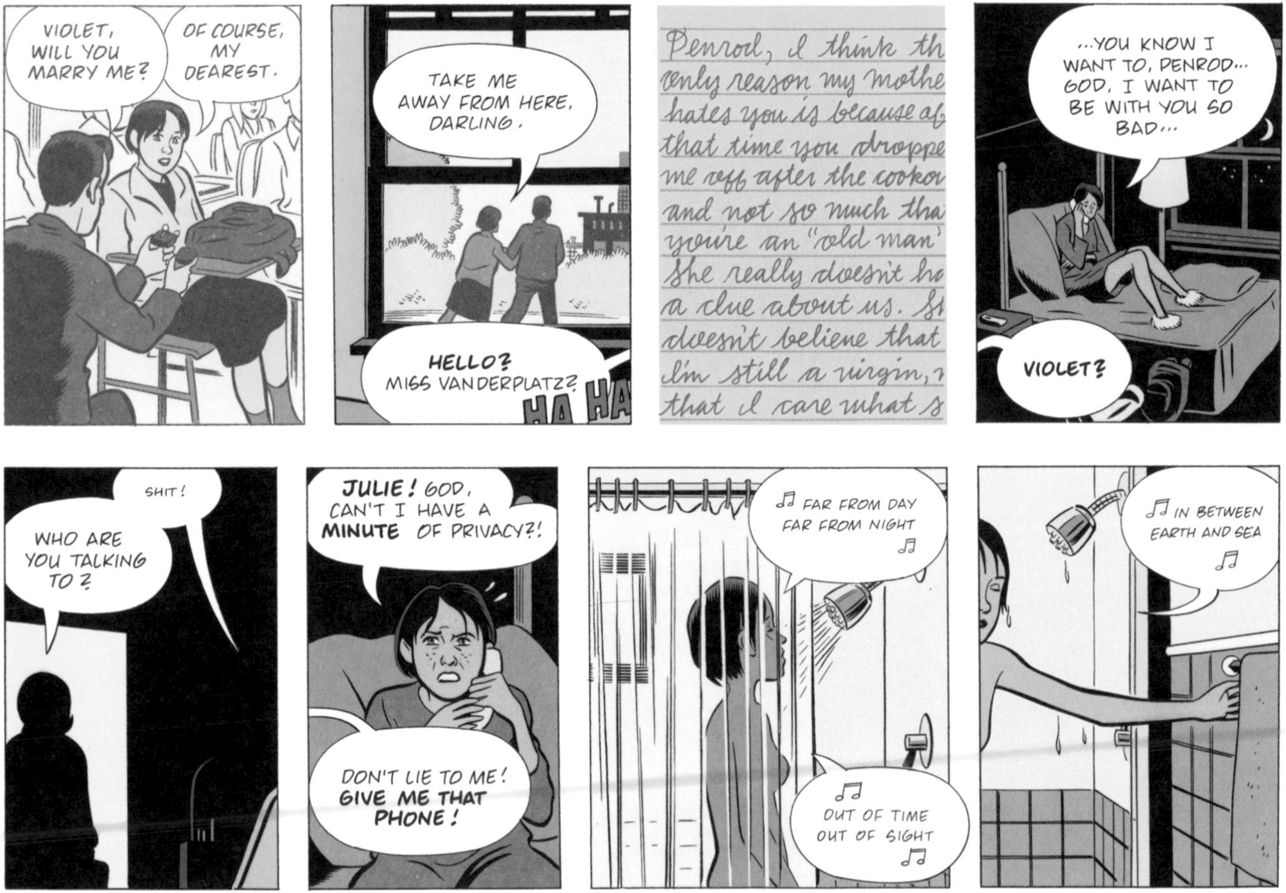
VIOLET, WILL YOU MARRY ME?
OF COURSE, MY DEAREST.
TAKE ME AWAY FROM HERE, DARLING.
HELLO? MISS VANDERPLATZ?
HA HA
Penrod, I think th
only reason my mothe
hates you is because af
that time you droppe
me off after the cooko
and not so much tha
you're an "old man"
She really doesn't ha
a clue about us. Sh
doesn't believe that
I'm still a virgin, n
that I care what s
...YOU KNOW I WANT TO, PENROD... GOD, I WANT TO BE WITH YOU SO BAD...
VIOLET?
WHO ARE YOU TALKING TO?
SHIT!
JULIE! GOD, CAN'T I HAVE A MINUTE OF PRIVACY?!
DON'T LIE TO ME! GIVE ME THAT PHONE!
♫ FAR FROM DAY FAR FROM NIGHT ♫
♫ OUT OF TIME OUT OF SIGHT ♫
♫ IN BETWEEN EARTH AND SEA ♫

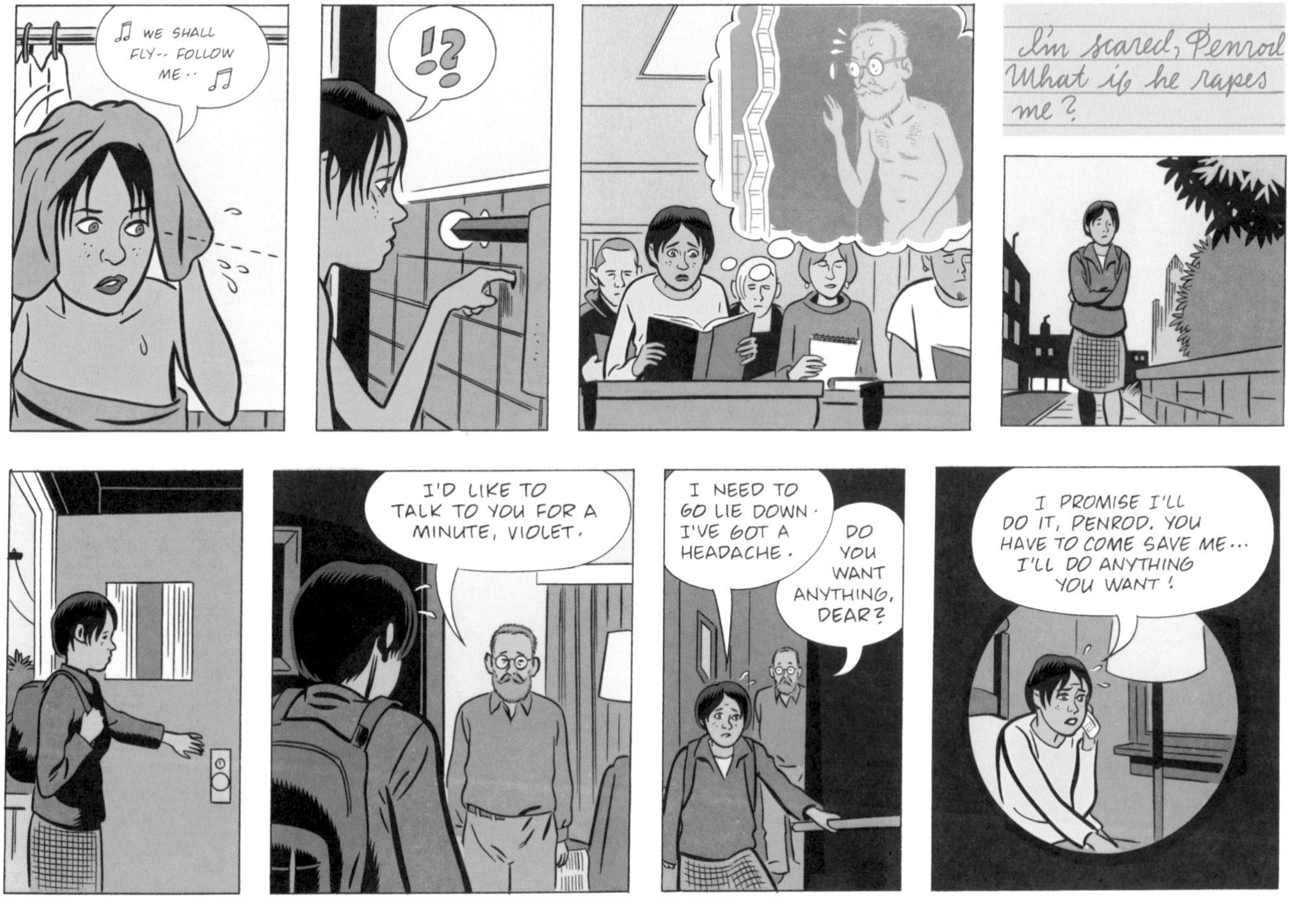
♫ WE SHALL FLY-- FOLLOW ME.. ♫
!?
I'm scared, Penrod
What if he rapes me?
I'D LIKE TO TALK TO YOU FOR A MINUTE, VIOLET.
I NEED TO GO LIE DOWN. I'VE GOT A HEADACHE.
DO YOU WANT ANYTHING, DEAR?
I PROMISE I'LL DO IT, PENROD. YOU HAVE TO COME SAVE ME... I'LL DO ANYTHING YOU WANT!

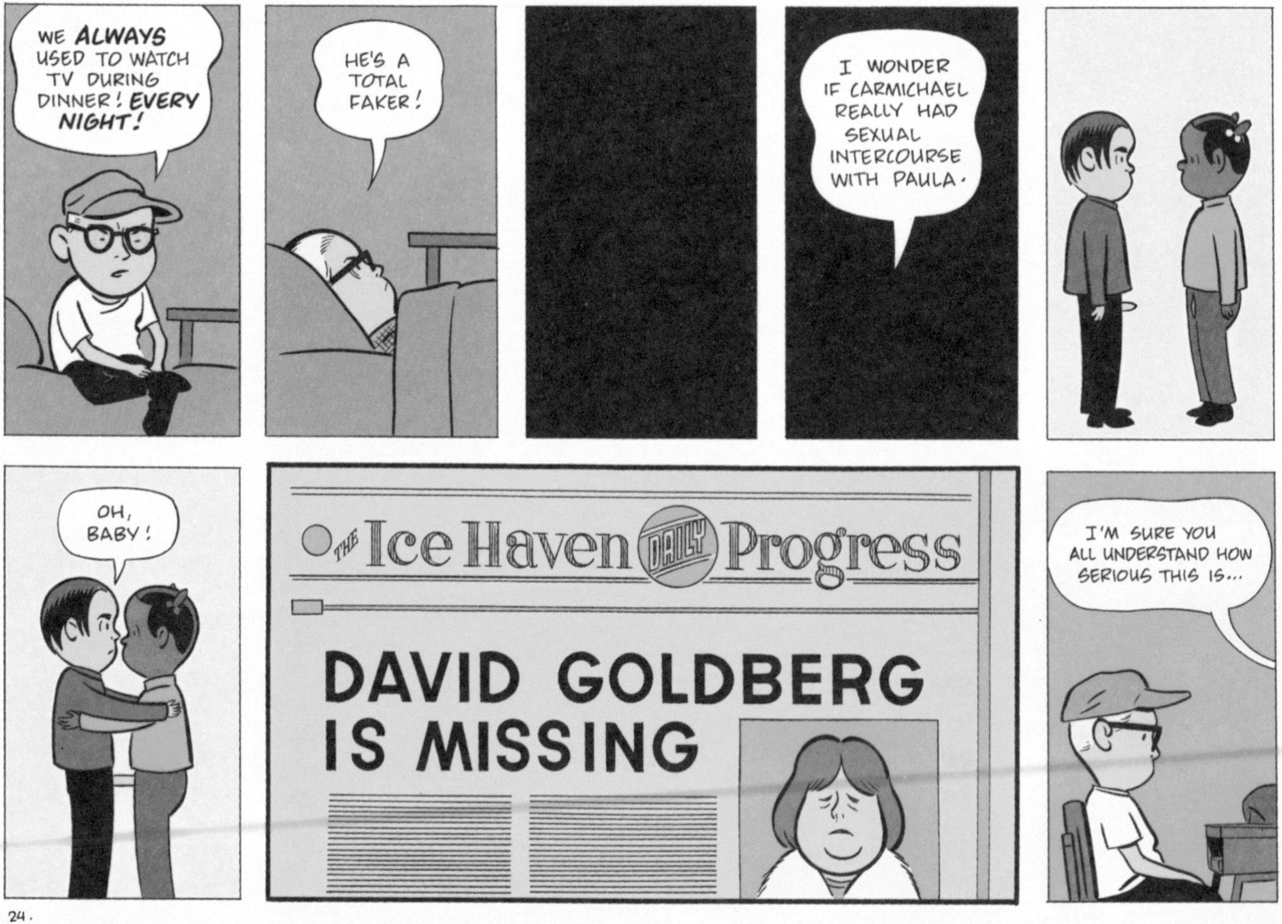
WE ALWAYS USED TO WATCH TV DURING DINNER! EVERY NIGHT!
HE'S A TOTAL FAKER!
I WONDER IF CARMICHAEL REALLY HAD SEXUAL INTERCOURSE WITH PAULA.
OH, BABY!
THE Ice Haven DAILY Progress
DAVID GOLDBERG IS MISSING
I'M SURE YOU ALL UNDERSTAND HOW SERIOUS THIS IS...

IF ANY OF YOU HAVE ANY INFORMATION ABOUT DAVID, YOU NEED TO TELL IT TO ME OR PRINCIPAL JAFFE IMMEDIATELY...

AFTER LUNCH TODAY THERE WILL BE AN ASSEMBLY WITH NURSE HEALY WHO WILL TALK TO US ABOUT COPING WITH GRIEF AND TERROR...

AND TOMORROW WE HOPE TO HAVE ANOTHER VISIT FROM OFFICER KAUFMAN WHO WILL TELL YOU HOW TO STOP THIS FROM HAPPENING TO YOU...

CHARLES!

I GUESS YOU HEARD ABOUT YOUR LITTLE FRIEND.

WHO DO YOU THINK DID IT?

I HAVE NO IDEA.

25.

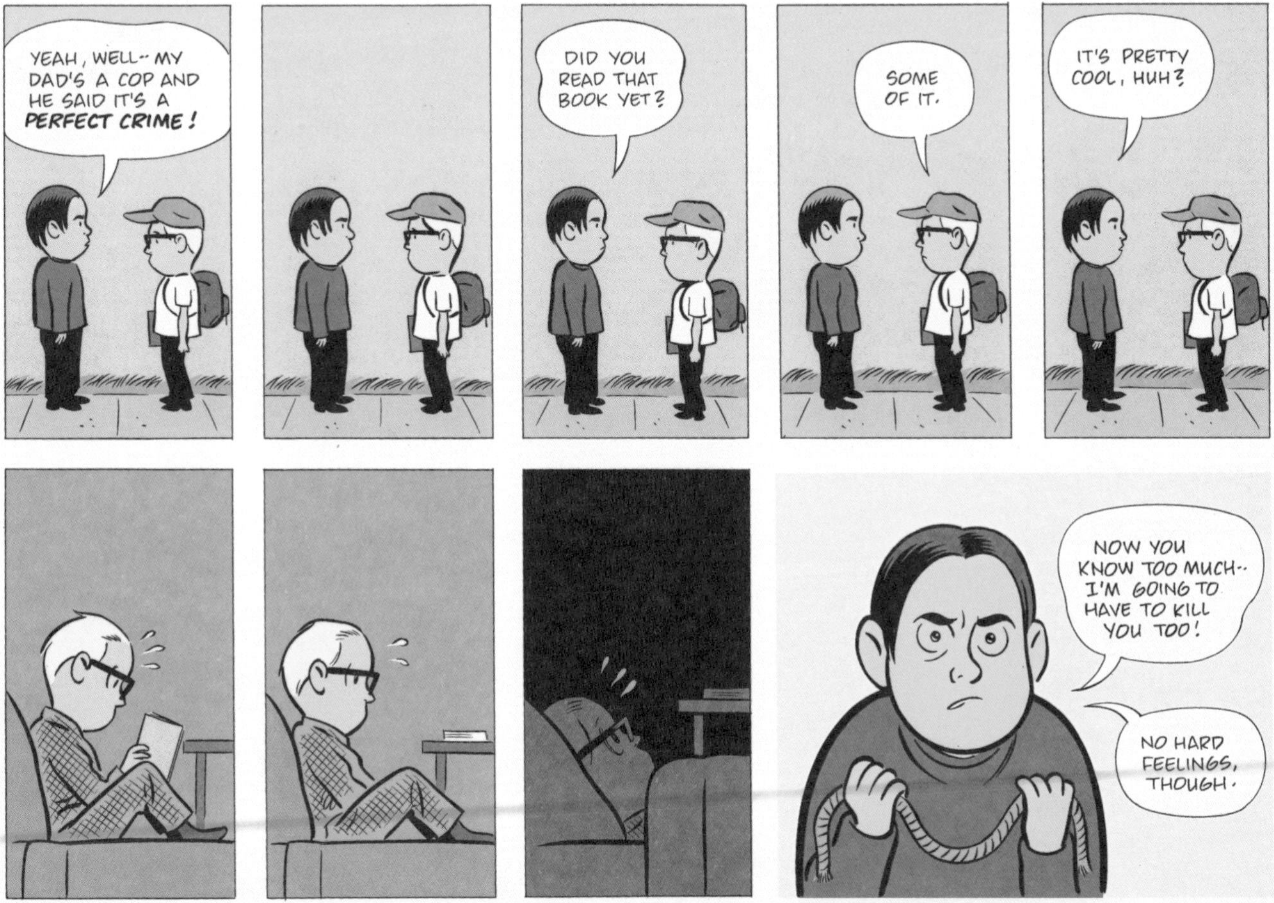
YEAH, WELL-- MY DAD'S A COP AND HE SAID IT'S A **PERFECT CRIME!**
DID YOU READ THAT BOOK YET?
SOME OF IT.
IT'S PRETTY COOL, HUH?
NOW YOU KNOW TOO MUCH-- I'M GOING TO HAVE TO KILL YOU TOO!
NO HARD FEELINGS, THOUGH.

OR...

WHY DO YOU HAVE THIS BOOK? I SUSPECT YOU'RE IN CAHOOTS WITH THE MURDERER!

LEOPOLD AND DEB

SHRED SHRED

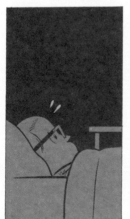

≡SIGH≡

DO YOU LIKE IT, BABY? UGN! UGN!

OH YEAH, UGN!

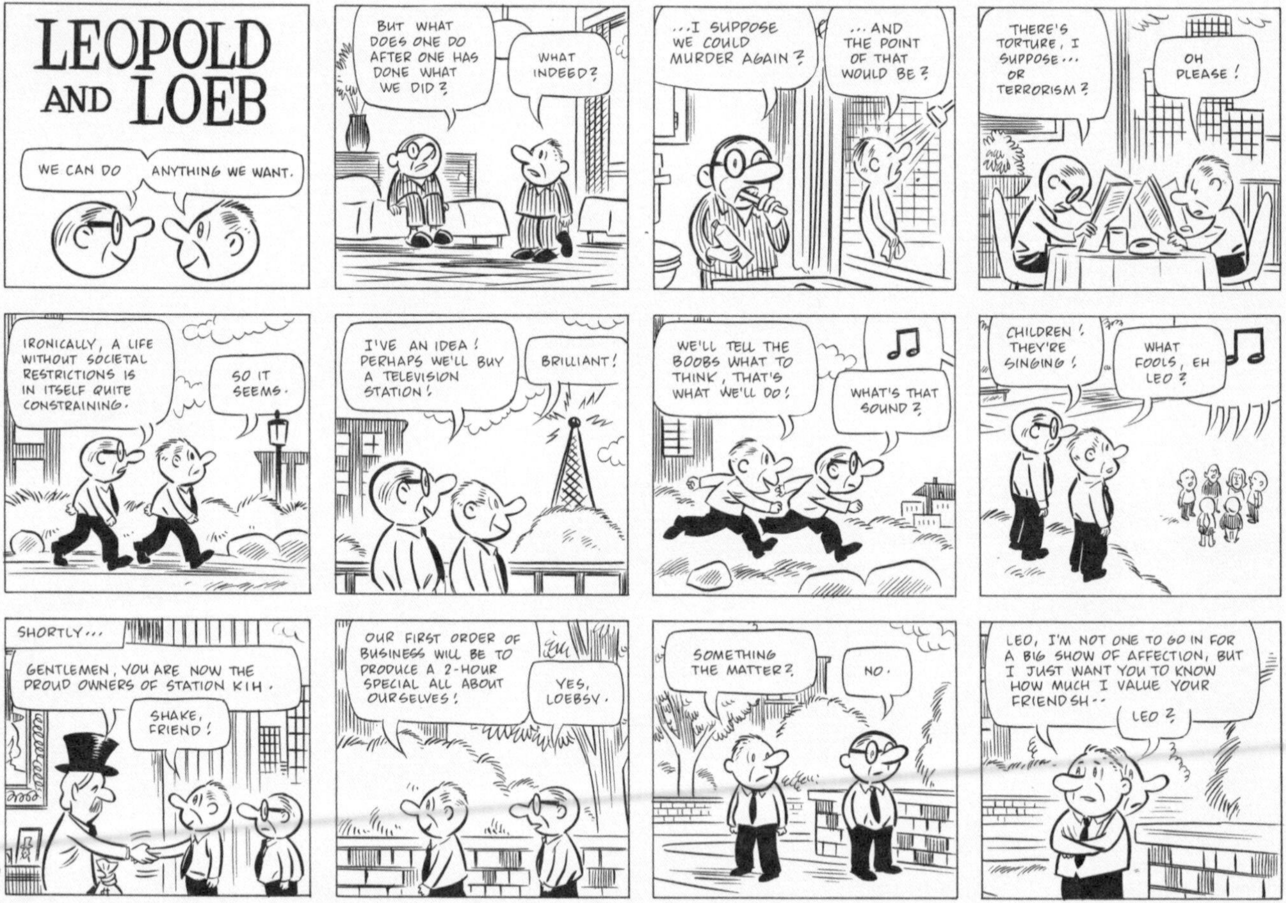
LEOPOLD AND LOEB
WE CAN DO
ANYTHING WE WANT.
BUT WHAT DOES ONE DO AFTER ONE HAS DONE WHAT WE DID?
WHAT INDEED?
...I SUPPOSE WE COULD MURDER AGAIN?
...AND THE POINT OF THAT WOULD BE?
THERE'S TORTURE, I SUPPOSE... OR TERRORISM?
OH PLEASE!
IRONICALLY, A LIFE WITHOUT SOCIETAL RESTRICTIONS IS IN ITSELF QUITE CONSTRAINING.
SO IT SEEMS.
I'VE AN IDEA! PERHAPS WE'LL BUY A TELEVISION STATION!
BRILLIANT!
WE'LL TELL THE BOOBS WHAT TO THINK, THAT'S WHAT WE'LL DO!
WHAT'S THAT SOUND?
CHILDREN! THEY'RE SINGING!
WHAT FOOLS, EH LEO?
SHORTLY...
GENTLEMEN, YOU ARE NOW THE PROUD OWNERS OF STATION KIH.
SHAKE, FRIEND!
OUR FIRST ORDER OF BUSINESS WILL BE TO PRODUCE A 2-HOUR SPECIAL ALL ABOUT OURSELVES!
YES, LOEBSY.
SOMETHING THE MATTER?
NO.
LEO, I'M NOT ONE TO GO IN FOR A BIG SHOW OF AFFECTION, BUT I JUST WANT YOU TO KNOW HOW MUCH I VALUE YOUR FRIENDSH--
LEO?

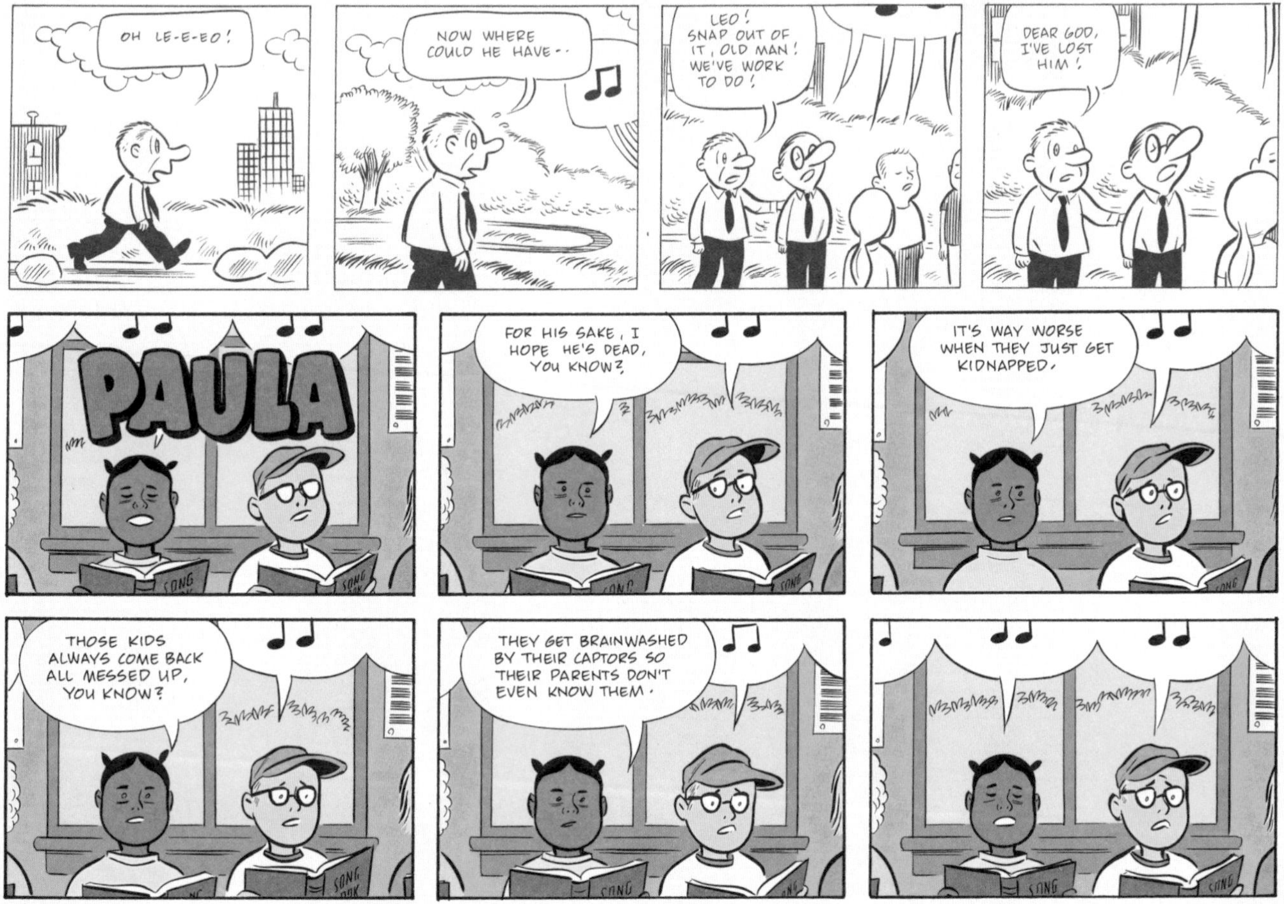
OH LE-E-EO!
NOW WHERE COULD HE HAVE--
LEO! SNAP OUT OF IT, OLD MAN! WE'VE WORK TO DO!
DEAR GOD, I'VE LOST HIM!
PAULA
FOR HIS SAKE, I HOPE HE'S DEAD, YOU KNOW?
IT'S WAY WORSE WHEN THEY JUST GET KIDNAPPED.
THOSE KIDS ALWAYS COME BACK ALL MESSED UP, YOU KNOW?
THEY GET BRAINWASHED BY THEIR CAPTORS SO THEIR PARENTS DON'T EVEN KNOW THEM.

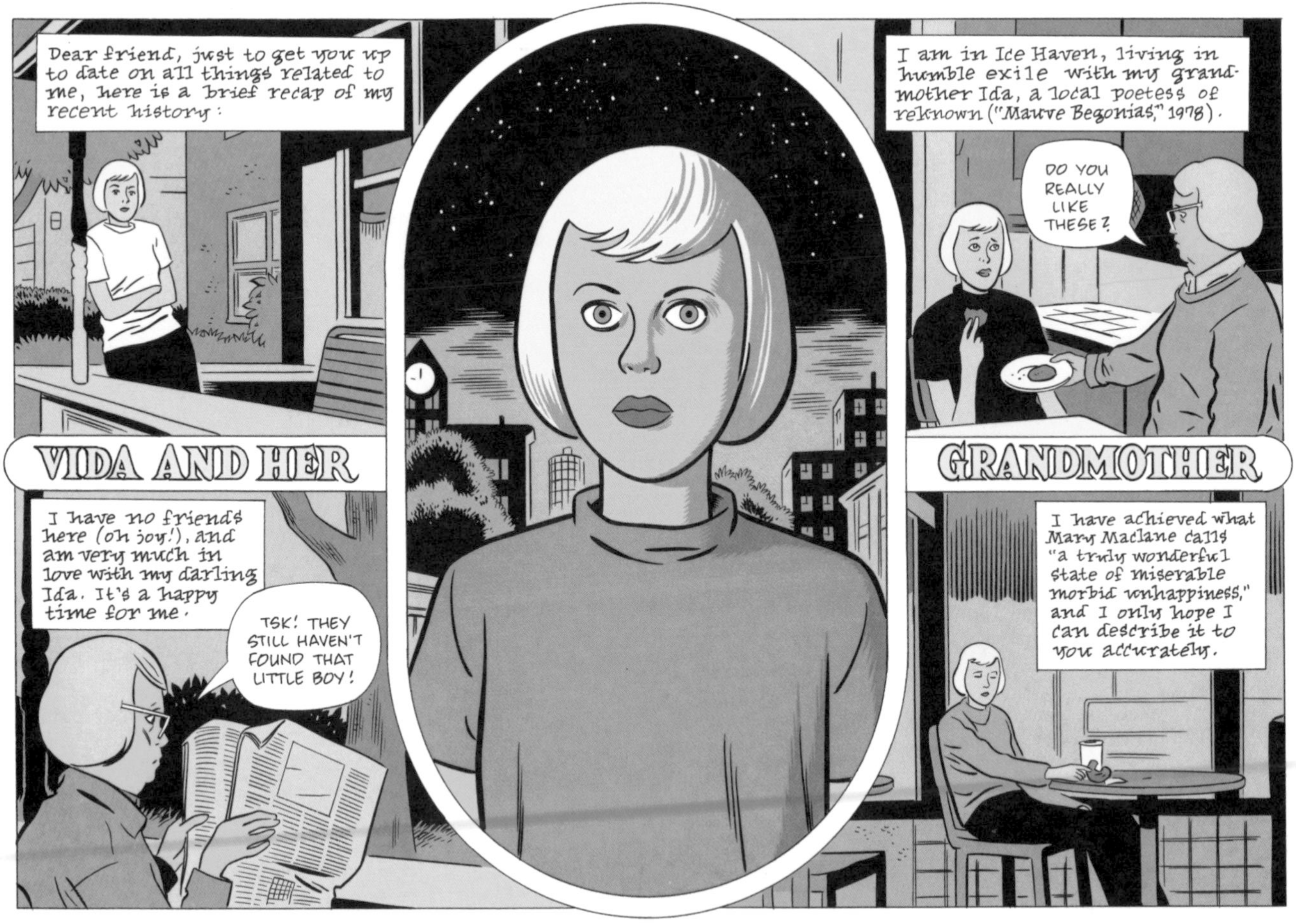

Dear friend, just to get you up to date on all things related to me, here is a brief recap of my recent history:
I am in Ice Haven, living in humble exile with my grandmother Ida, a local poetess of reknown ("Mauve Begonias," 1978).
DO YOU REALLY LIKE THESE?
VIDA AND HER GRANDMOTHER
I have no friends here (oh joy!), and am very much in love with my darling Ida. It's a happy time for me.
TSK! THEY STILL HAVEN'T FOUND THAT LITTLE BOY!
I have achieved what Mary MacLane calls "a truly wonderful state of miserable morbid unhappiness," and I only hope I can describe it to you accurately.

Those of you who read the first issue of my magazine (thus far available only at Pete's Books in Ice Haven; zero copies sold) will recall that I grew up in Chicago and attended a well-regarded private school on the south side.

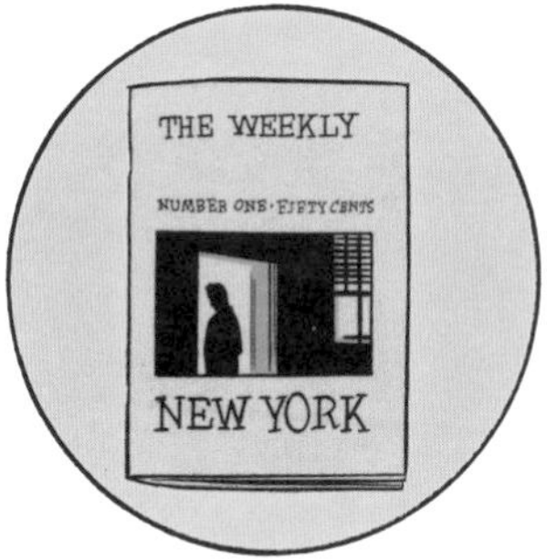
THE WEEKLY
NUMBER ONE · FIFTY CENTS
NEW YORK

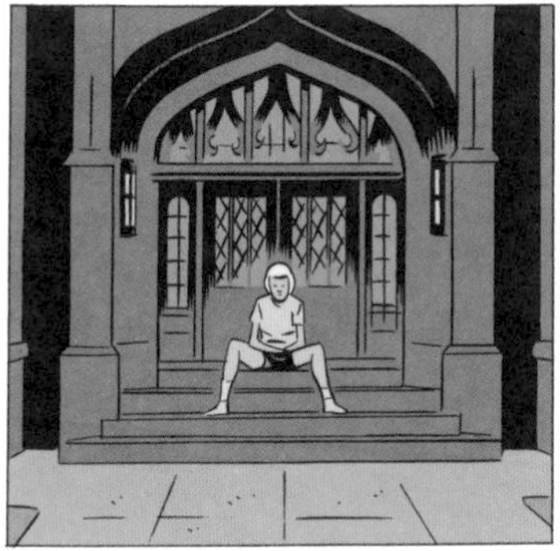

From there (forgive me for repeating myself) I spent four years at a prestigious University and then a year in New York, where no one showed any interest whatsoever in my poetry ("too prose-y") or my short fiction ("hard to swallow").

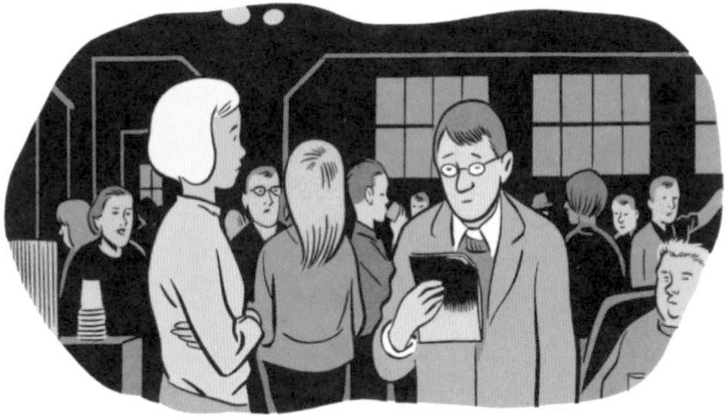

Also I had my first (and last) "serious" "relationship" with a "man" & was soundly forsaken (see issue #1 for details).

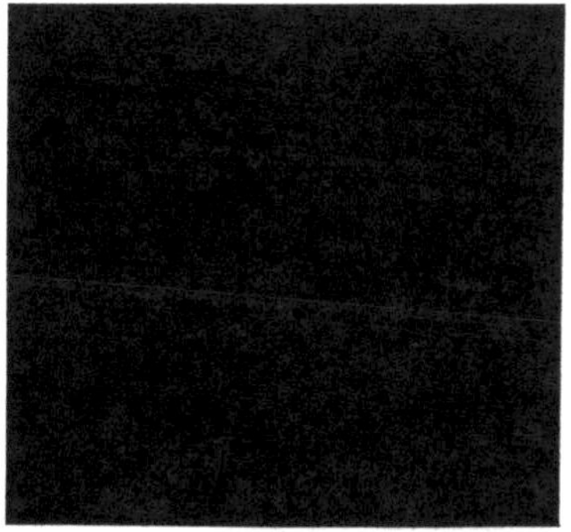

I have assigned myself the weekly output of one 16-page magazine (prose and poetry). The second issue was to have been subtitled "Ice Haven for Beginners," but I was derailed by an unexpected discovery.

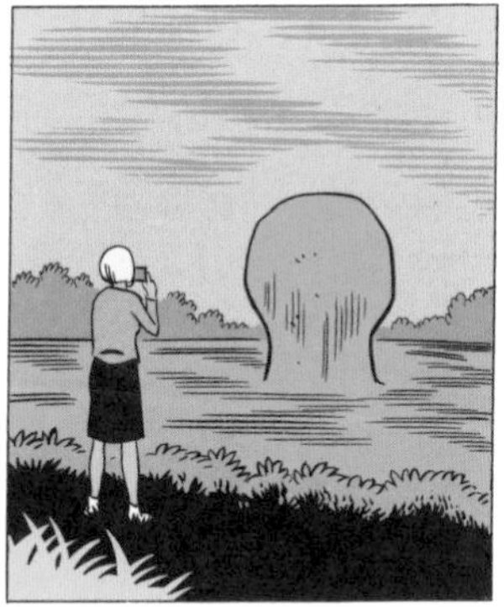

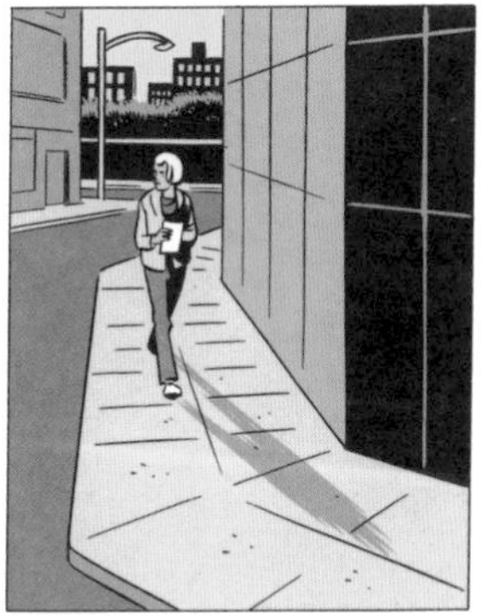

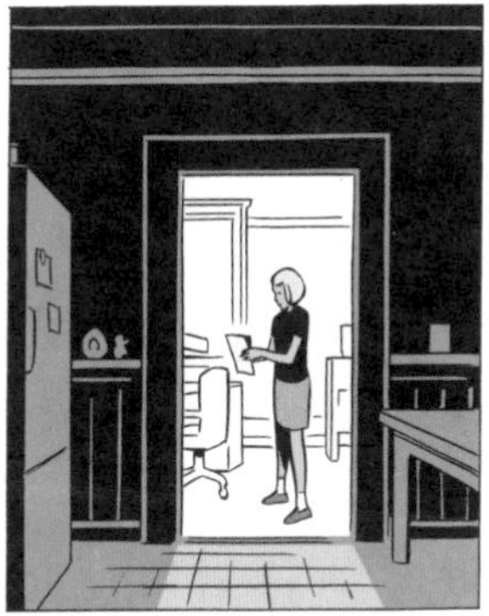

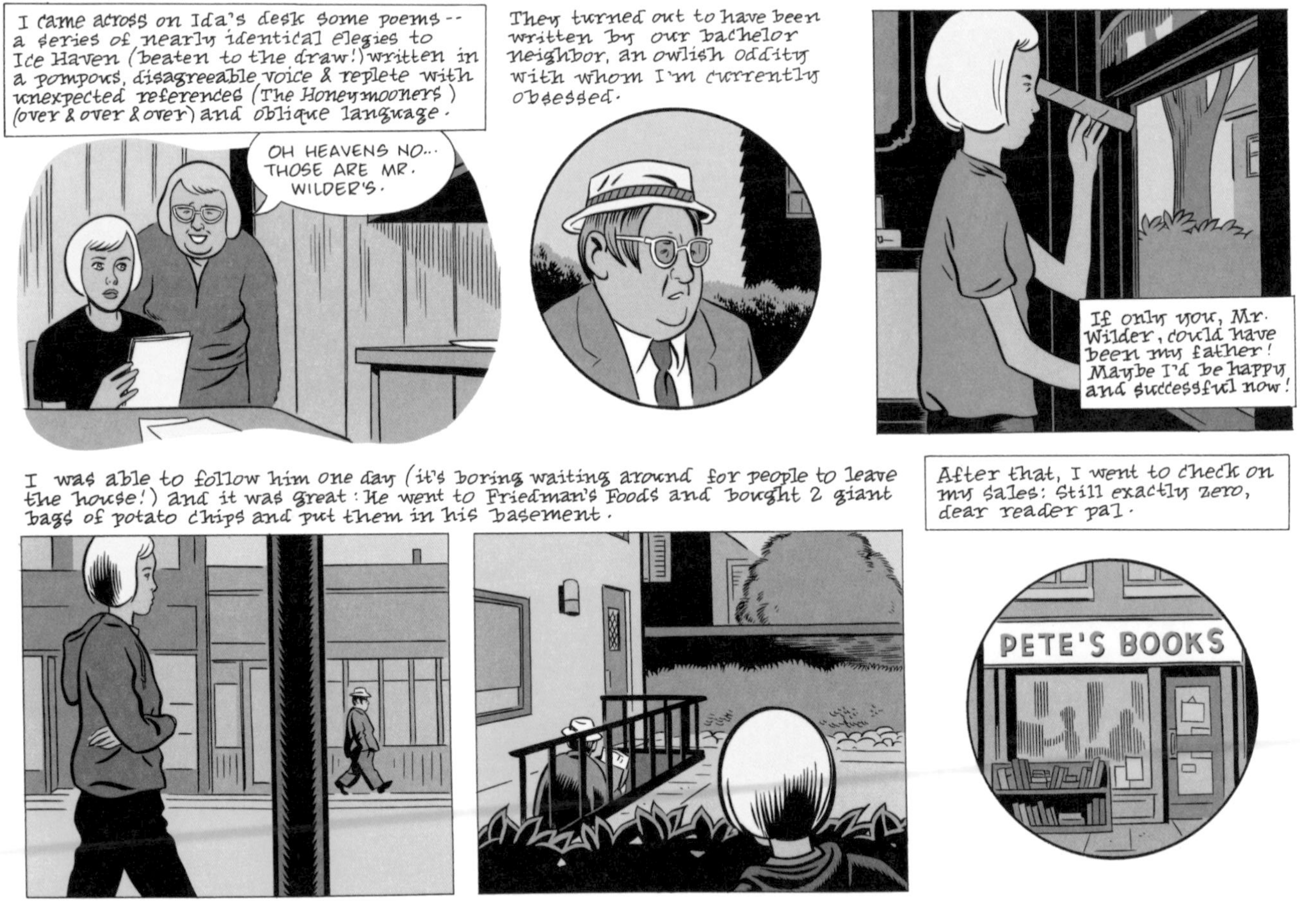
I came across on Ida's desk some poems -- a series of nearly identical elegies to Ice Haven (beaten to the draw!) written in a pompous, disagreeable voice & replete with unexpected references (The Honeymooners) (over & over & over) and oblique language.
OH HEAVENS NO... THOSE ARE MR. WILDER'S.
They turned out to have been written by our bachelor neighbor, an owlish oddity with whom I'm currently obsessed.
If only you, Mr. Wilder, could have been my father! Maybe I'd be happy and successful now!
I was able to follow him one day (it's boring waiting around for people to leave the house!) and it was great: He went to Friedman's Foods and bought 2 giant bags of potato chips and put them in his basement.
After that, I went to check on my sales: Still exactly zero, dear reader pal.
PETE'S BOOKS

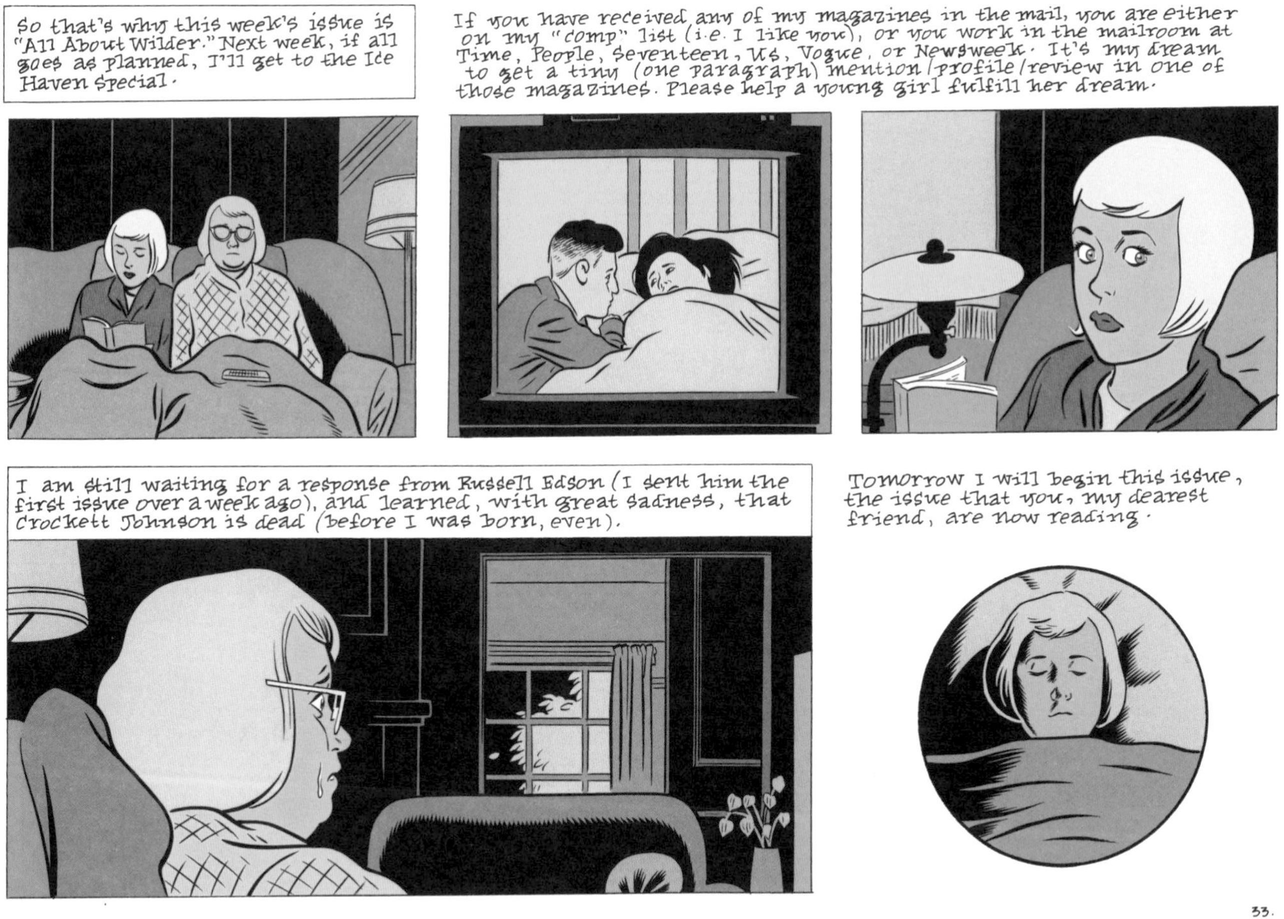
So that's why this week's issue is "All About Wilder." Next week, if all goes as planned, I'll get to the Ice Haven Special.
If you have received any of my magazines in the mail, you are either on my "comp" list (i.e. I like you), or you work in the mailroom at Time, People, Seventeen, Us, Vogue, or Newsweek. It's my dream to get a tiny (one paragraph) mention/profile/review in one of those magazines. Please help a young girl fulfill her dream.
I am still waiting for a response from Russell Edson (I sent him the first issue over a week ago), and learned, with great sadness, that Crockett Johnson is dead (before I was born, even).
Tomorrow I will begin this issue, the issue that you, my dearest friend, are now reading.

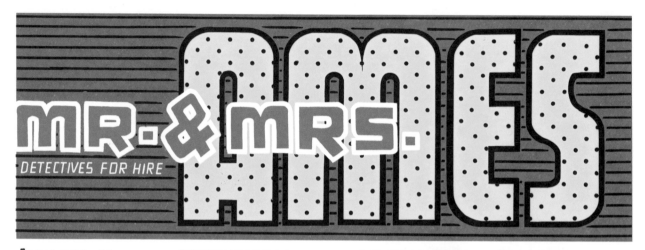

MR. & MRS. AMES

DETECTIVES FOR HIRE

IT WAS 2 PM. WE HAD BEEN CALLED TO *ICE HAVEN* BY MRS. NATALIE GOLDBERG TO INVESTIGATE THE DISAPPEARANCE OF HER SON...

WHY DID YOU TELL HIM TO MEET US HERE WHEN YOU KNOW I HATE CHINESE FOOD?

MAYBE *I'D* LIKE CHINESE FOOD ONCE IN A WHILE.

WELL WE'RE HERE -- LIVE IT UP!

SEEMS LIKE A CUTE TOWN.

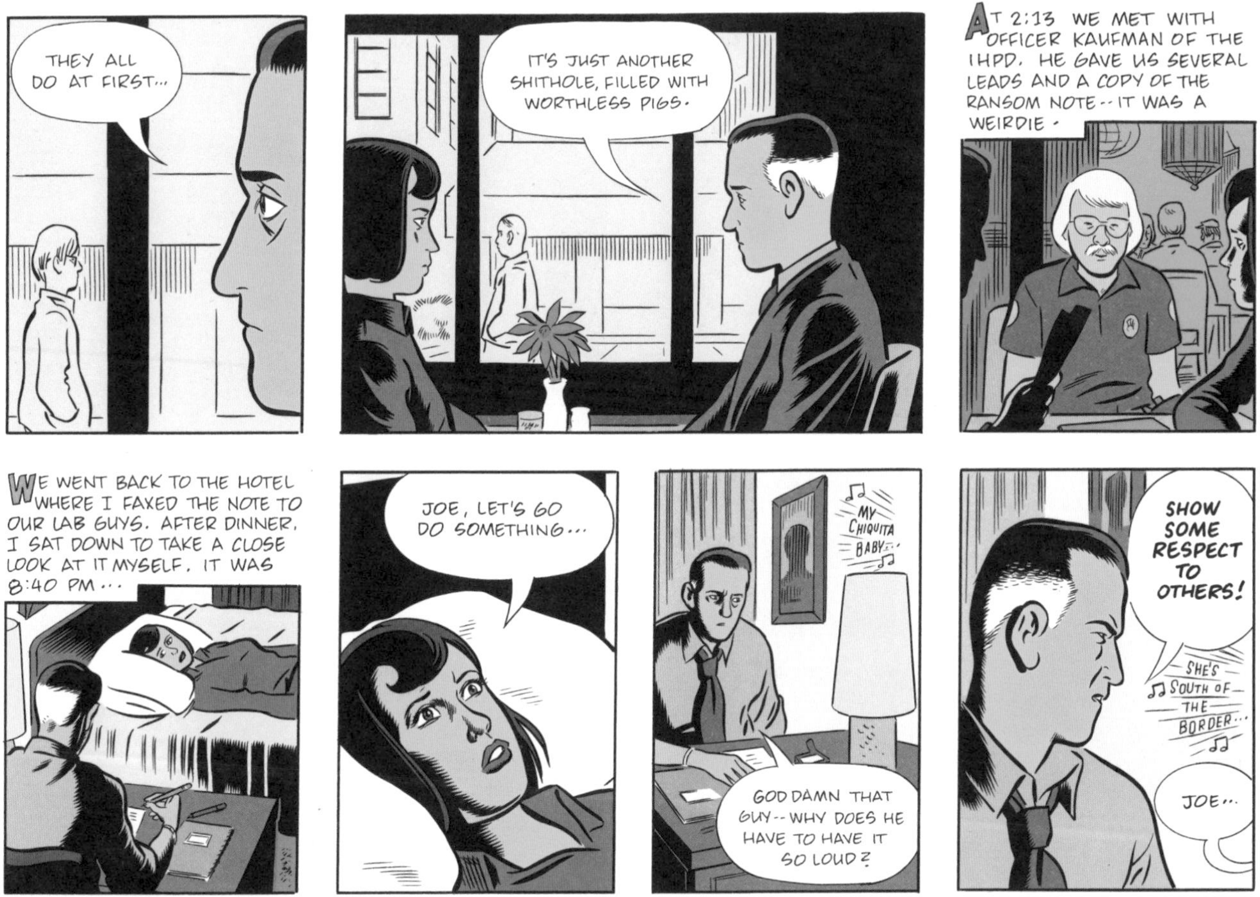
THEY ALL DO AT FIRST...
IT'S JUST ANOTHER SHITHOLE, FILLED WITH WORTHLESS PIGS.
AT 2:13 WE MET WITH OFFICER KAUFMAN OF THE IHPD. HE GAVE US SEVERAL LEADS AND A COPY OF THE RANSOM NOTE -- IT WAS A WEIRDIE.
WE WENT BACK TO THE HOTEL WHERE I FAXED THE NOTE TO OUR LAB GUYS. AFTER DINNER, I SAT DOWN TO TAKE A CLOSE LOOK AT IT MYSELF. IT WAS 8:40 PM...
JOE, LET'S GO DO SOMETHING...
MY CHIQUITA BABY...
GOD DAMN THAT GUY -- WHY DOES HE HAVE TO HAVE IT SO LOUD?
SHOW SOME RESPECT TO OTHERS!
SHE'S SOUTH OF THE BORDER...
JOE...

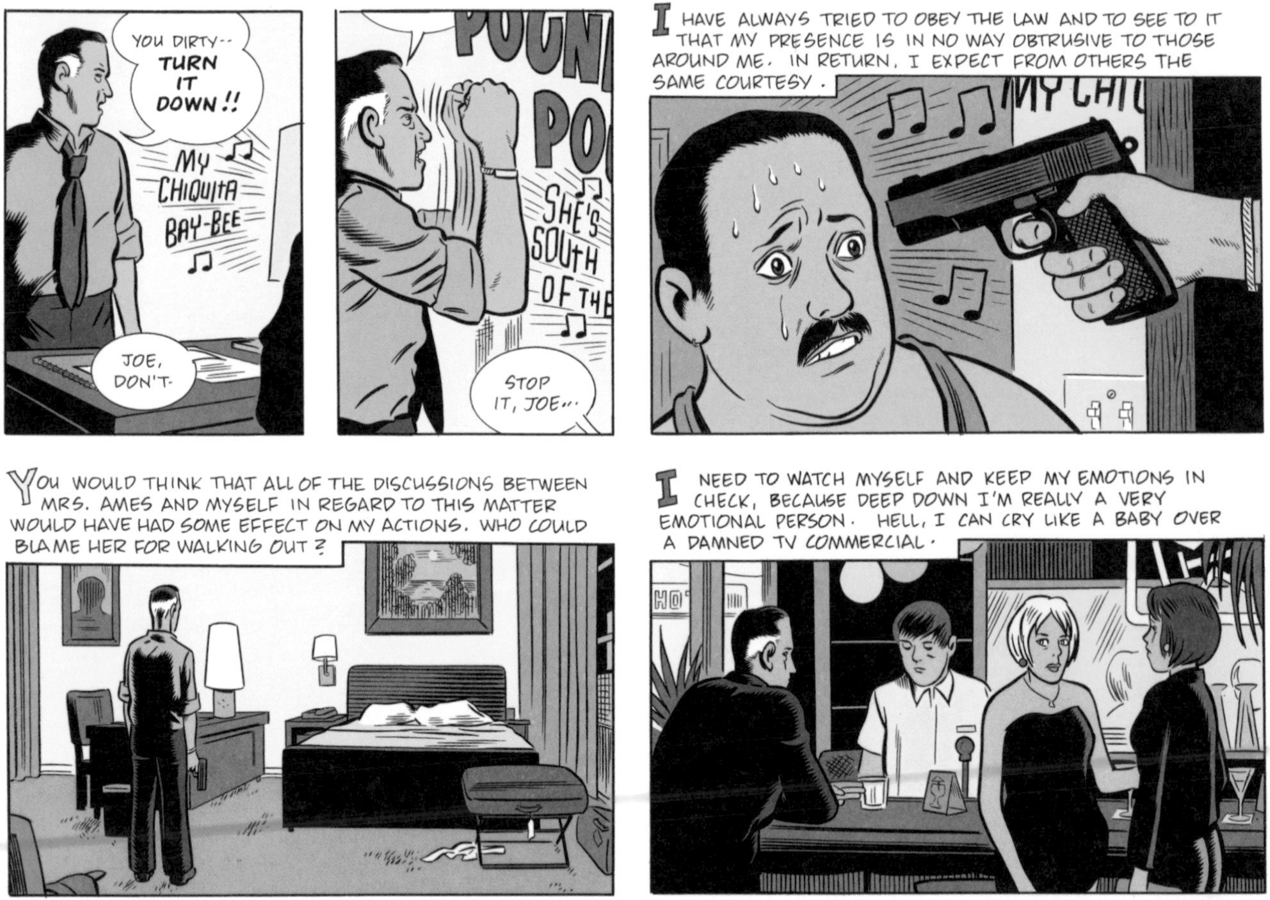
YOU DIRTY-- **TURN IT DOWN!!**
MY CHIQUITA BAY-BEE
JOE, DON'T-
SHE'S SOUTH OF TH
STOP IT, JOE...
I HAVE ALWAYS TRIED TO OBEY THE LAW AND TO SEE TO IT THAT MY PRESENCE IS IN NO WAY OBTRUSIVE TO THOSE AROUND ME. IN RETURN, I EXPECT FROM OTHERS THE SAME COURTESY.
YOU WOULD THINK THAT ALL OF THE DISCUSSIONS BETWEEN MRS. AMES AND MYSELF IN REGARD TO THIS MATTER WOULD HAVE HAD SOME EFFECT ON MY ACTIONS. WHO COULD BLAME HER FOR WALKING OUT?
I NEED TO WATCH MYSELF AND KEEP MY EMOTIONS IN CHECK, BECAUSE DEEP DOWN I'M REALLY A VERY EMOTIONAL PERSON. HELL, I CAN CRY LIKE A BABY OVER A DAMNED TV COMMERCIAL.

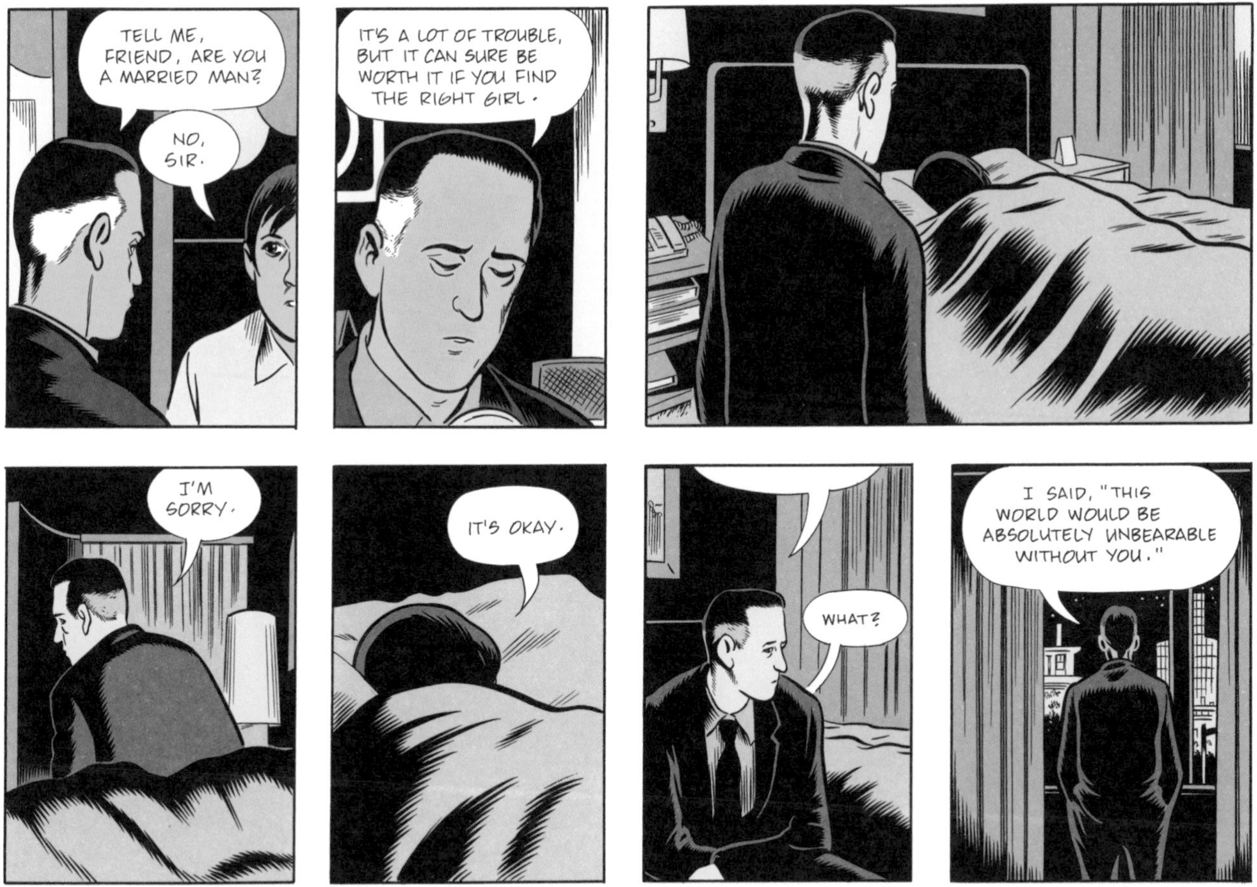
TELL ME, FRIEND, ARE YOU A MARRIED MAN?
NO, SIR.
IT'S A LOT OF TROUBLE, BUT IT CAN SURE BE WORTH IT IF YOU FIND THE RIGHT GIRL.
I'M SORRY.
IT'S OKAY.
WHAT?
I SAID, "THIS WORLD WOULD BE ABSOLUTELY UNBEARABLE WITHOUT YOU."

Charles

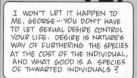

I WON'T LET IT HAPPEN TO ME, GEORGE... YOU DON'T HAVE TO LET SEXUAL DESIRE CONTROL YOUR LIFE. DESIRE IS NATURE'S WAY OF FURTHERING THE SPECIES AT THE COST OF THE INDIVIDUAL, AND WHAT GOOD IS A SPECIES OF THWARTED INDIVIDUALS?

I SUPPORT ANYTHING THAT GOES AGAINST NATURE. NATURE IS EVIL. ONLY HUMAN CONSCIOUSNESS IS HEROIC, ESPECIALLY WHEN IT FINDS A WAY TO OUTWIT NATURE.

CHARLES'S LITTLE NEIGHBOR, GEORGE

HAVE YOU EVER WITNESSED A SPECTACLE AS AWFUL AS THAT OF A NOBLE STALLION BEING ATTACKED BY A SWARM OF HORSEFLIES? THE POOR BEAST, UNABLE TO ELUDE THE BLOODSUCKERS, CAN DO NOTHING BUT SUFFER AS THEY HAVE THEIR WAY WITH HIM -- THAT'S NATURE!

NATURE IS NOT BEAUTIFUL. ONLY THE ARTIFICIAL AND THE MAN-MADE CAN BE TRULY BEAUTIFUL.

GEORGE!

WHEN I GROW UP, I WON'T NEED TO GET MARRIED. THERE WILL BE VIRTUAL REALITY GOGGLES TO TAKE CARE OF MY SEXUAL NEEDS, AND WHO KNOWS WHAT ELSE. WHEN OUR DNA LEARNS THAT IT CAN NO LONGER RELY ON PROGRAMMED URGES TO FURTHER THE SPECIES, IT WILL GIVE UP IN DEFEAT, AND SEXUAL DESIRE WILL RECEDE LIKE POLIO OR SMALLPOX.

WILL THIS PUT AN END TO OUR ONGOING SELF-DESTRUCTION? DOES ALL VIOLENCE RISE FROM DISTORTED SEXUAL IMPULSES? AND WHAT IS THE EQUIVALENT OF VIRTUAL REALITY WHEN IT COMES TO REROUTING VIOLENT INCLINATIONS?

BYE CHARLES!

MURDER IS THOUGHT TO BE A "CRIME AGAINST NATURE." HOW ABSURD! SENSELESS VIOLENCE IS AS NATURAL AS AN OAK TREE! NATURE WANTS US TO DIE! NATURE LAUGHS AT OUR SUFFERING!

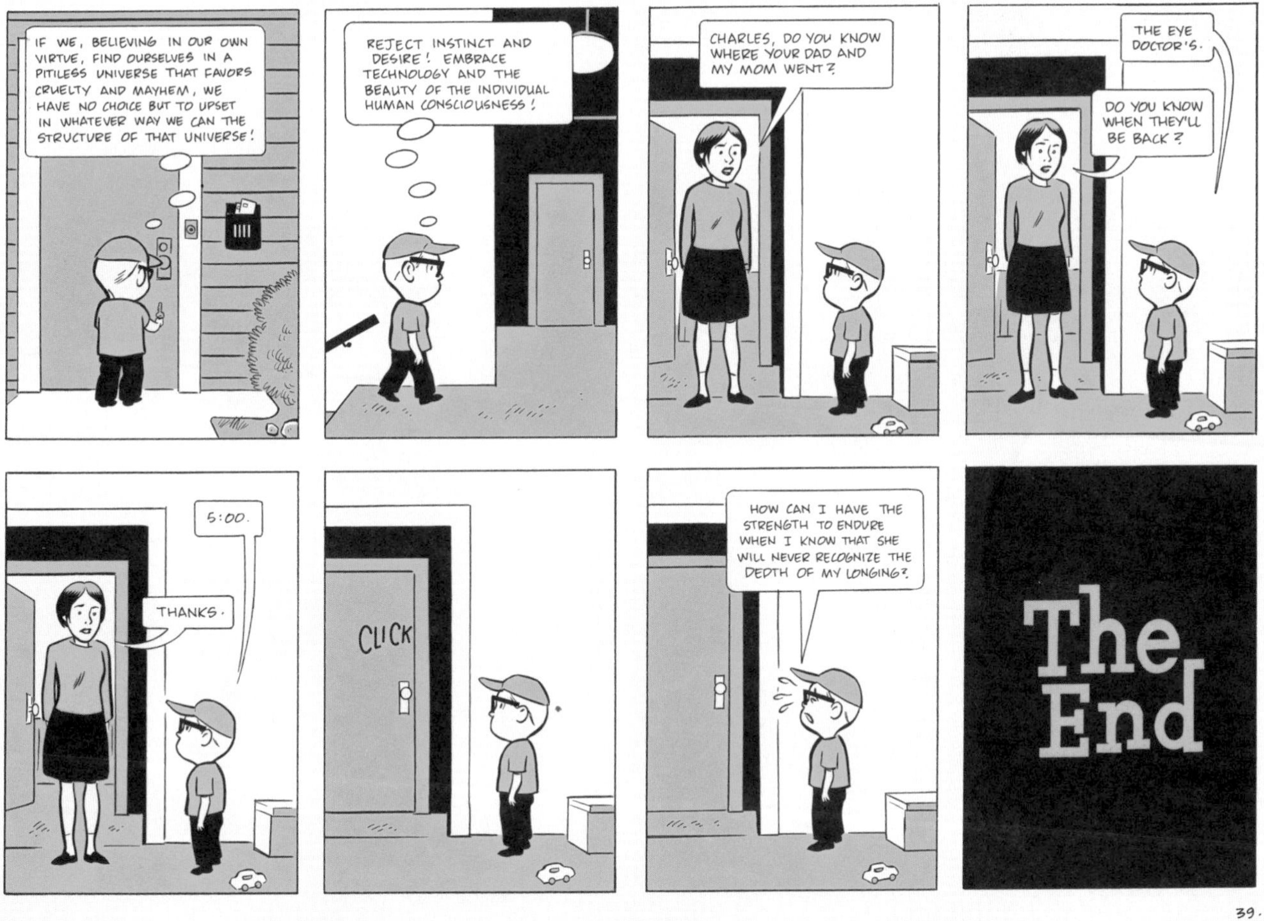
IF WE, BELIEVING IN OUR OWN VIRTUE, FIND OURSELVES IN A PITILESS UNIVERSE THAT FAVORS CRUELTY AND MAYHEM, WE HAVE NO CHOICE BUT TO UPSET IN WHATEVER WAY WE CAN THE STRUCTURE OF THAT UNIVERSE!
REJECT INSTINCT AND DESIRE! EMBRACE TECHNOLOGY AND THE BEAUTY OF THE INDIVIDUAL HUMAN CONSCIOUSNESS!
CHARLES, DO YOU KNOW WHERE YOUR DAD AND MY MOM WENT?
THE EYE DOCTOR'S.
DO YOU KNOW WHEN THEY'LL BE BACK?
5:00.
THANKS.
CLICK
HOW CAN I HAVE THE STRENGTH TO ENDURE WHEN I KNOW THAT SHE WILL NEVER RECOGNIZE THE DEPTH OF MY LONGING?
The End

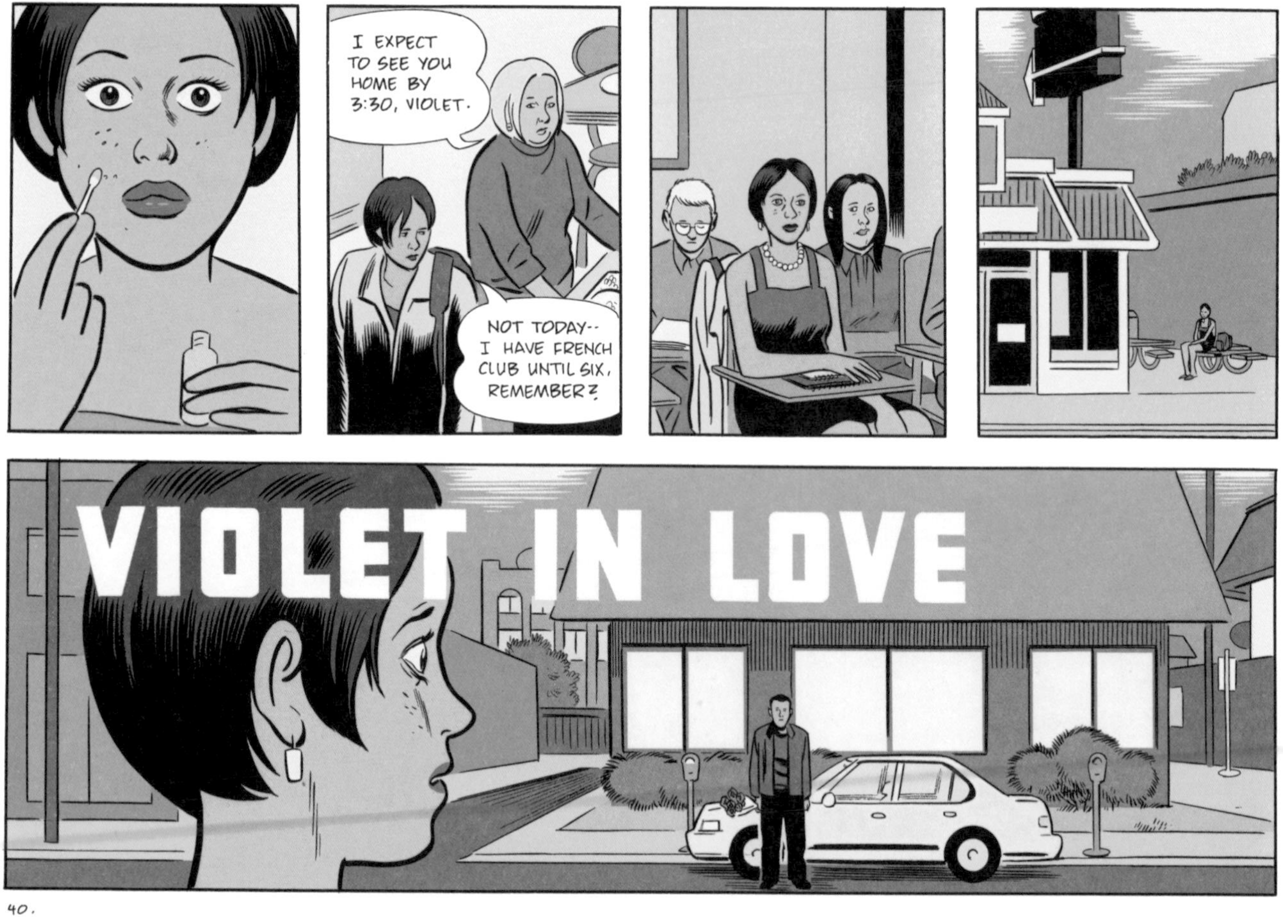
I EXPECT TO SEE YOU HOME BY 3:30, VIOLET.
NOT TODAY-- I HAVE FRENCH CLUB UNTIL SIX, REMEMBER?
VIOLET IN LOVE

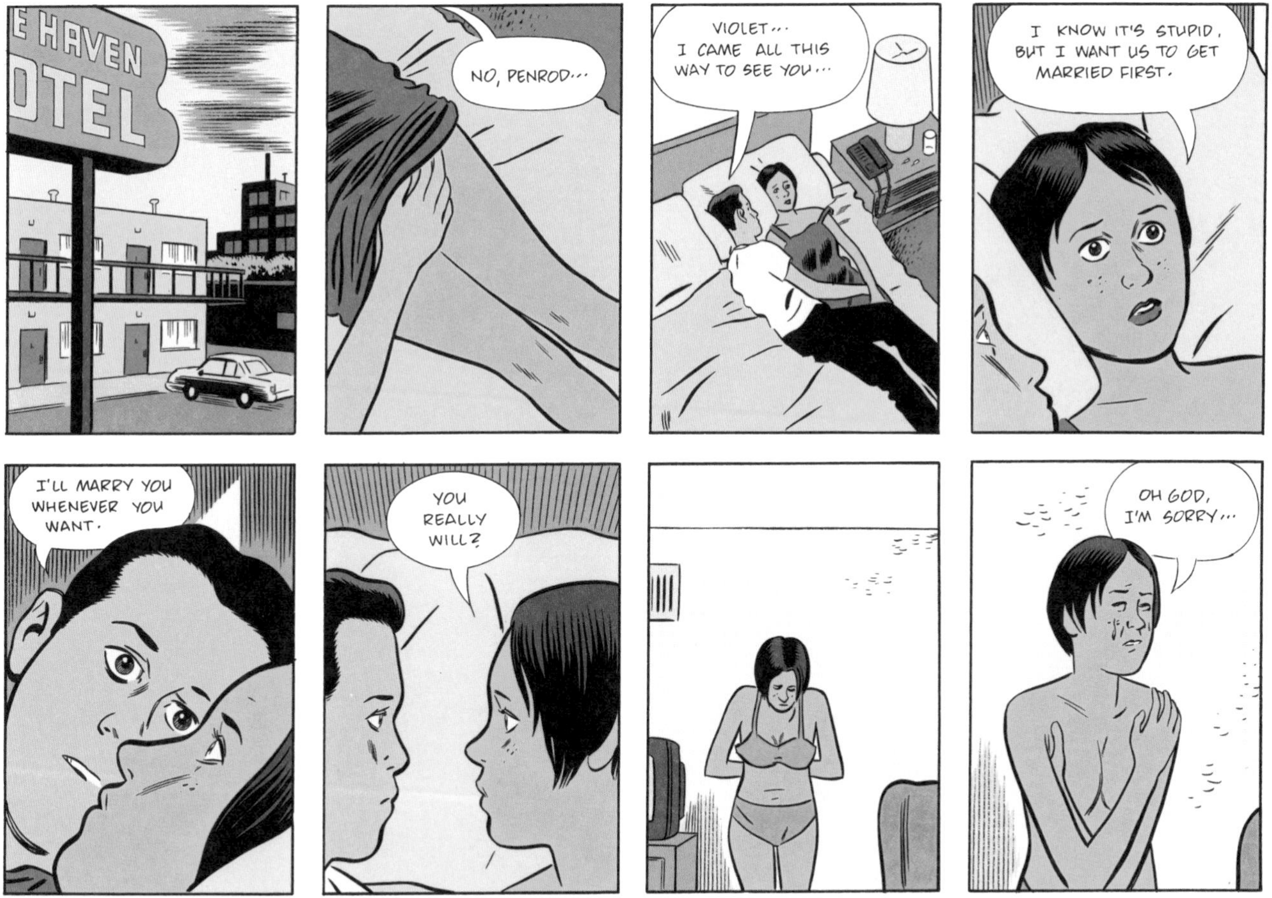
E HAVEN
OTEL
NO, PENROD...
VIOLET... I CAME ALL THIS WAY TO SEE YOU...
I KNOW IT'S STUPID, BUT I WANT US TO GET MARRIED FIRST.
I'LL MARRY YOU WHENEVER YOU WANT.
YOU REALLY WILL?
OH GOD, I'M SORRY...

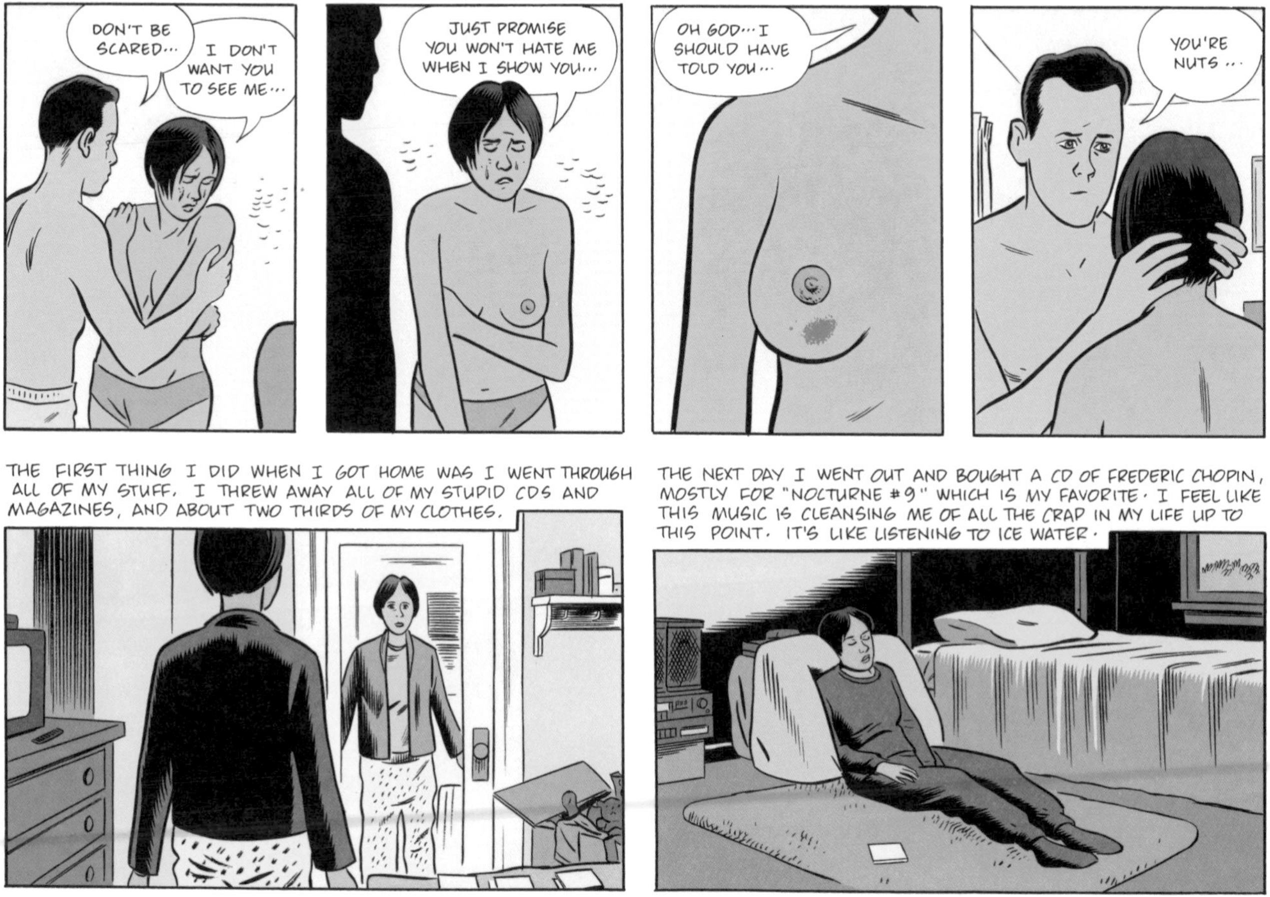
DON'T BE SCARED...
I DON'T WANT YOU TO SEE ME...
JUST PROMISE YOU WON'T HATE ME WHEN I SHOW YOU...
OH GOD... I SHOULD HAVE TOLD YOU...
YOU'RE NUTS ...
THE FIRST THING I DID WHEN I GOT HOME WAS I WENT THROUGH ALL OF MY STUFF. I THREW AWAY ALL OF MY STUPID CDS AND MAGAZINES, AND ABOUT TWO THIRDS OF MY CLOTHES.
THE NEXT DAY I WENT OUT AND BOUGHT A CD OF FREDERIC CHOPIN, MOSTLY FOR "NOCTURNE #9" WHICH IS MY FAVORITE. I FEEL LIKE THIS MUSIC IS CLEANSING ME OF ALL THE CRAP IN MY LIFE UP TO THIS POINT. IT'S LIKE LISTENING TO ICE WATER.

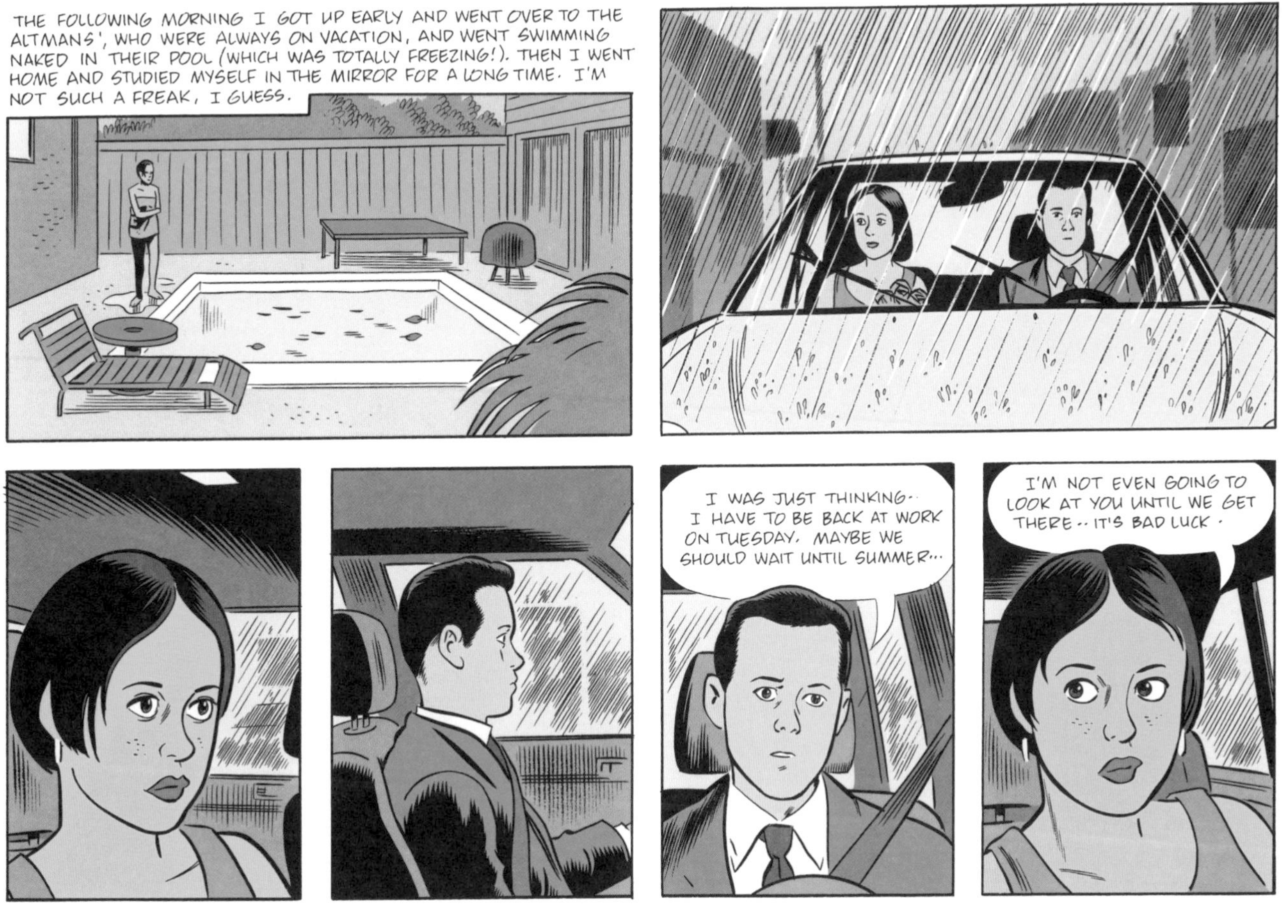
THE FOLLOWING MORNING I GOT UP EARLY AND WENT OVER TO THE ALTMANS', WHO WERE ALWAYS ON VACATION, AND WENT SWIMMING NAKED IN THEIR POOL (WHICH WAS TOTALLY FREEZING!). THEN I WENT HOME AND STUDIED MYSELF IN THE MIRROR FOR A LONG TIME. I'M NOT SUCH A FREAK, I GUESS.
I WAS JUST THINKING.. I HAVE TO BE BACK AT WORK ON TUESDAY. MAYBE WE SHOULD WAIT UNTIL SUMMER...
I'M NOT EVEN GOING TO LOOK AT YOU UNTIL WE GET THERE.. IT'S BAD LUCK.

I GUESS I DON'T NEED TO TELL YOU BUT MY LIFE HAS BEEN PRETTY HORRIBLE UP TO THIS POINT. MY REAL DAD LEFT WHEN I WAS LIKE FOUR AND MY MOM IS PRETTY MUCH A TOTAL SELFISH BITCH.

MY FRIEND JULIE THINKS IT'S CRAZY TO GET MARRIED, BUT SHE'S KIND OF BIASED AGAINST MEN. I DON'T KNOW, I MEAN, I DON'T BELIEVE IN GOD AND ALL THAT, BUT DESPITE ALL THE CRAP I'VE BEEN THROUGH IN MY LIFE, I STILL BELIEVE IN TRUE LOVE.

I'M SURE THAT SOUNDS REALLY STUPID, BUT I REALLY DO. SO MAYBE I'M STUPID.

MAYBE THIS IS A BIG MISTAKE. I WONDER WHAT PENROD IS THINKING? WHAT ARE YOU THINKING, PENROD?

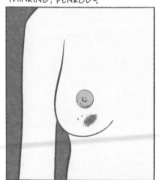

I GUESS HE WOULDN'T BE HERE IF HE DIDN'T REALLY LOVE ME. I LOVE YOU TOO, PENROD.

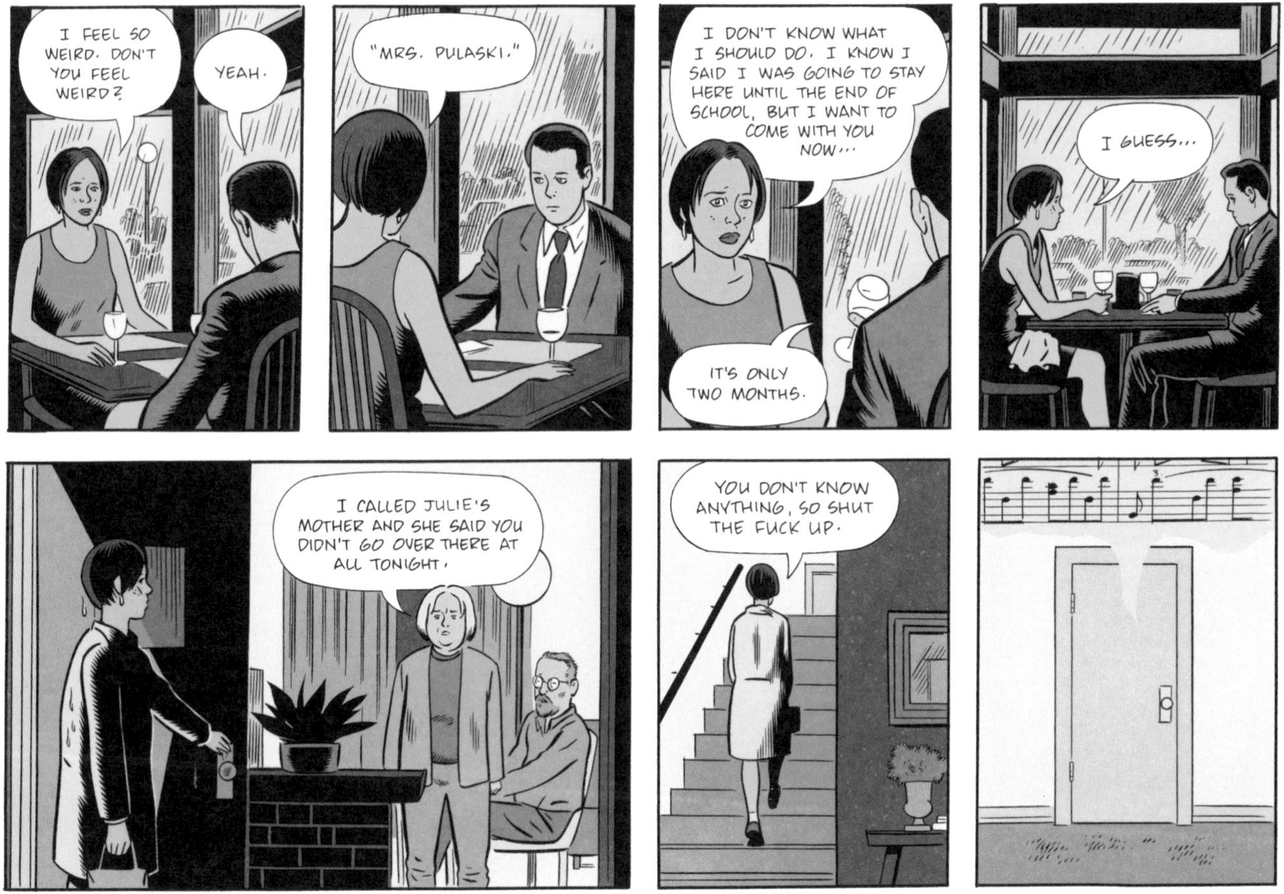
I FEEL SO WEIRD. DON'T YOU FEEL WEIRD?
YEAH.
"MRS. PULASKI."
I DON'T KNOW WHAT I SHOULD DO. I KNOW I SAID I WAS GOING TO STAY HERE UNTIL THE END OF SCHOOL, BUT I WANT TO COME WITH YOU NOW...
IT'S ONLY TWO MONTHS.
I GUESS...
I CALLED JULIE'S MOTHER AND SHE SAID YOU DIDN'T GO OVER THERE AT ALL TONIGHT.
YOU DON'T KNOW ANYTHING, SO SHUT THE FUCK UP.

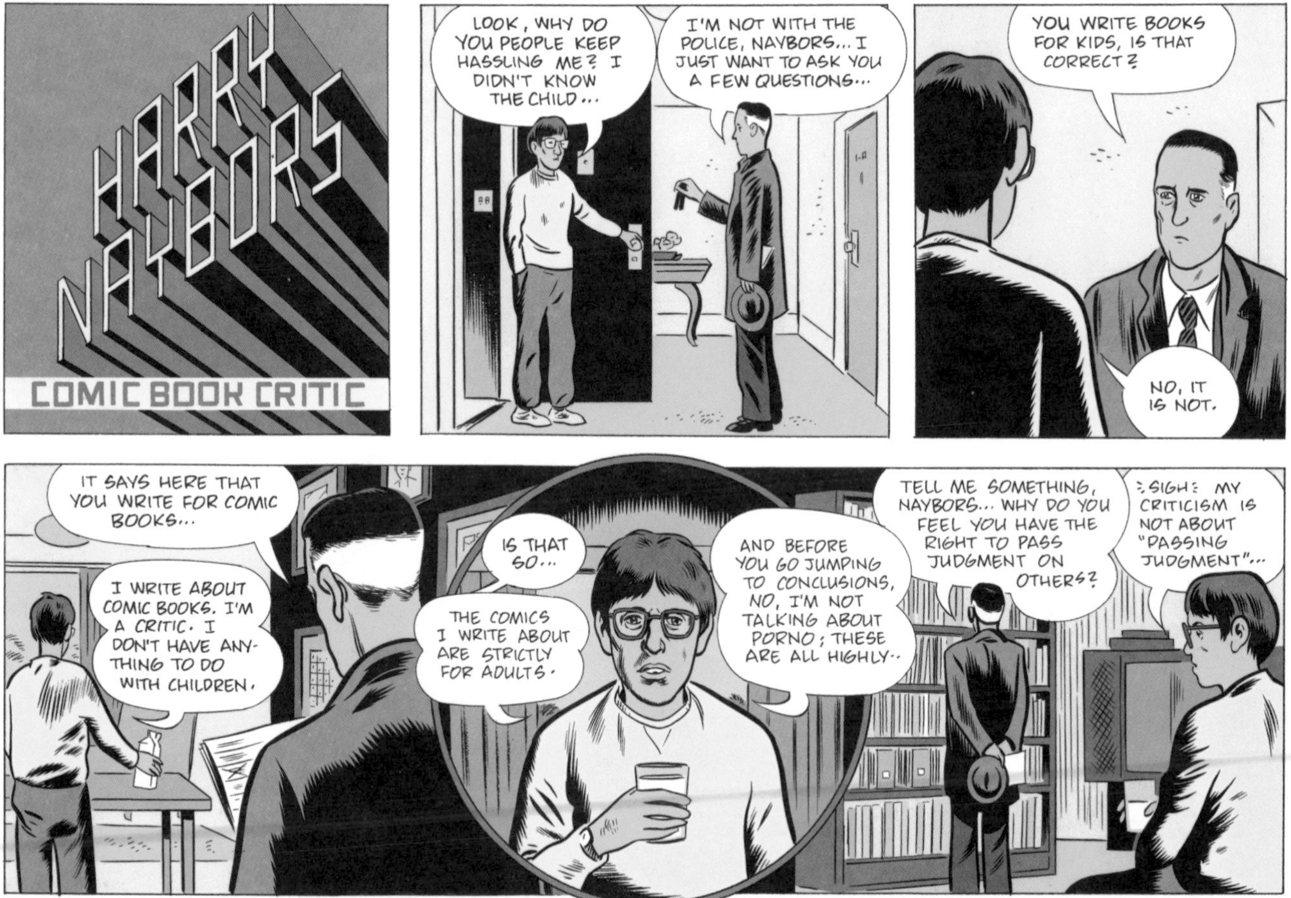
HARRY NAYBORS
COMIC BOOK CRITIC
LOOK, WHY DO YOU PEOPLE KEEP HASSLING ME? I DIDN'T KNOW THE CHILD...
I'M NOT WITH THE POLICE, NAYBORS... I JUST WANT TO ASK YOU A FEW QUESTIONS...
YOU WRITE BOOKS FOR KIDS, IS THAT CORRECT?
NO, IT IS NOT.
IT SAYS HERE THAT YOU WRITE FOR COMIC BOOKS...
I WRITE ABOUT COMIC BOOKS. I'M A CRITIC. I DON'T HAVE ANYTHING TO DO WITH CHILDREN.
IS THAT SO...
THE COMICS I WRITE ABOUT ARE STRICTLY FOR ADULTS.
AND BEFORE YOU GO JUMPING TO CONCLUSIONS, NO, I'M NOT TALKING ABOUT PORNO; THESE ARE ALL HIGHLY..
TELL ME SOMETHING, NAYBORS... WHY DO YOU FEEL YOU HAVE THE RIGHT TO PASS JUDGMENT ON OTHERS?
:SIGH: MY CRITICISM IS NOT ABOUT "PASSING JUDGMENT"...

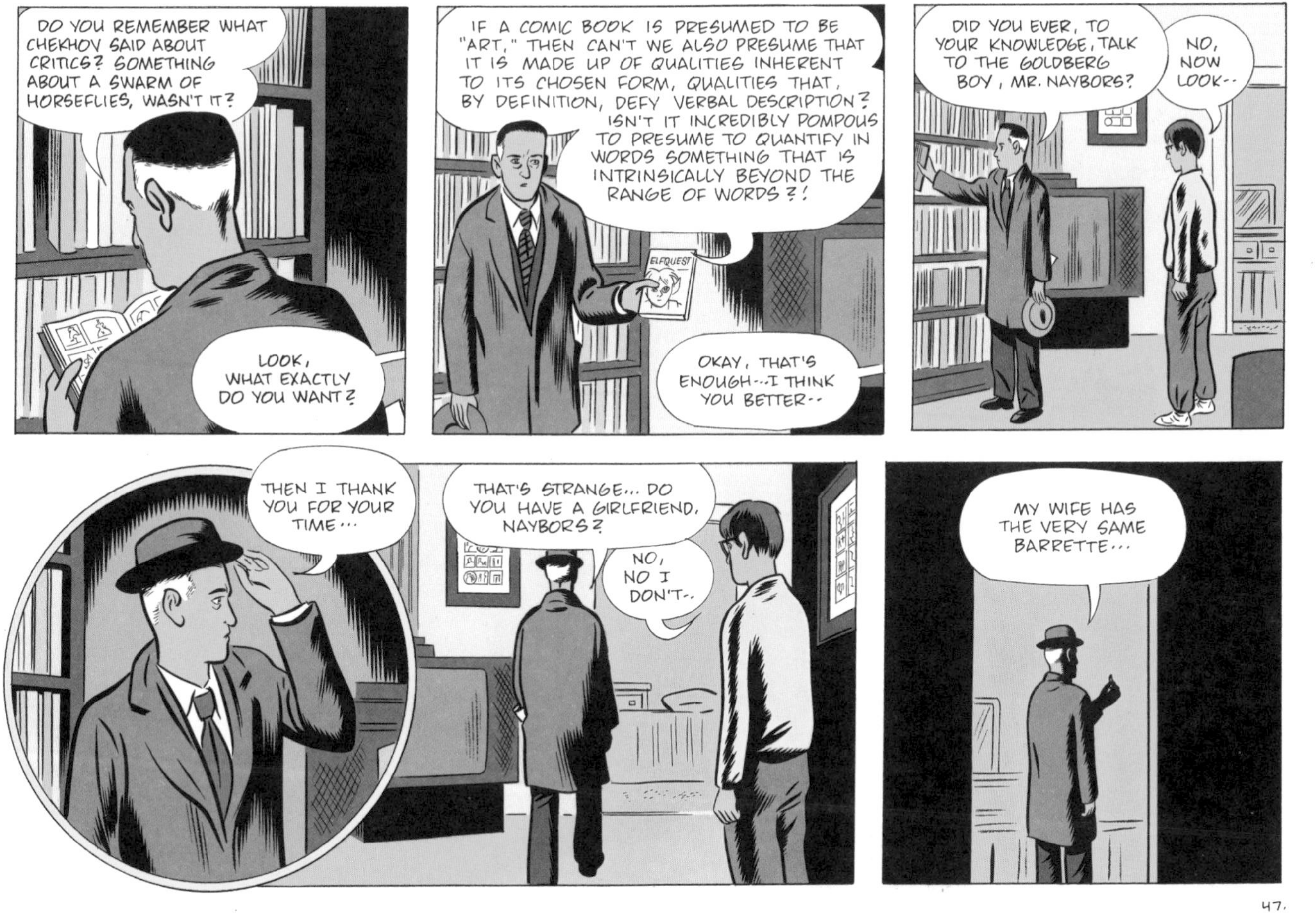
DO YOU REMEMBER WHAT CHEKHOV SAID ABOUT CRITICS? SOMETHING ABOUT A SWARM OF HORSEFLIES, WASN'T IT?
LOOK, WHAT EXACTLY DO YOU WANT?
IF A COMIC BOOK IS PRESUMED TO BE "ART," THEN CAN'T WE ALSO PRESUME THAT IT IS MADE UP OF QUALITIES INHERENT TO ITS CHOSEN FORM, QUALITIES THAT, BY DEFINITION, DEFY VERBAL DESCRIPTION? ISN'T IT INCREDIBLY POMPOUS TO PRESUME TO QUANTIFY IN WORDS SOMETHING THAT IS INTRINSICALLY BEYOND THE RANGE OF WORDS?!
ELFQUEST
OKAY, THAT'S ENOUGH--I THINK YOU BETTER--
DID YOU EVER, TO YOUR KNOWLEDGE, TALK TO THE GOLDBERG BOY, MR. NAYBORS?
NO, NOW LOOK--
THEN I THANK YOU FOR YOUR TIME...
THAT'S STRANGE... DO YOU HAVE A GIRLFRIEND, NAYBORS?
NO, NO I DON'T-.
MY WIFE HAS THE VERY SAME BARRETTE...

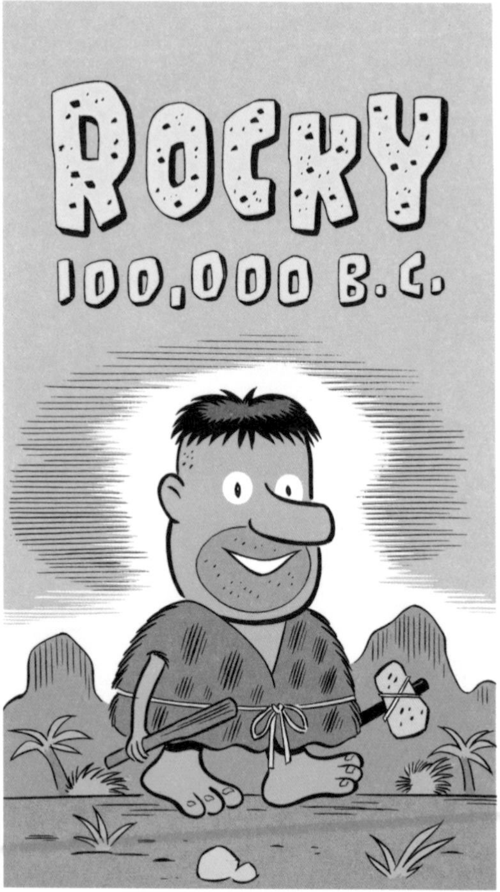
ROCKY
100,000 B.C.

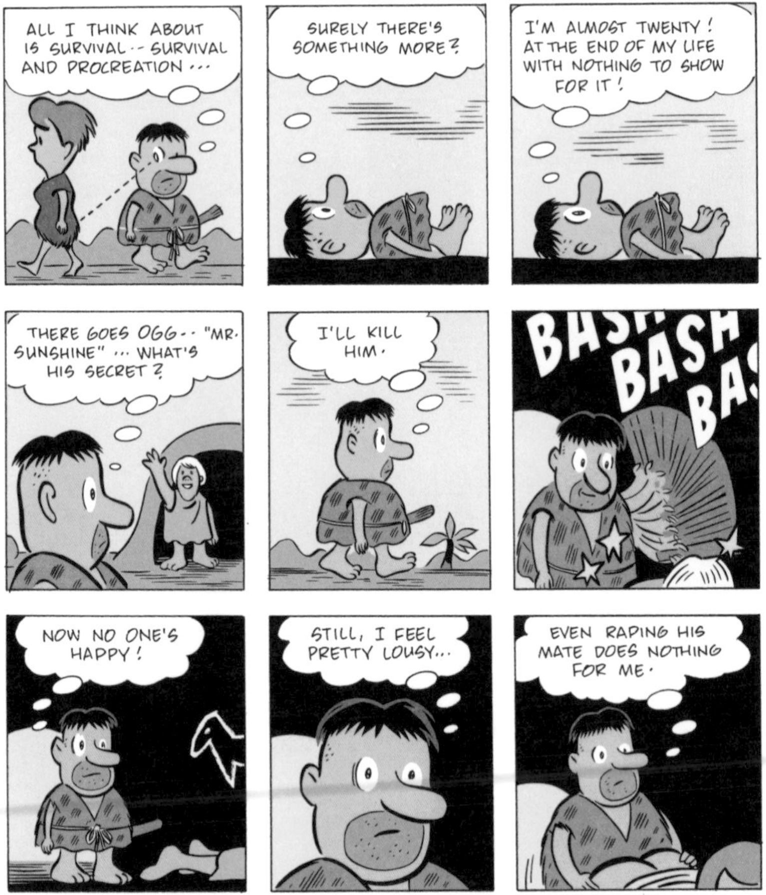
ALL I THINK ABOUT IS SURVIVAL -- SURVIVAL AND PROCREATION ...
SURELY THERE'S SOMETHING MORE?
I'M ALMOST TWENTY! AT THE END OF MY LIFE WITH NOTHING TO SHOW FOR IT!
THERE GOES OGG -- "MR. SUNSHINE" ... WHAT'S HIS SECRET?
I'LL KILL HIM.
BASH
BASH
NOW NO ONE'S HAPPY!
STILL, I FEEL PRETTY LOUSY...
EVEN RAPING HIS MATE DOES NOTHING FOR ME.

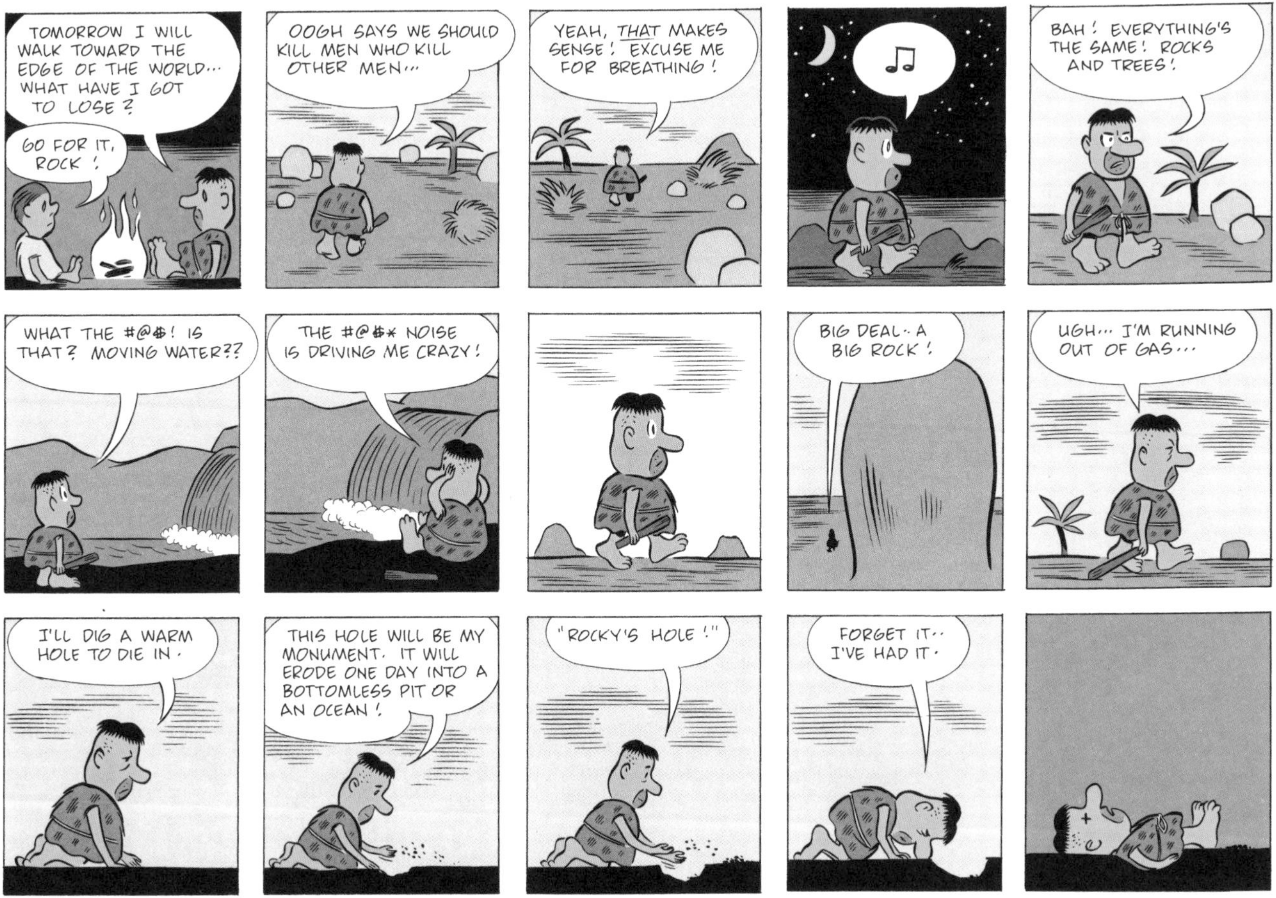
TOMORROW I WILL WALK TOWARD THE EDGE OF THE WORLD... WHAT HAVE I GOT TO LOSE?
GO FOR IT, ROCK!
OOGH SAYS WE SHOULD KILL MEN WHO KILL OTHER MEN...
YEAH, THAT MAKES SENSE! EXCUSE ME FOR BREATHING!
♫
BAH! EVERYTHING'S THE SAME! ROCKS AND TREES!
WHAT THE #@$! IS THAT? MOVING WATER??
THE #@$* NOISE IS DRIVING ME CRAZY!
BIG DEAL.. A BIG ROCK!
UGH... I'M RUNNING OUT OF GAS...
I'LL DIG A WARM HOLE TO DIE IN.
THIS HOLE WILL BE MY MONUMENT. IT WILL ERODE ONE DAY INTO A BOTTOMLESS PIT OR AN OCEAN!
"ROCKY'S HOLE!"
FORGET IT.. I'VE HAD IT.

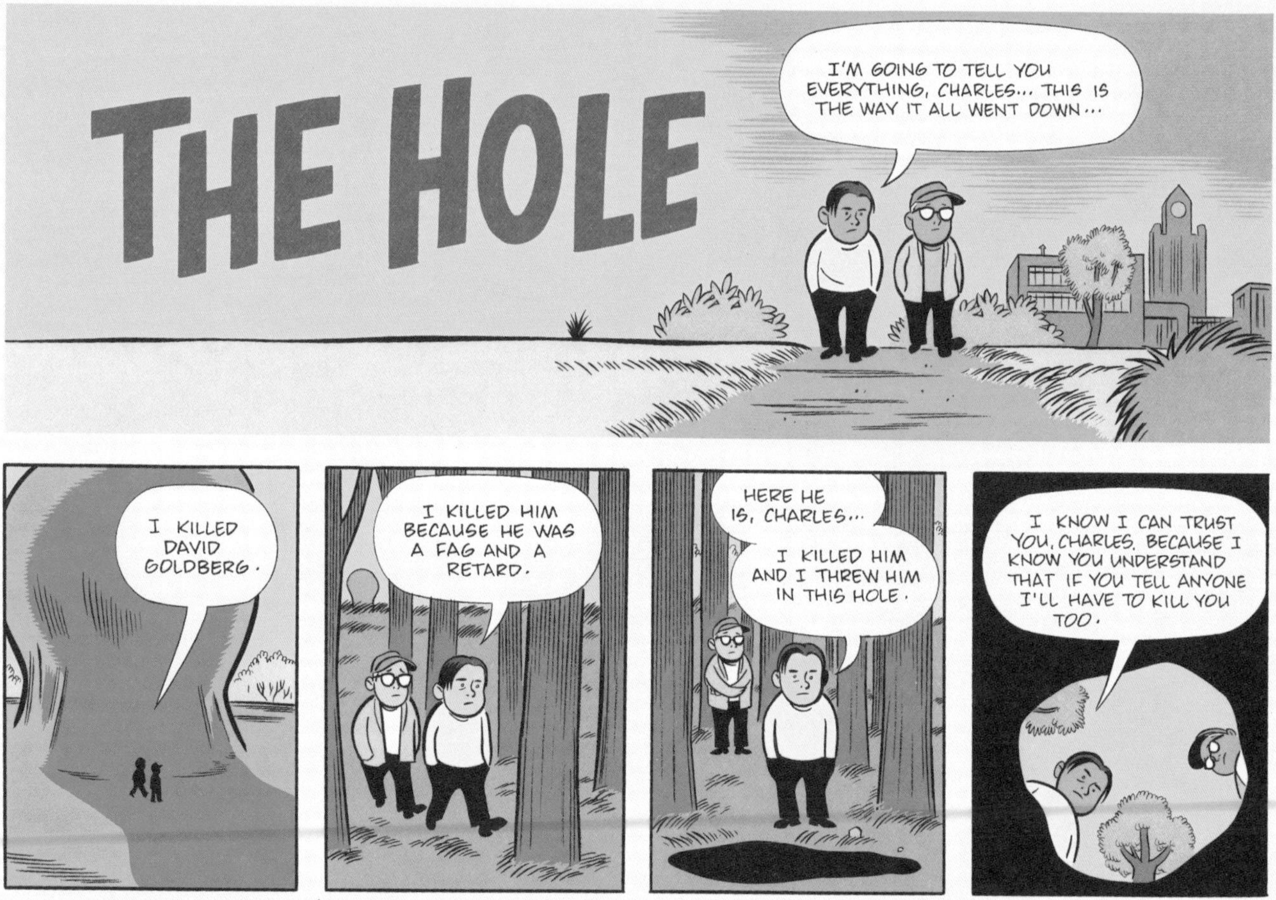
THE HOLE
I'M GOING TO TELL YOU EVERYTHING, CHARLES... THIS IS THE WAY IT ALL WENT DOWN...
I KILLED DAVID GOLDBERG.
I KILLED HIM BECAUSE HE WAS A FAG AND A RETARD.
HERE HE IS, CHARLES...
I KILLED HIM AND I THREW HIM IN THIS HOLE.
I KNOW I CAN TRUST YOU, CHARLES, BECAUSE I KNOW YOU UNDERSTAND THAT IF YOU TELL ANYONE I'LL HAVE TO KILL YOU TOO.

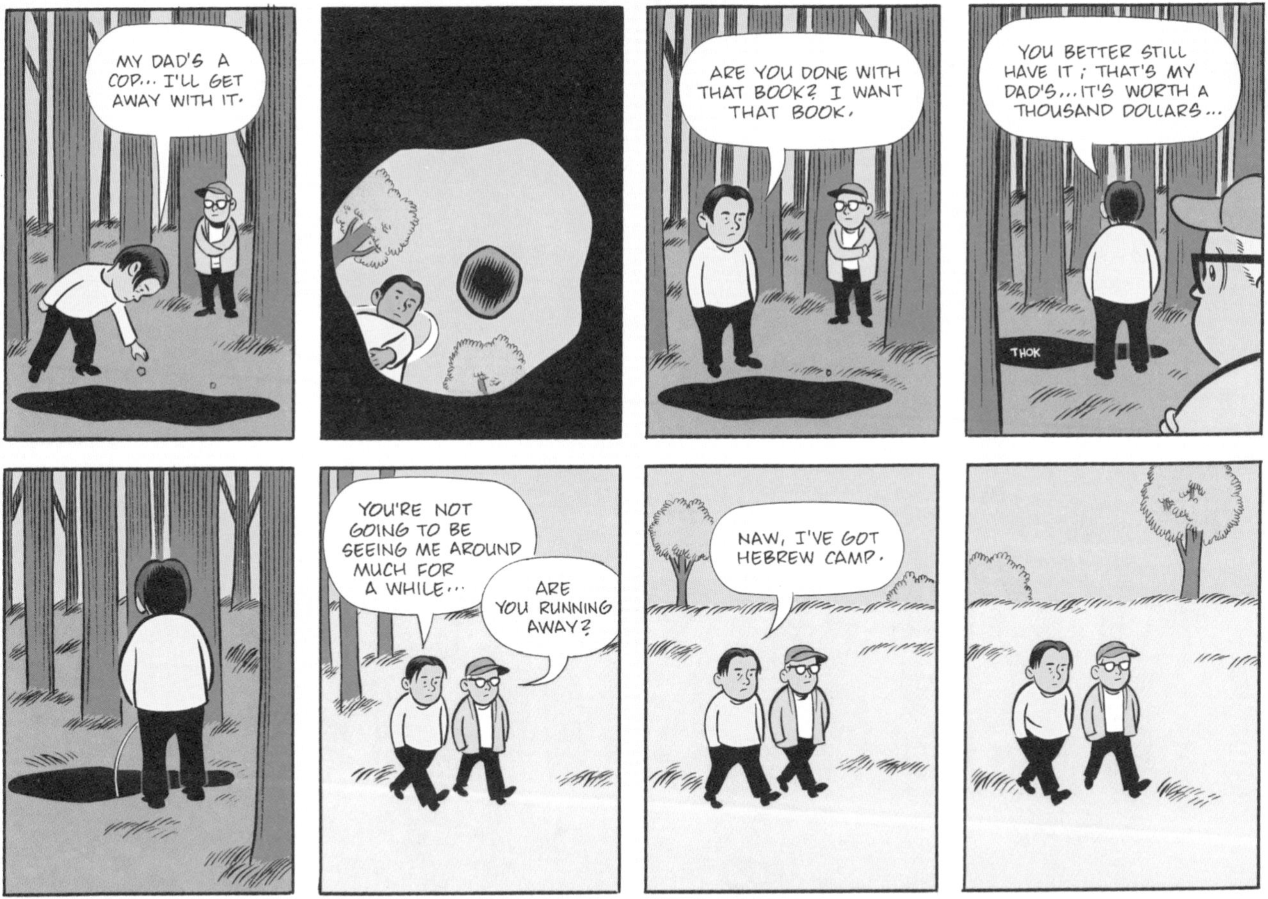
MY DAD'S A COP... I'LL GET AWAY WITH IT.
ARE YOU DONE WITH THAT BOOK? I WANT THAT BOOK.
YOU BETTER STILL HAVE IT ; THAT'S MY DAD'S... IT'S WORTH A THOUSAND DOLLARS...
THOK
YOU'RE NOT GOING TO BE SEEING ME AROUND MUCH FOR A WHILE...
ARE YOU RUNNING AWAY?
NAW, I'VE GOT HEBREW CAMP.

I'M THE GRANDDAUGHTER OF MRS. WENTZ, AND I'D . . . I'M YOUR NEW NEIGHBOR...
I'M A BIG FAN OF YOUR WORK AND I'D LIKE TO PRESENT YOU WITH THIS TOKEN OF MY ESTEEM... PRESENT TO YOU THIS...
I'M A STRUGGLING WRITER, AND I'D LIKE FOR YOU TO... I'M A BIG FAN OF YOU... OF YOUR WRITING, AND I...

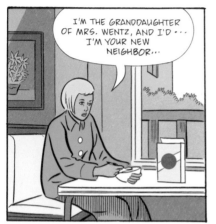

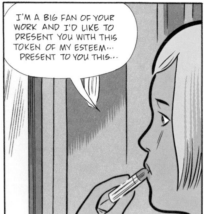

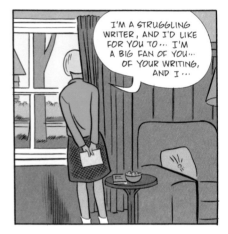

SEERSUCKER

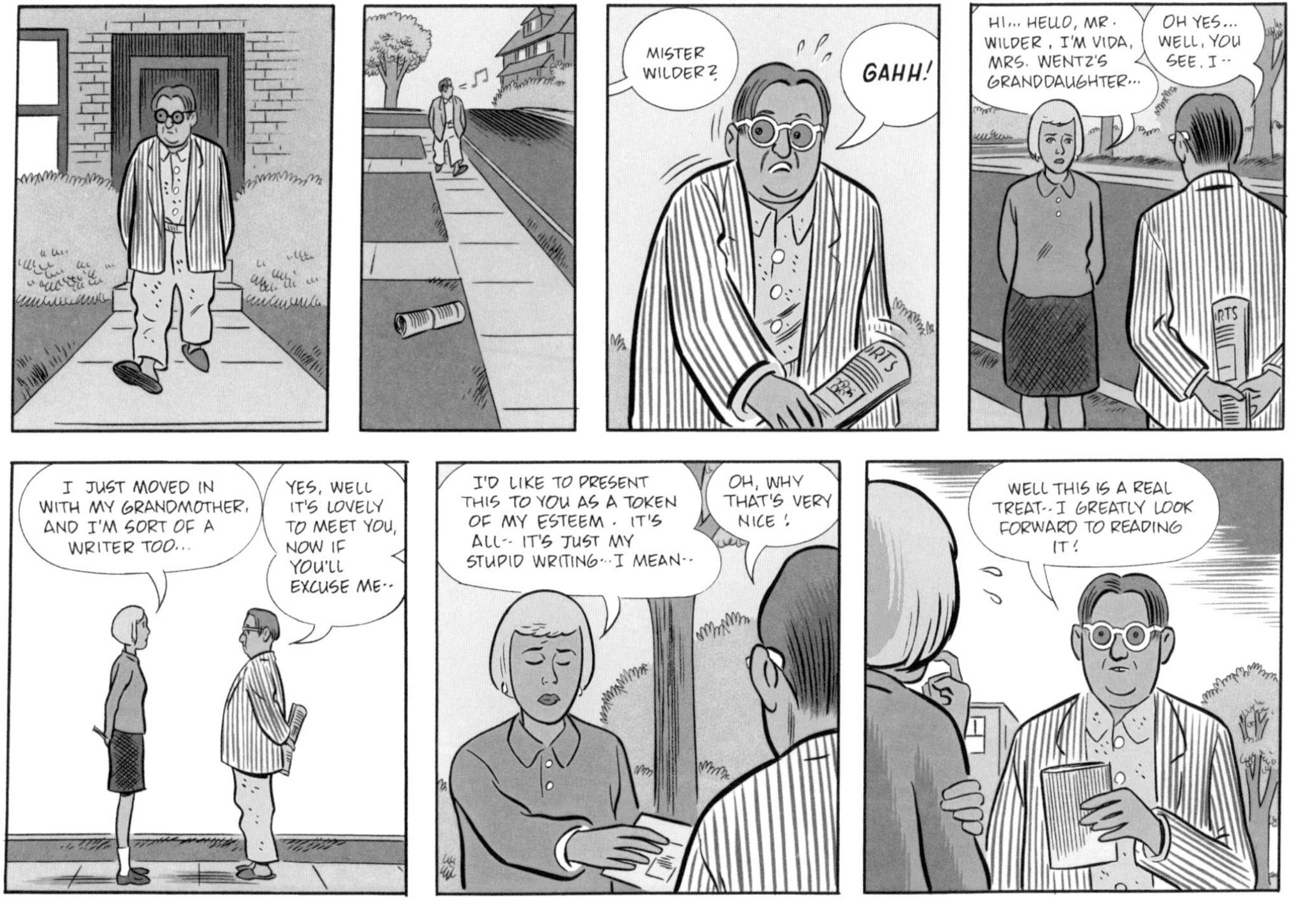
MISTER WILDER?
GAHH!
HI... HELLO, MR. WILDER, I'M VIDA, MRS. WENTZ'S GRANDDAUGHTER...
OH YES... WELL, YOU SEE, I--
RTS
I JUST MOVED IN WITH MY GRANDMOTHER, AND I'M SORT OF A WRITER TOO...
YES, WELL IT'S LOVELY TO MEET YOU, NOW IF YOU'LL EXCUSE ME--
I'D LIKE TO PRESENT THIS TO YOU AS A TOKEN OF MY ESTEEM. IT'S ALL-- IT'S JUST MY STUPID WRITING--I MEAN--
OH, WHY THAT'S VERY NICE!
WELL THIS IS A REAL TREAT--I GREATLY LOOK FORWARD TO READING IT!

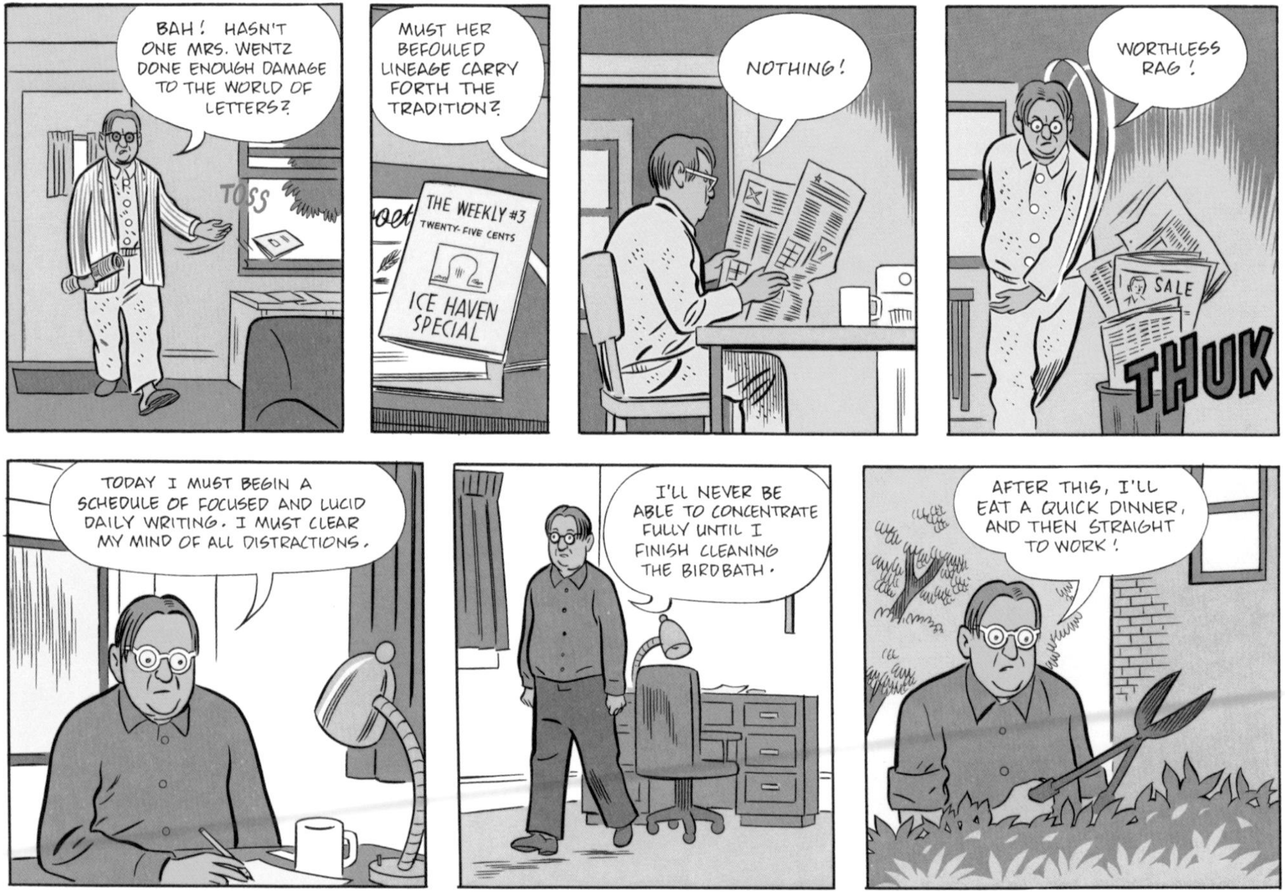
BAH! HASN'T ONE MRS. WENTZ DONE ENOUGH DAMAGE TO THE WORLD OF LETTERS?
TOSS
MUST HER BEFOULED LINEAGE CARRY FORTH THE TRADITION?
THE WEEKLY #3
TWENTY-FIVE CENTS
ICE HAVEN SPECIAL
NOTHING!
WORTHLESS RAG!
SALE
THUK
TODAY I MUST BEGIN A SCHEDULE OF FOCUSED AND LUCID DAILY WRITING. I MUST CLEAR MY MIND OF ALL DISTRACTIONS.
I'LL NEVER BE ABLE TO CONCENTRATE FULLY UNTIL I FINISH CLEANING THE BIRDBATH.
AFTER THIS, I'LL EAT A QUICK DINNER, AND THEN STRAIGHT TO WORK!

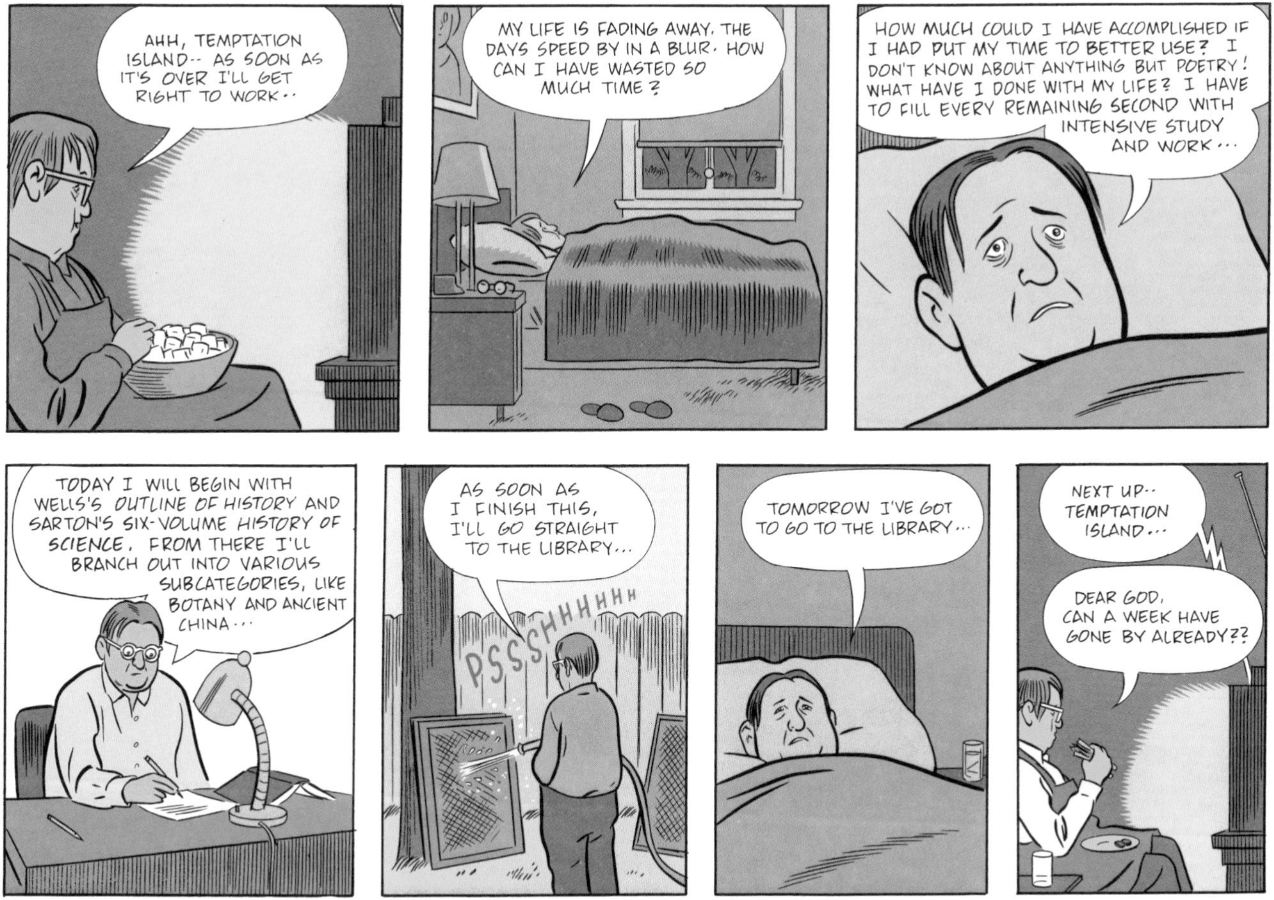
AHH, TEMPTATION ISLAND-- AS SOON AS IT'S OVER I'LL GET RIGHT TO WORK..
MY LIFE IS FADING AWAY. THE DAYS SPEED BY IN A BLUR. HOW CAN I HAVE WASTED SO MUCH TIME?
HOW MUCH COULD I HAVE ACCOMPLISHED IF I HAD PUT MY TIME TO BETTER USE? I DON'T KNOW ABOUT ANYTHING BUT POETRY! WHAT HAVE I DONE WITH MY LIFE? I HAVE TO FILL EVERY REMAINING SECOND WITH INTENSIVE STUDY AND WORK...
TODAY I WILL BEGIN WITH WELLS'S OUTLINE OF HISTORY AND SARTON'S SIX-VOLUME HISTORY OF SCIENCE. FROM THERE I'LL BRANCH OUT INTO VARIOUS SUBCATEGORIES, LIKE BOTANY AND ANCIENT CHINA...
AS SOON AS I FINISH THIS, I'LL GO STRAIGHT TO THE LIBRARY...
PSSSHHHHHH
TOMORROW I'VE GOT TO GO TO THE LIBRARY...
NEXT UP.. TEMPTATION ISLAND...
DEAR GOD, CAN A WEEK HAVE GONE BY ALREADY??

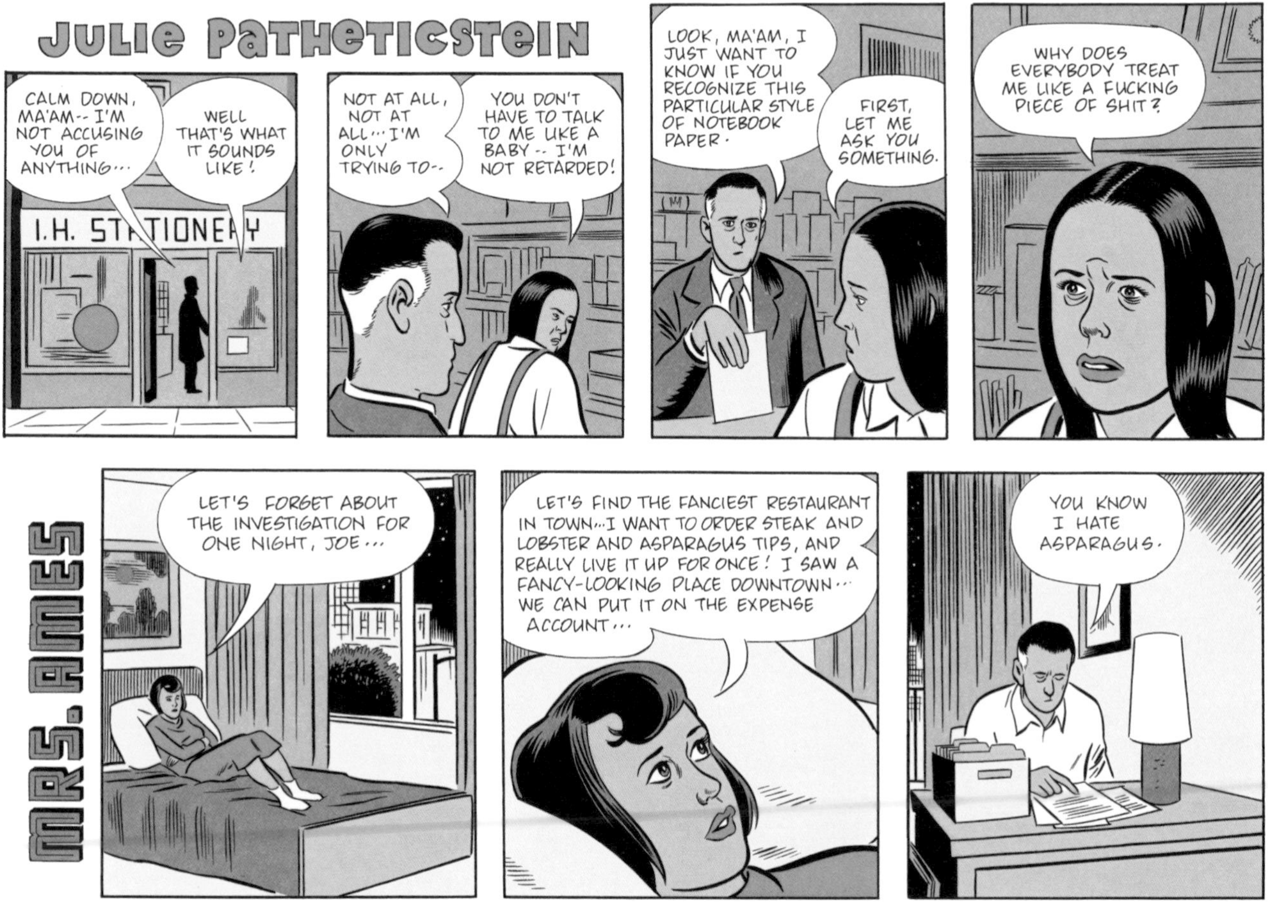
JULIE PATHETICSTEIN
CALM DOWN, MA'AM -- I'M NOT ACCUSING YOU OF ANYTHING...
WELL THAT'S WHAT IT SOUNDS LIKE!
I.H. STATIONERY
NOT AT ALL, NOT AT ALL... I'M ONLY TRYING TO--
YOU DON'T HAVE TO TALK TO ME LIKE A BABY -- I'M NOT RETARDED!
LOOK, MA'AM, I JUST WANT TO KNOW IF YOU RECOGNIZE THIS PARTICULAR STYLE OF NOTEBOOK PAPER.
FIRST, LET ME ASK YOU SOMETHING.
WHY DOES EVERYBODY TREAT ME LIKE A FUCKING PIECE OF SHIT?
MRS. AMES
LET'S FORGET ABOUT THE INVESTIGATION FOR ONE NIGHT, JOE...
LET'S FIND THE FANCIEST RESTAURANT IN TOWN... I WANT TO ORDER STEAK AND LOBSTER AND ASPARAGUS TIPS, AND REALLY LIVE IT UP FOR ONCE! I SAW A FANCY-LOOKING PLACE DOWNTOWN... WE CAN PUT IT ON THE EXPENSE ACCOUNT...
YOU KNOW I HATE ASPARAGUS.

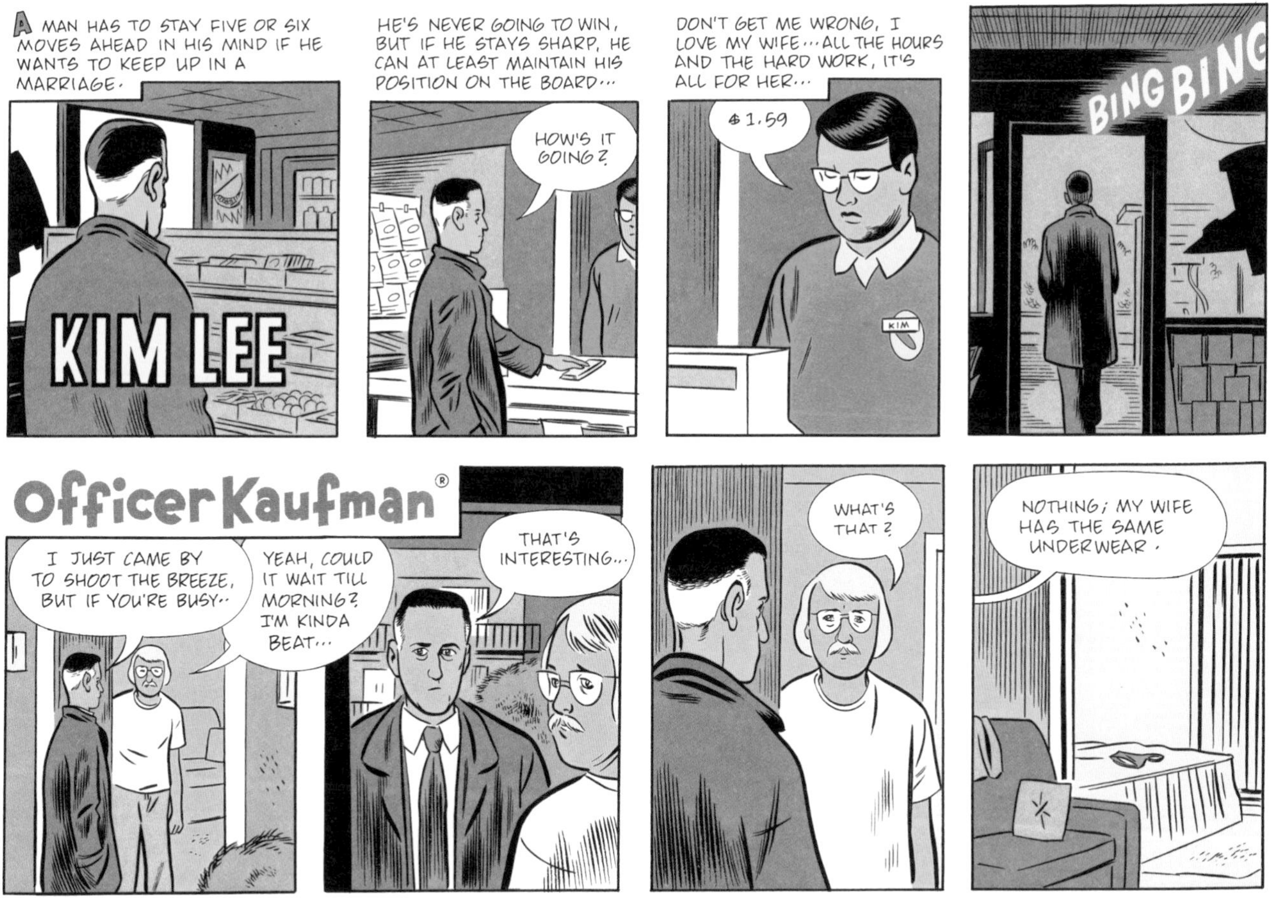
A MAN HAS TO STAY FIVE OR SIX MOVES AHEAD IN HIS MIND IF HE WANTS TO KEEP UP IN A MARRIAGE.
KIM LEE
HE'S NEVER GOING TO WIN, BUT IF HE STAYS SHARP, HE CAN AT LEAST MAINTAIN HIS POSITION ON THE BOARD...
HOW'S IT GOING?
DON'T GET ME WRONG, I LOVE MY WIFE... ALL THE HOURS AND THE HARD WORK, IT'S ALL FOR HER...
$ 1.59
KIM
BING BING
Officer Kaufman®
I JUST CAME BY TO SHOOT THE BREEZE, BUT IF YOU'RE BUSY..
YEAH, COULD IT WAIT TILL MORNING? I'M KINDA BEAT...
THAT'S INTERESTING...
WHAT'S THAT?
NOTHING; MY WIFE HAS THE SAME UNDERWEAR.

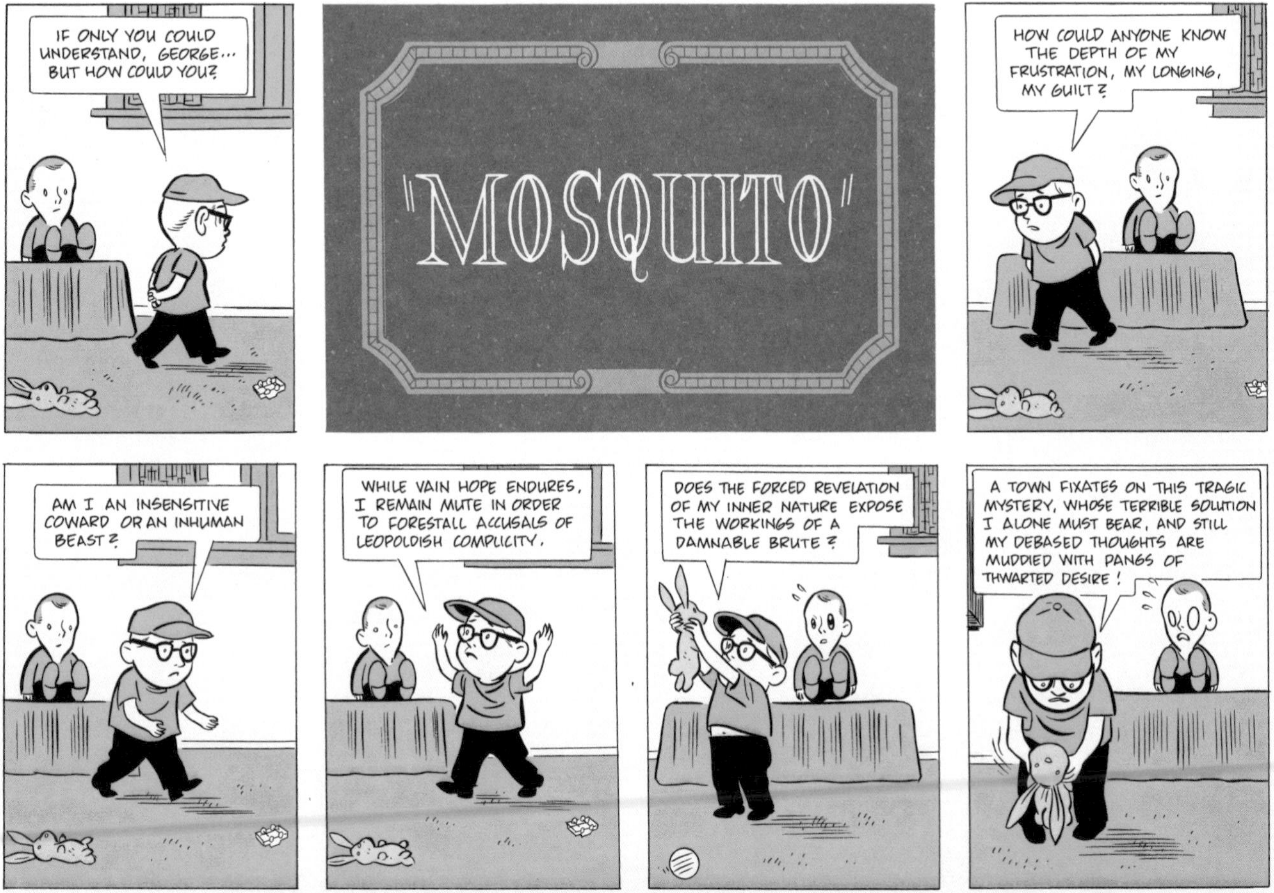
IF ONLY YOU COULD UNDERSTAND, GEORGE... BUT HOW COULD YOU?
"MOSQUITO"
HOW COULD ANYONE KNOW THE DEPTH OF MY FRUSTRATION, MY LONGING, MY GUILT?
AM I AN INSENSITIVE COWARD OR AN INHUMAN BEAST?
WHILE VAIN HOPE ENDURES, I REMAIN MUTE IN ORDER TO FORESTALL ACCUSALS OF LEOPOLDISH COMPLICITY.
DOES THE FORCED REVELATION OF MY INNER NATURE EXPOSE THE WORKINGS OF A DAMNABLE BRUTE?
A TOWN FIXATES ON THIS TRAGIC MYSTERY, WHOSE TERRIBLE SOLUTION I ALONE MUST BEAR, AND STILL MY DEBASED THOUGHTS ARE MUDDIED WITH PANGS OF THWARTED DESIRE!

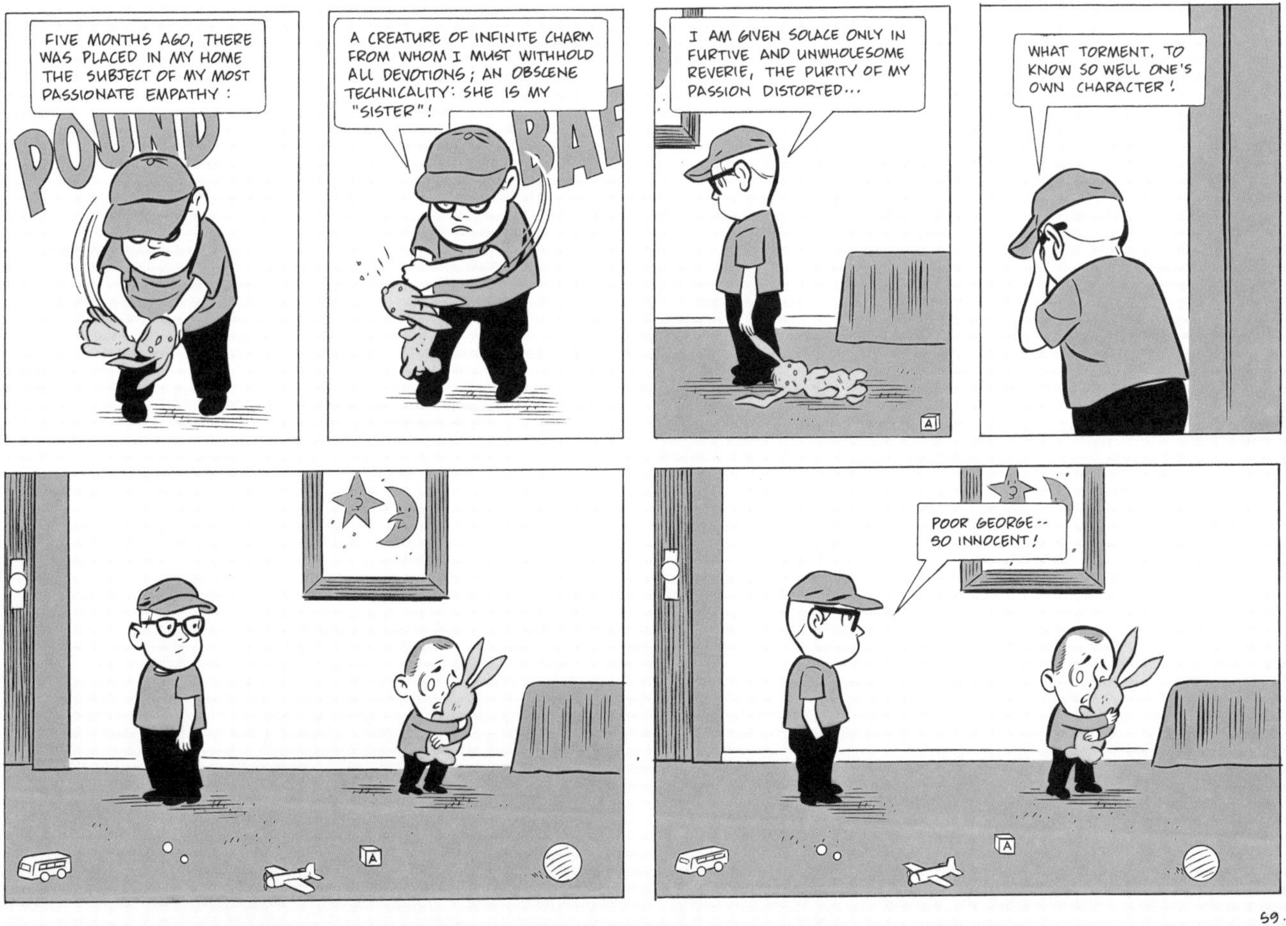
FIVE MONTHS AGO, THERE WAS PLACED IN MY HOME THE SUBJECT OF MY MOST PASSIONATE EMPATHY :
POUND
A CREATURE OF INFINITE CHARM FROM WHOM I MUST WITHHOLD ALL DEVOTIONS ; AN OBSCENE TECHNICALITY: SHE IS MY "SISTER"!
BAF
I AM GIVEN SOLACE ONLY IN FURTIVE AND UNWHOLESOME REVERIE, THE PURITY OF MY PASSION DISTORTED...
A
WHAT TORMENT, TO KNOW SO WELL ONE'S OWN CHARACTER!
A
POOR GEORGE -- SO INNOCENT!
A

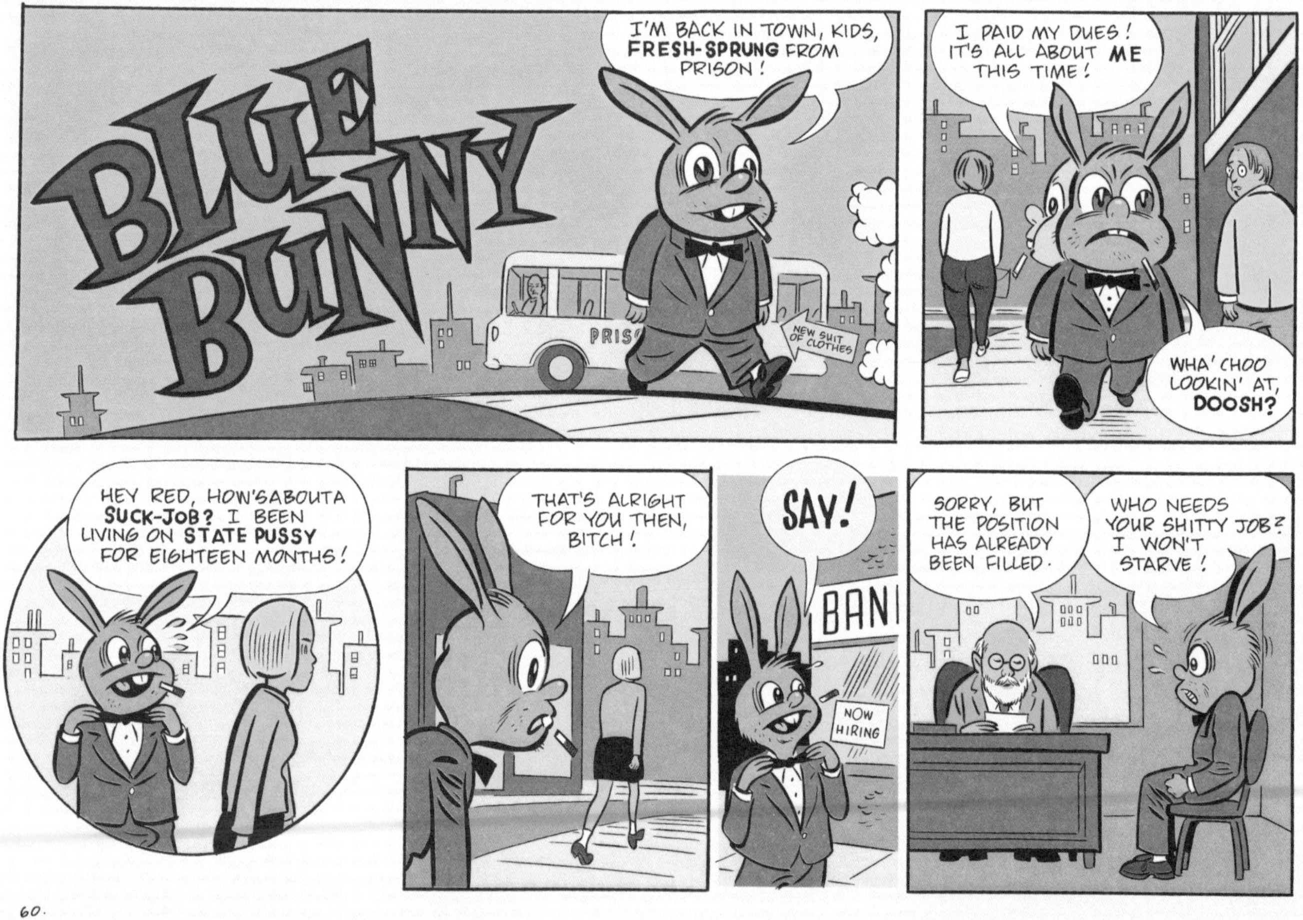
BLUE BUNNY
I'M BACK IN TOWN, KIDS, FRESH-SPRUNG FROM PRISON!
PRIS
NEW SUIT OF CLOTHES
I PAID MY DUES! IT'S ALL ABOUT ME THIS TIME!
WHA' CHOO LOOKIN' AT, DOOSH?
HEY RED, HOW'SABOUTA SUCK-JOB? I BEEN LIVING ON STATE PUSSY FOR EIGHTEEN MONTHS!
THAT'S ALRIGHT FOR YOU THEN, BITCH!
SAY!
BAN
NOW HIRING
SORRY, BUT THE POSITION HAS ALREADY BEEN FILLED.
WHO NEEDS YOUR SHITTY JOB? I WON'T STARVE!

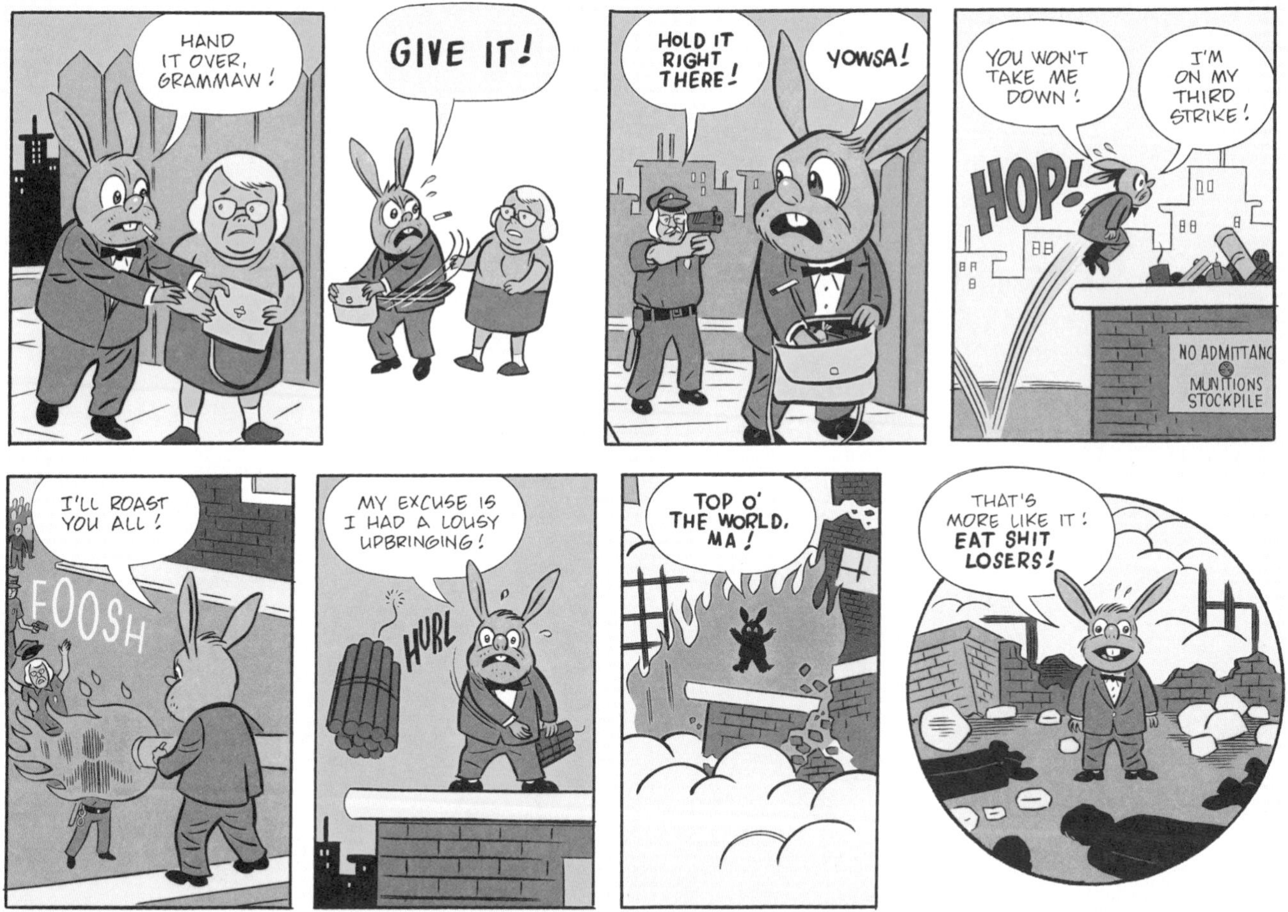
HAND IT OVER, GRAMMAW!
GIVE IT!
HOLD IT RIGHT THERE!
YOWSA!
YOU WON'T TAKE ME DOWN!
I'M ON MY THIRD STRIKE!
HOP!
NO ADMITTANC
MUNITIONS STOCKPILE
I'LL ROAST YOU ALL!
FOOSH
MY EXCUSE IS I HAD A LOUSY UPBRINGING!
HURL
TOP O' THE WORLD, MA!
THAT'S MORE LIKE IT! EAT SHIT LOSERS!

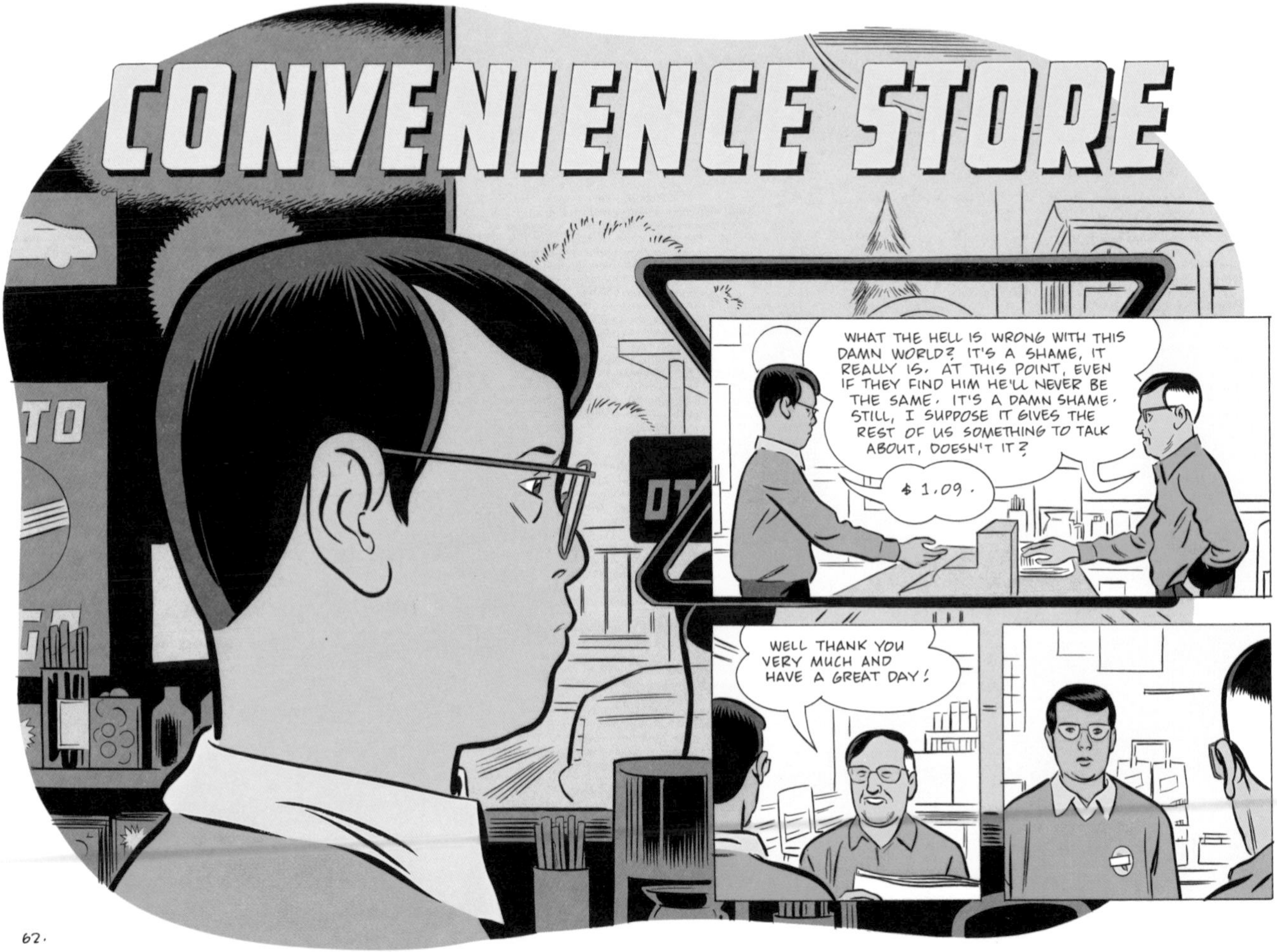
CONVENIENCE STORE
WHAT THE HELL IS WRONG WITH THIS DAMN WORLD? IT'S A SHAME, IT REALLY IS. AT THIS POINT, EVEN IF THEY FIND HIM HE'LL NEVER BE THE SAME. IT'S A DAMN SHAME. STILL, I SUPPOSE IT GIVES THE REST OF US SOMETHING TO TALK ABOUT, DOESN'T IT?
$ 1.09.
WELL THANK YOU VERY MUCH AND HAVE A GREAT DAY!

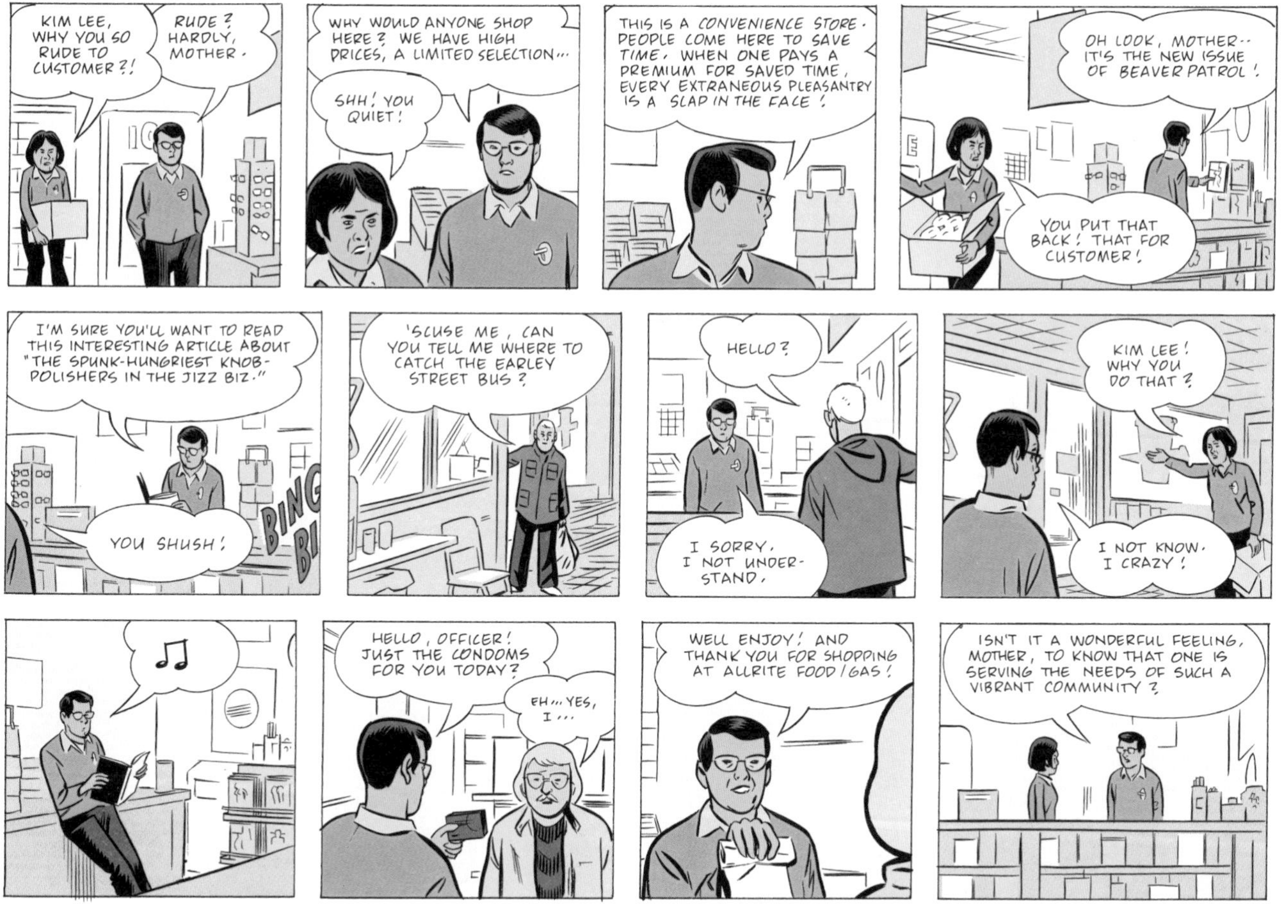
KIM LEE, WHY YOU SO RUDE TO CUSTOMER?!
RUDE? HARDLY, MOTHER.
WHY WOULD ANYONE SHOP HERE? WE HAVE HIGH PRICES, A LIMITED SELECTION...
SHH! YOU QUIET!
THIS IS A CONVENIENCE STORE. PEOPLE COME HERE TO SAVE TIME. WHEN ONE PAYS A PREMIUM FOR SAVED TIME, EVERY EXTRANEOUS PLEASANTRY IS A SLAP IN THE FACE!
OH LOOK, MOTHER.. IT'S THE NEW ISSUE OF BEAVER PATROL!
YOU PUT THAT BACK! THAT FOR CUSTOMER!
I'M SURE YOU'LL WANT TO READ THIS INTERESTING ARTICLE ABOUT "THE SPUNK-HUNGRIEST KNOB-POLISHERS IN THE JIZZ BIZ."
YOU SHUSH!
BING
'SCUSE ME, CAN YOU TELL ME WHERE TO CATCH THE EARLEY STREET BUS?
HELLO?
I SORRY. I NOT UNDER-STAND.
KIM LEE! WHY YOU DO THAT?
I NOT KNOW. I CRAZY!
♫
HELLO, OFFICER! JUST THE CONDOMS FOR YOU TODAY?
EH... YES, I...
WELL ENJOY! AND THANK YOU FOR SHOPPING AT ALLRITE FOOD/GAS!
ISN'T IT A WONDERFUL FEELING, MOTHER, TO KNOW THAT ONE IS SERVING THE NEEDS OF SUCH A VIBRANT COMMUNITY?

Random Wilder IN TOILET TIME

I CAN'T HOLD OUT MUCH LONGER!

NOT A MOMENT TOO SOON!

SURELY THERE'S SOMETHING IN THIS HOUSE I HAVEN'T READ!

RIFFLE

I'D SETTLE FOR A GARDENING CATALOG!

C'MON... C'MON!

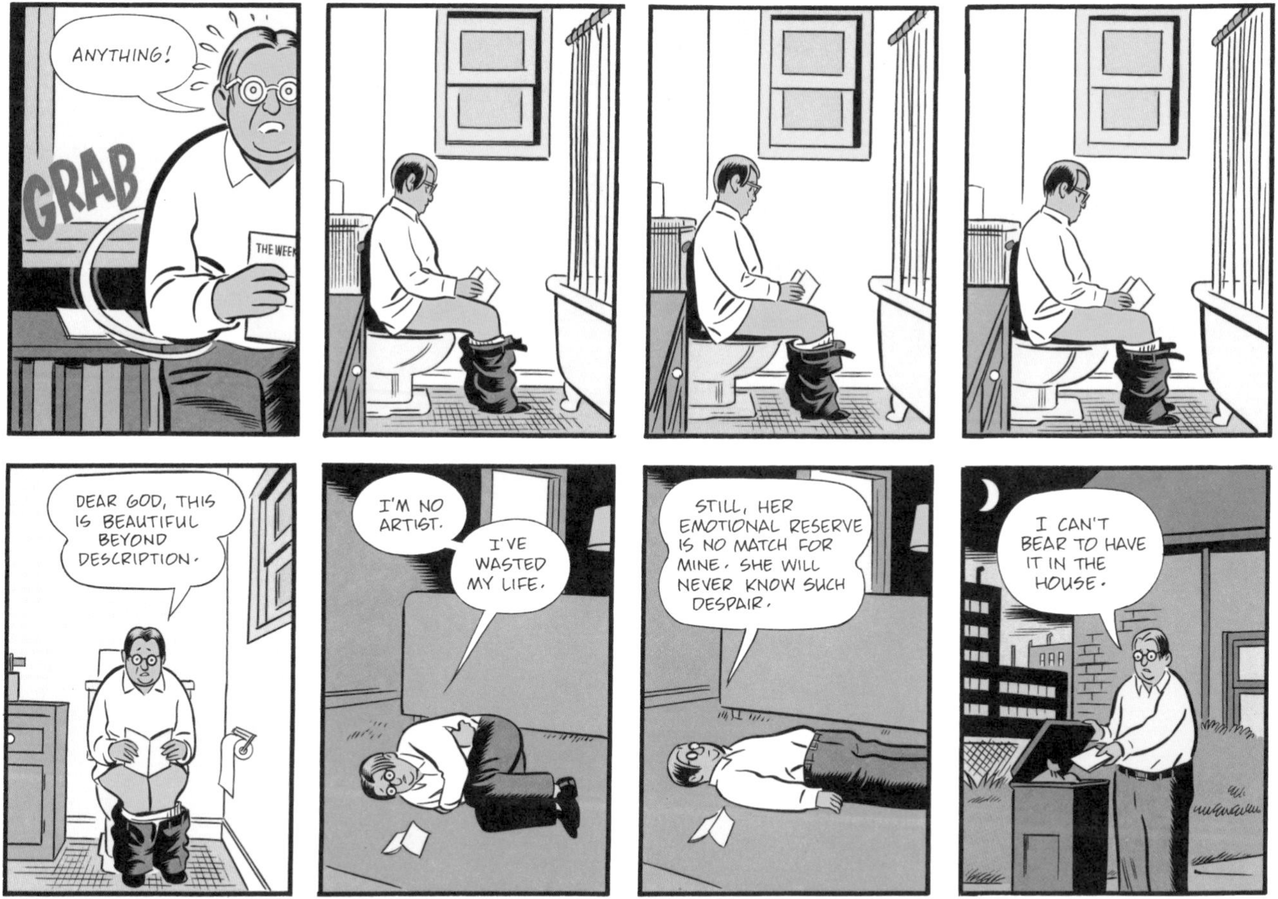
ANYTHING!
GRAB
THE WEEK
DEAR GOD, THIS IS BEAUTIFUL BEYOND DESCRIPTION.
I'M NO ARTIST.
I'VE WASTED MY LIFE.
STILL, HER EMOTIONAL RESERVE IS NO MATCH FOR MINE. SHE WILL NEVER KNOW SUCH DESPAIR.
I CAN'T BEAR TO HAVE IT IN THE HOUSE.

CHARLES and his THERAPIST

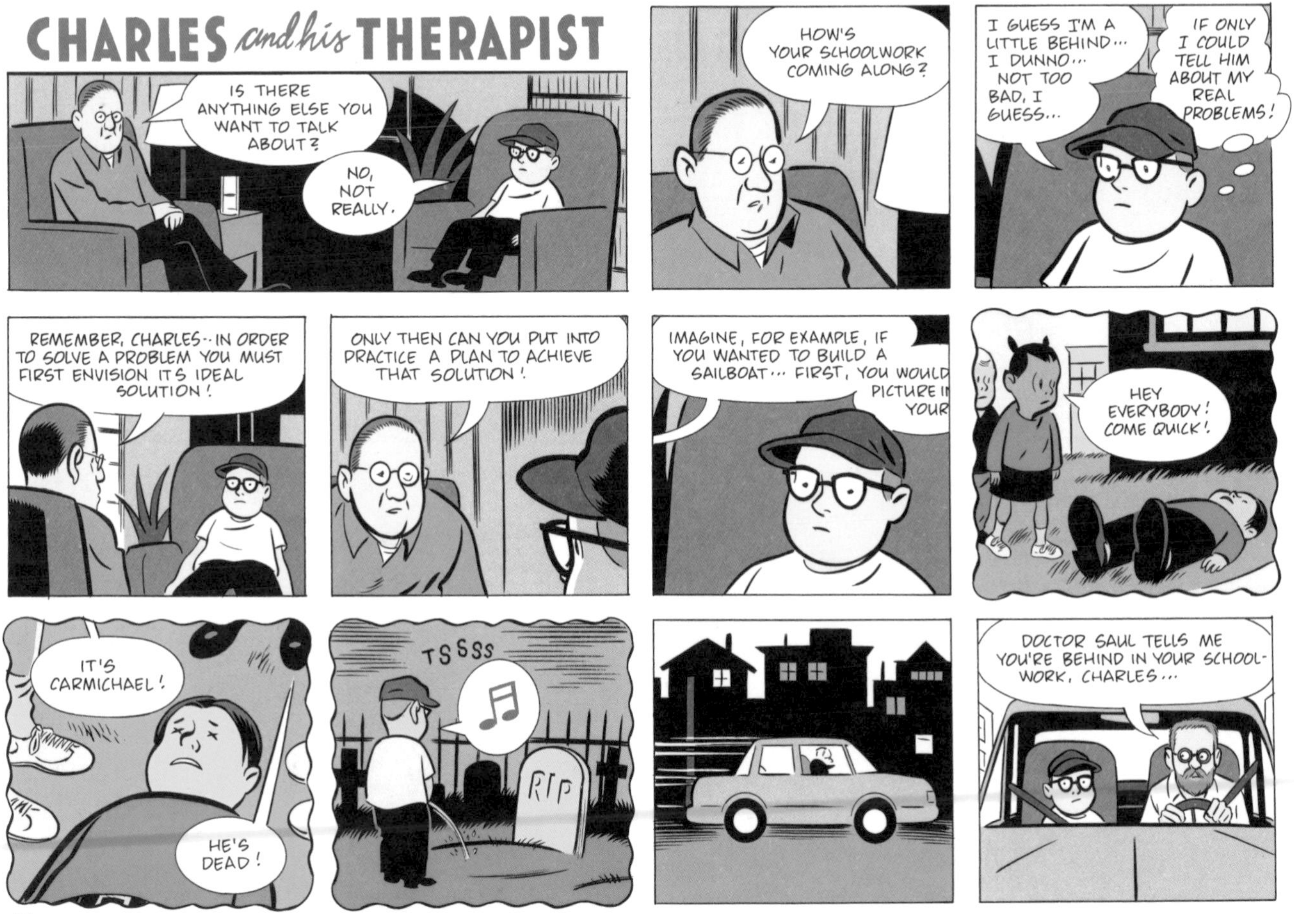
IS THERE ANYTHING ELSE YOU WANT TO TALK ABOUT?
NO, NOT REALLY.
HOW'S YOUR SCHOOLWORK COMING ALONG?
I GUESS I'M A LITTLE BEHIND... I DUNNO... NOT TOO BAD, I GUESS...
IF ONLY I COULD TELL HIM ABOUT MY REAL PROBLEMS!
REMEMBER, CHARLES.. IN ORDER TO SOLVE A PROBLEM YOU MUST FIRST ENVISION ITS IDEAL SOLUTION!
ONLY THEN CAN YOU PUT INTO PRACTICE A PLAN TO ACHIEVE THAT SOLUTION!
IMAGINE, FOR EXAMPLE, IF YOU WANTED TO BUILD A SAILBOAT... FIRST, YOU WOULD PICTURE IN YOUR
HEY EVERYBODY! COME QUICK!
IT'S CARMICHAEL!
HE'S DEAD!
TSSSS
RIP
DOCTOR SAUL TELLS ME YOU'RE BEHIND IN YOUR SCHOOL-WORK, CHARLES...

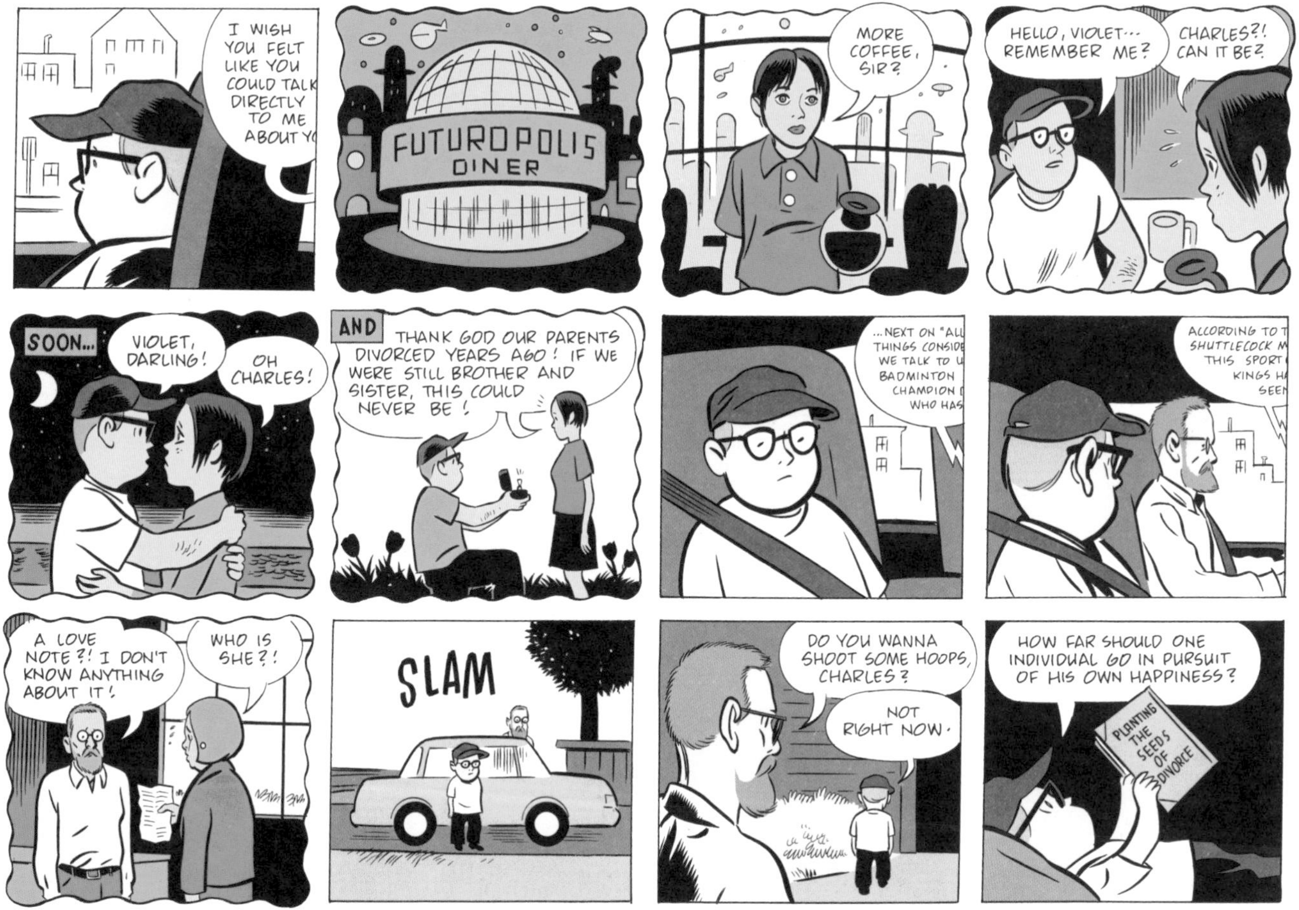
I WISH YOU FELT LIKE YOU COULD TALK DIRECTLY TO ME ABOUT YO
FUTUROPOLIS DINER
MORE COFFEE, SIR?
HELLO, VIOLET... REMEMBER ME?
CHARLES?! CAN IT BE?
SOON...
VIOLET, DARLING!
OH CHARLES!
AND
THANK GOD OUR PARENTS DIVORCED YEARS AGO! IF WE WERE STILL BROTHER AND SISTER, THIS COULD NEVER BE!
...NEXT ON "ALL THINGS CONSIDE WE TALK TO U BADMINTON CHAMPION WHO HAS
ACCORDING TO T SHUTTLECOCK M THIS SPORT KINGS HA SEEN
A LOVE NOTE?! I DON'T KNOW ANYTHING ABOUT IT!
WHO IS SHE?!
SLAM
DO YOU WANNA SHOOT SOME HOOPS, CHARLES?
NOT RIGHT NOW.
HOW FAR SHOULD ONE INDIVIDUAL GO IN PURSUIT OF HIS OWN HAPPINESS?
PLANTING THE SEEDS OF DIVORCE

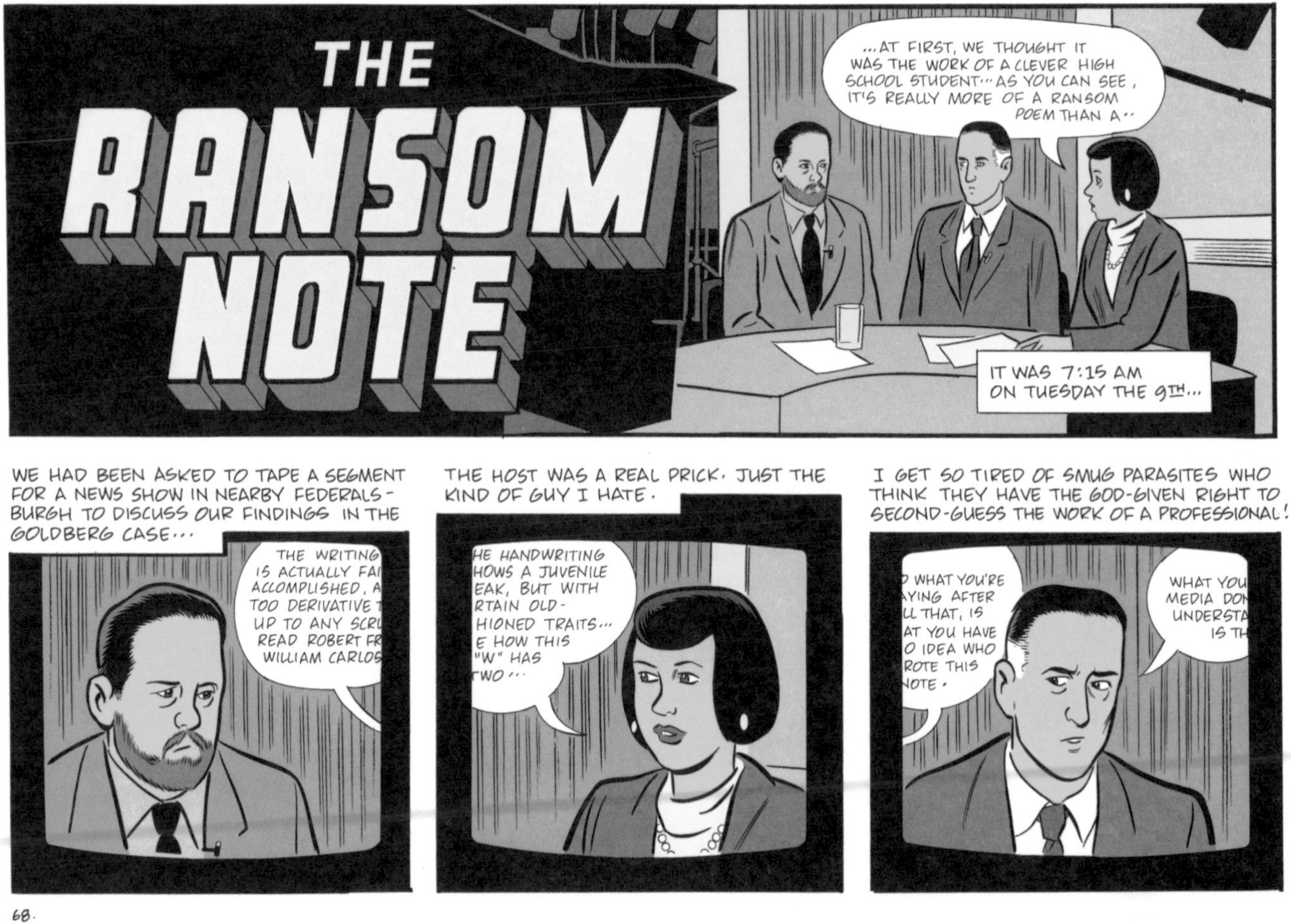
THE RANSOM NOTE
...AT FIRST, WE THOUGHT IT WAS THE WORK OF A CLEVER HIGH SCHOOL STUDENT... AS YOU CAN SEE, IT'S REALLY MORE OF A RANSOM POEM THAN A...
IT WAS 7:15 AM ON TUESDAY THE 9TH...
WE HAD BEEN ASKED TO TAPE A SEGMENT FOR A NEWS SHOW IN NEARBY FEDERALSBURGH TO DISCUSS OUR FINDINGS IN THE GOLDBERG CASE...
THE WRITING IS ACTUALLY FAI ACCOMPLISHED, A TOO DERIVATIVE T UP TO ANY SCRU READ ROBERT FR WILLIAM CARLOS
THE HOST WAS A REAL PRICK. JUST THE KIND OF GUY I HATE.
HE HANDWRITING HOWS A JUVENILE EAK, BUT WITH RTAIN OLD-HIONED TRAITS... E HOW THIS "W" HAS TWO...
I GET SO TIRED OF SMUG PARASITES WHO THINK THEY HAVE THE GOD-GIVEN RIGHT TO SECOND-GUESS THE WORK OF A PROFESSIONAL!
WHAT YOU'RE AYING AFTER LL THAT, IS AT YOU HAVE O IDEA WHO ROTE THIS NOTE.
WHAT YOU MEDIA DON UNDERSTA IS TH

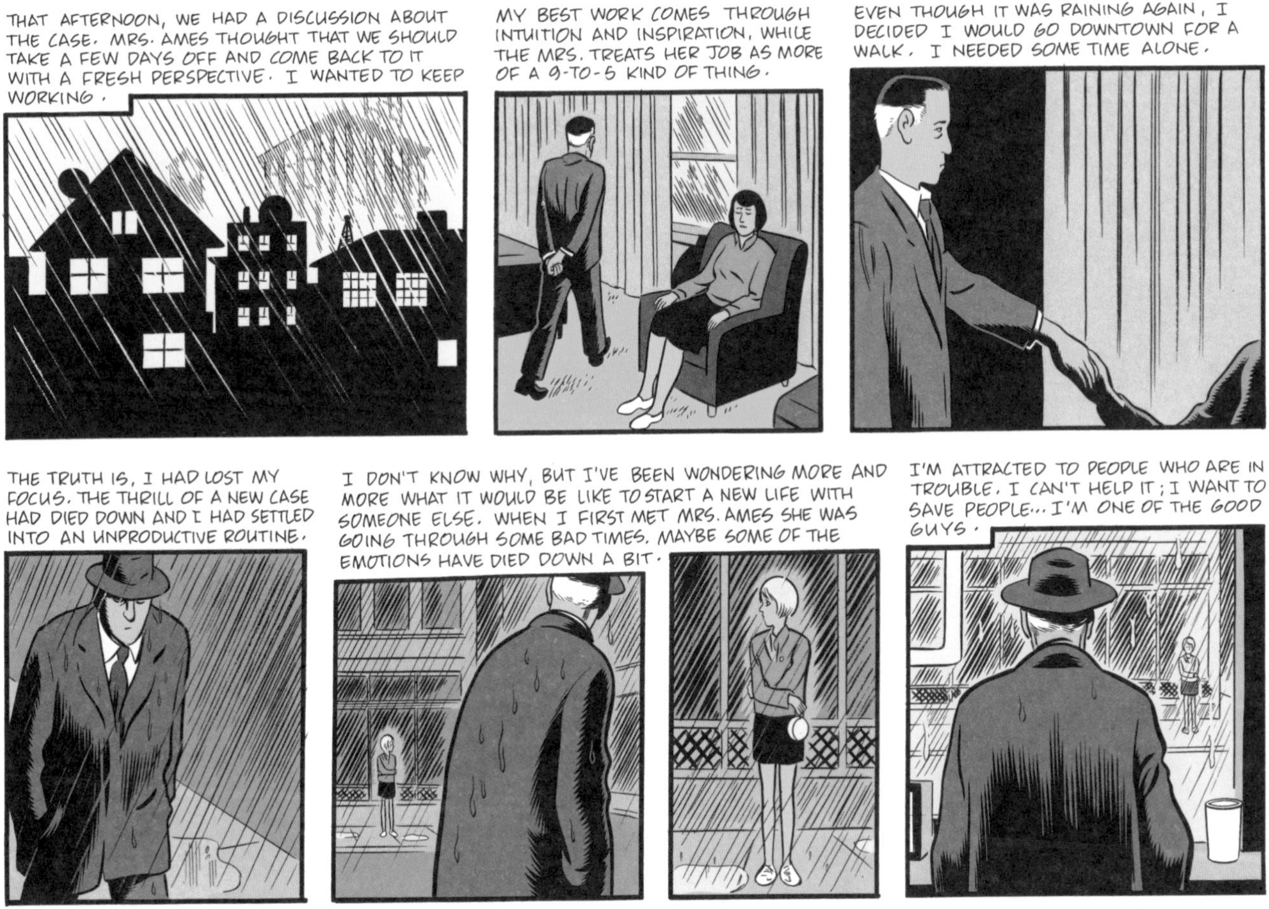
THAT AFTERNOON, WE HAD A DISCUSSION ABOUT THE CASE. MRS. AMES THOUGHT THAT WE SHOULD TAKE A FEW DAYS OFF AND COME BACK TO IT WITH A FRESH PERSPECTIVE. I WANTED TO KEEP WORKING.
MY BEST WORK COMES THROUGH INTUITION AND INSPIRATION, WHILE THE MRS. TREATS HER JOB AS MORE OF A 9-TO-5 KIND OF THING.
EVEN THOUGH IT WAS RAINING AGAIN, I DECIDED I WOULD GO DOWNTOWN FOR A WALK. I NEEDED SOME TIME ALONE.
THE TRUTH IS, I HAD LOST MY FOCUS. THE THRILL OF A NEW CASE HAD DIED DOWN AND I HAD SETTLED INTO AN UNPRODUCTIVE ROUTINE.
I DON'T KNOW WHY, BUT I'VE BEEN WONDERING MORE AND MORE WHAT IT WOULD BE LIKE TO START A NEW LIFE WITH SOMEONE ELSE. WHEN I FIRST MET MRS. AMES SHE WAS GOING THROUGH SOME BAD TIMES. MAYBE SOME OF THE EMOTIONS HAVE DIED DOWN A BIT.
I'M ATTRACTED TO PEOPLE WHO ARE IN TROUBLE. I CAN'T HELP IT; I WANT TO SAVE PEOPLE... I'M ONE OF THE GOOD GUYS.

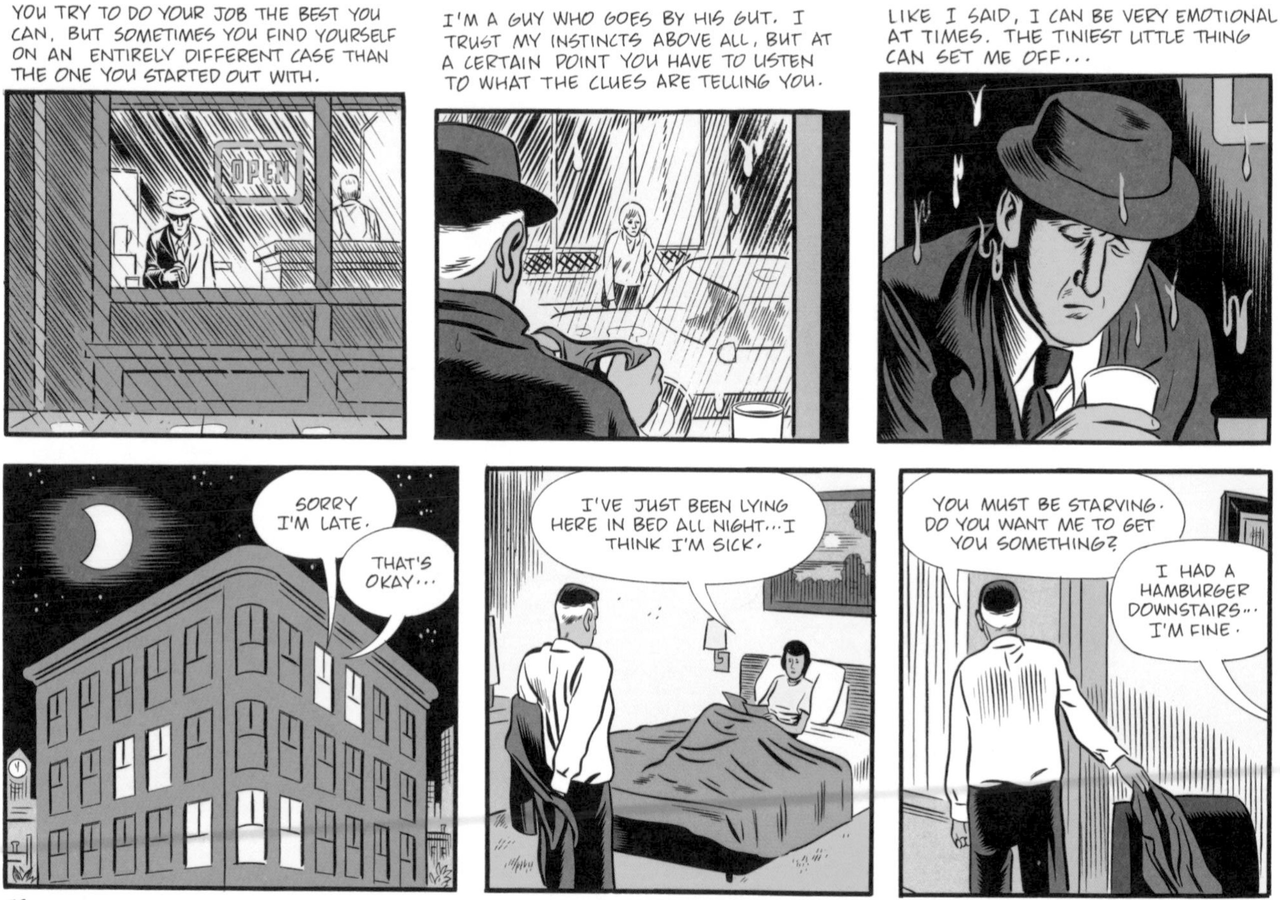
YOU TRY TO DO YOUR JOB THE BEST YOU CAN. BUT SOMETIMES YOU FIND YOURSELF ON AN ENTIRELY DIFFERENT CASE THAN THE ONE YOU STARTED OUT WITH.
OPEN
I'M A GUY WHO GOES BY HIS GUT. I TRUST MY INSTINCTS ABOVE ALL, BUT AT A CERTAIN POINT YOU HAVE TO LISTEN TO WHAT THE CLUES ARE TELLING YOU.
LIKE I SAID, I CAN BE VERY EMOTIONAL AT TIMES. THE TINIEST LITTLE THING CAN SET ME OFF...
SORRY I'M LATE.
THAT'S OKAY...
I'VE JUST BEEN LYING HERE IN BED ALL NIGHT... I THINK I'M SICK.
YOU MUST BE STARVING. DO YOU WANT ME TO GET YOU SOMETHING?
I HAD A HAMBURGER DOWNSTAIRS... I'M FINE.

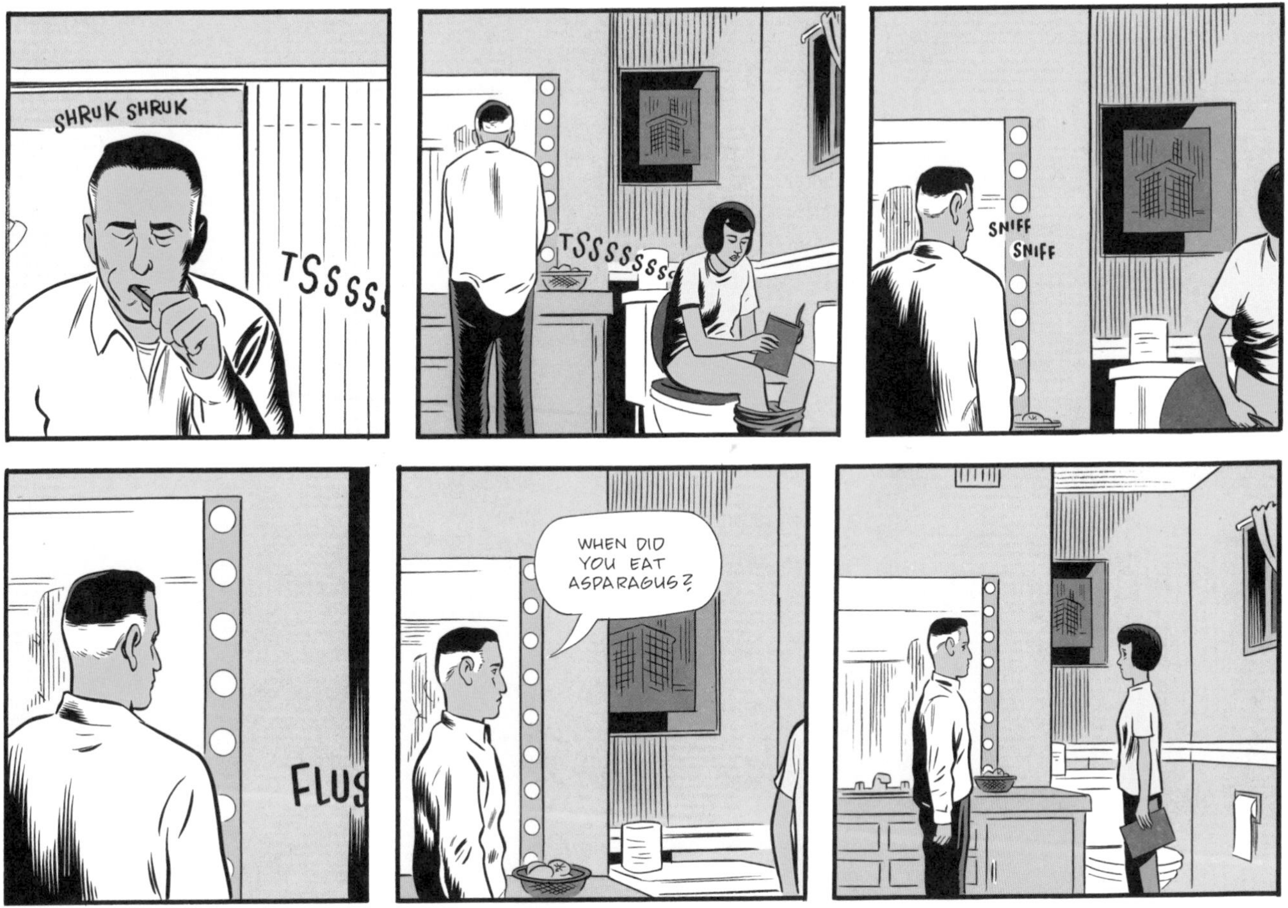
SHRUK SHRUK
TSSSSS
TSSSSSSSS
SNIFF
SNIFF
FLUS
WHEN DID YOU EAT ASPARAGUS?

WHY YOU DIRTY #@#!

RANDOM WILDER, AGAIN

SHUT UP SHUT UP SHUT UP!

CLICK!

"LIKE A DERIVATIVE HIGH-SCHOOLER"!

"POMPOUS AND IMITATIVE"!

SO MY WORK IS NOTHING BUT SHIT!

FINE!

WHY WON'T YOU FLUSH!?

JIGGLE JIGGLE

FLUSH, YOU TURDS!!

"STRICTLY AMATEUR"! "NOT A SINGLE ORIGINAL THOUGHT"!

START!

START, IDIOT!

VUHU VUHH VUHU VUH

WHY DOES EVERYTHING HAVE TO BE SUCH AN ORDEAL?

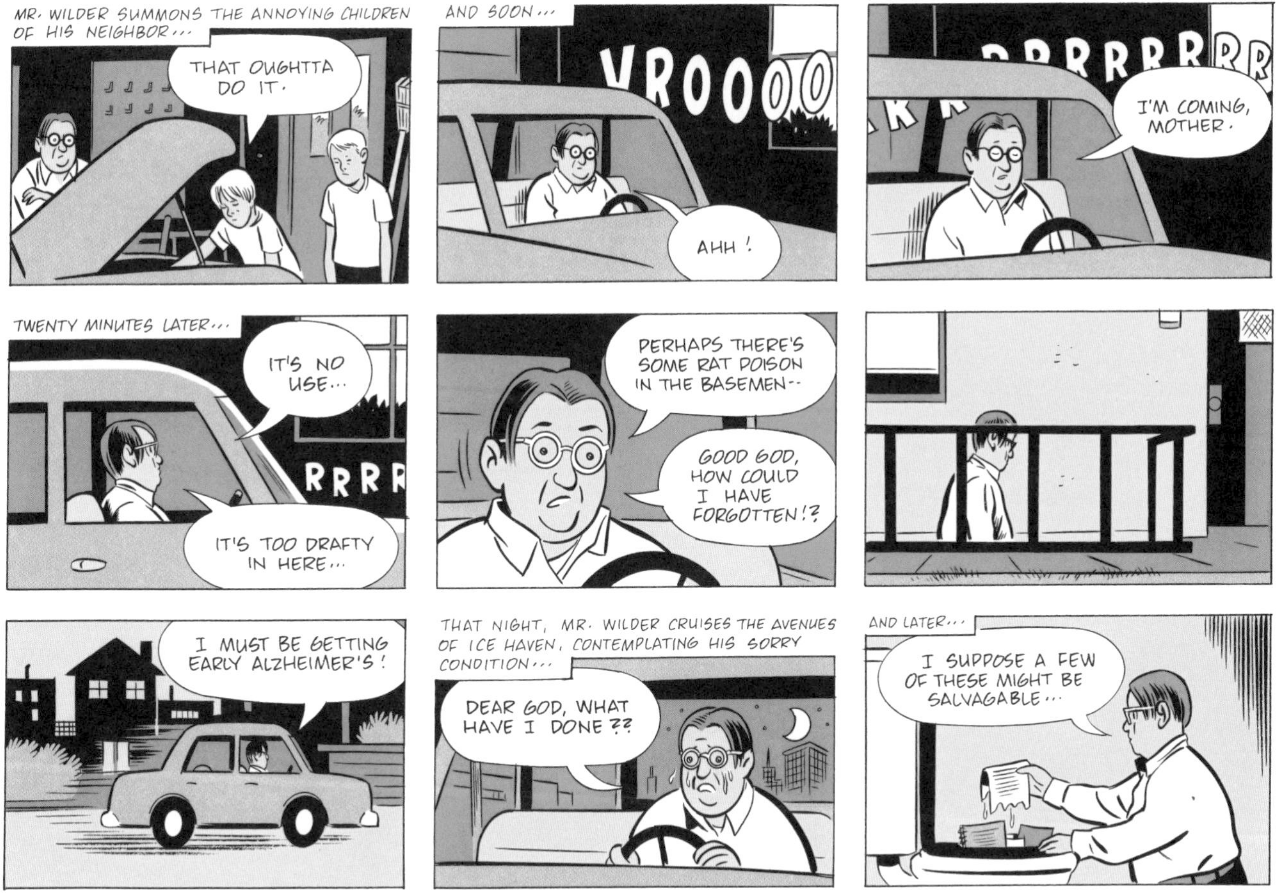
MR. WILDER SUMMONS THE ANNOYING CHILDREN OF HIS NEIGHBOR...
THAT OUGHTTA DO IT.
AND SOON...
VROOOOO
AHH!
RRRRRRRR
I'M COMING, MOTHER.
TWENTY MINUTES LATER...
IT'S NO USE...
RRRR
IT'S TOO DRAFTY IN HERE...
PERHAPS THERE'S SOME RAT POISON IN THE BASEMEN--
GOOD GOD, HOW COULD I HAVE FORGOTTEN!?
I MUST BE GETTING EARLY ALZHEIMER'S!
THAT NIGHT, MR. WILDER CRUISES THE AVENUES OF ICE HAVEN, CONTEMPLATING HIS SORRY CONDITION...
DEAR GOD, WHAT HAVE I DONE??
AND LATER...
I SUPPOSE A FEW OF THESE MIGHT BE SALVAGABLE...

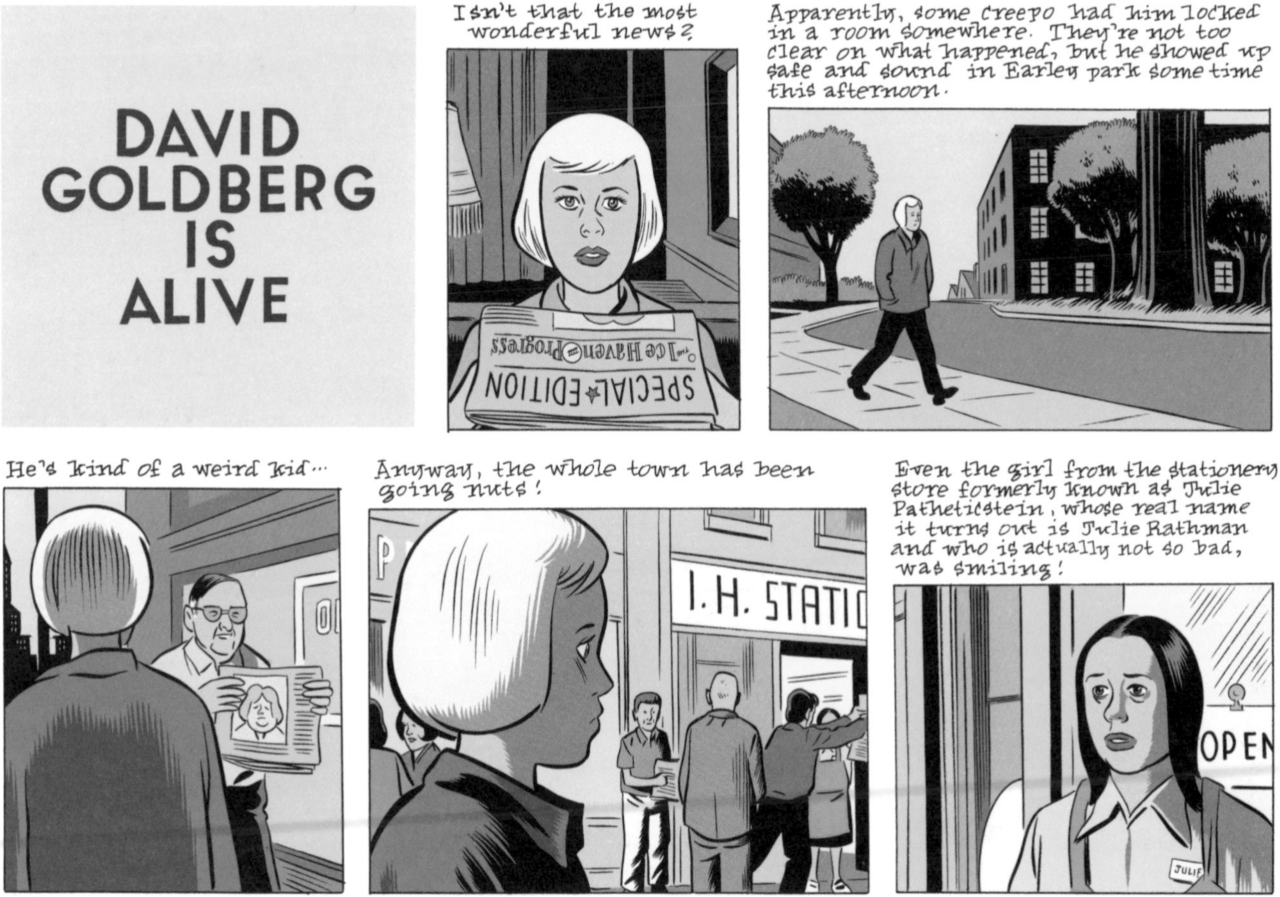
DAVID GOLDBERG IS ALIVE
Isn't that the most wonderful news?
The Ice Haven Progress
SPECIAL EDITION
Apparently, some creepo had him locked in a room somewhere. They're not too clear on what happened, but he showed up safe and sound in Earley park some time this afternoon.
He's kind of a weird kid...
Anyway, the whole town has been going nuts!
I. H. STATIO
Even the girl from the stationery store formerly known as Julie Patheticstein, whose real name it turns out is Julie Rathman and who is actually not so bad, was smiling!
OPEN
JULIE

As the news spread, a throng of Ice Havenites began to line Similar street. People were sobbing and hugging perfect strangers and running out into the street.

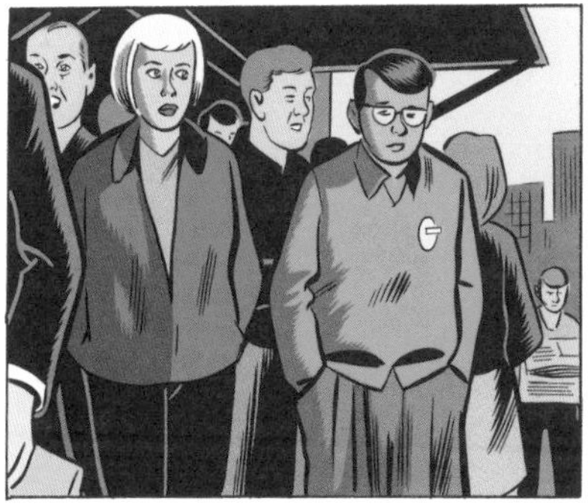

In all the excitement, the counter-man from Allrite Food Gas wandered toward me, as though he was actually going to talk to me for once!

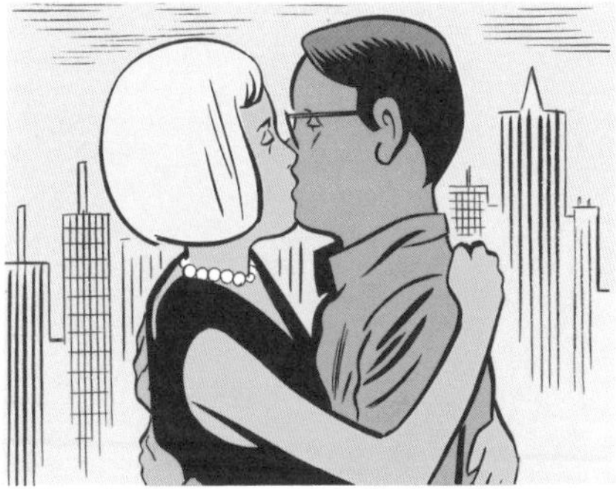

We embraced passionately and ran off together toward the park.

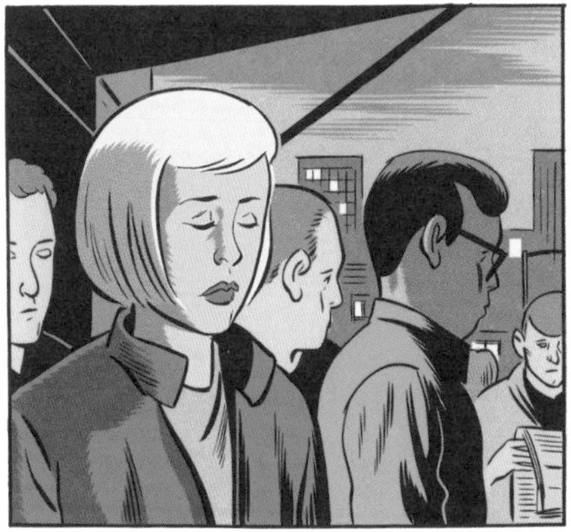

As evening fell, all the people of Ice Haven held hands and began to sing the most spine-chillingly beautiful song, like a beautiful hymn or the last part of Beethoven's Ninth Symphony, without any hint of embarrassment or uncertainty.

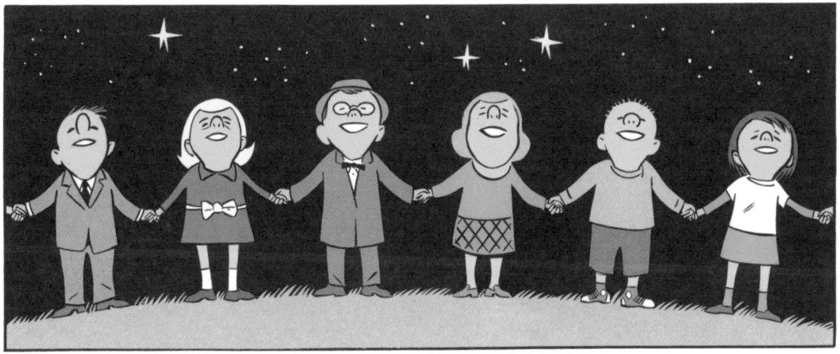

And before long I found myself singing loudest of all, ecstatic in glorious praise that our beloved home had been spared such tragedy!

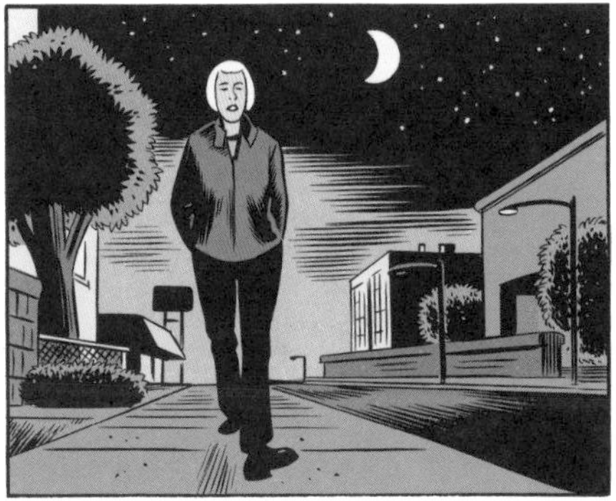

Our Children, Revisited

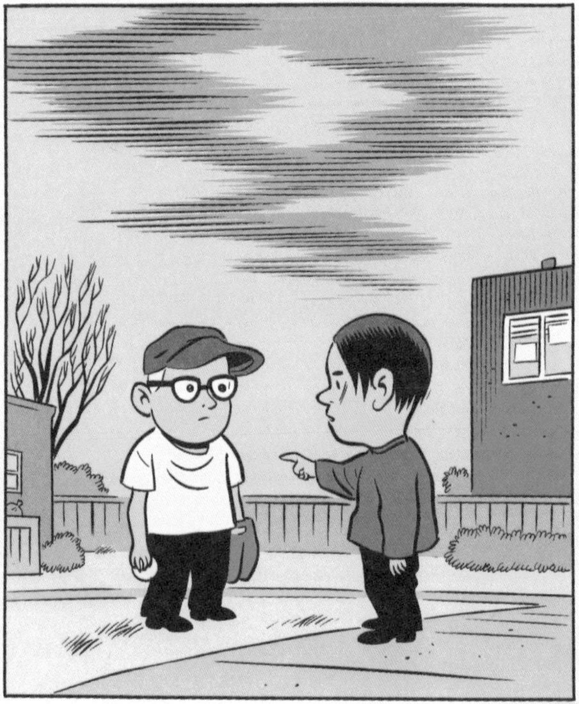

"YOU REALLY THOUGHT I KILLED HIM? MAN, NO OFFENSE, BUT WHAT A CHUMP!"

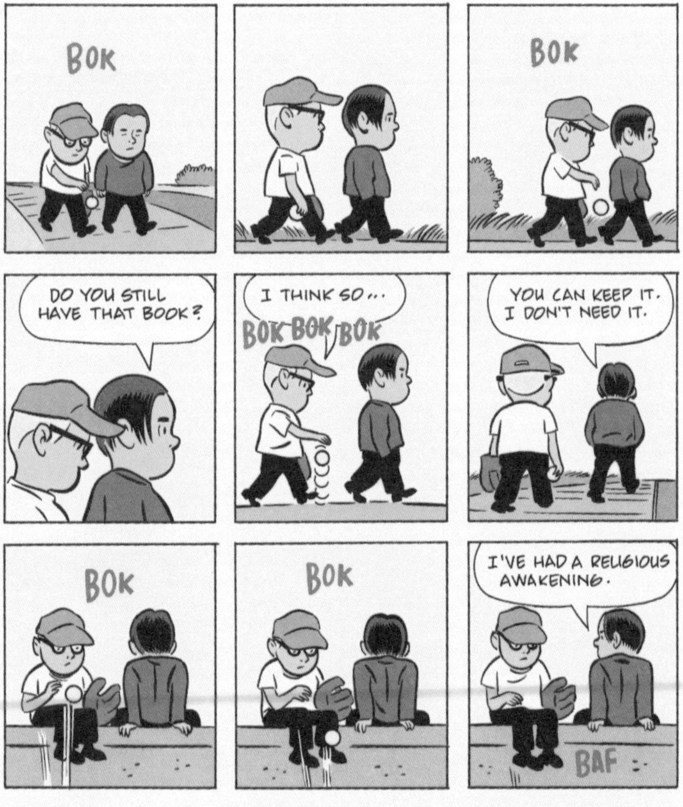

BOK
BOK
DO YOU STILL HAVE THAT BOOK?
I THINK SO...
BOK BOK BOK
YOU CAN KEEP IT. I DON'T NEED IT.
BOK
BOK
I'VE HAD A RELIGIOUS AWAKENING.
BAF

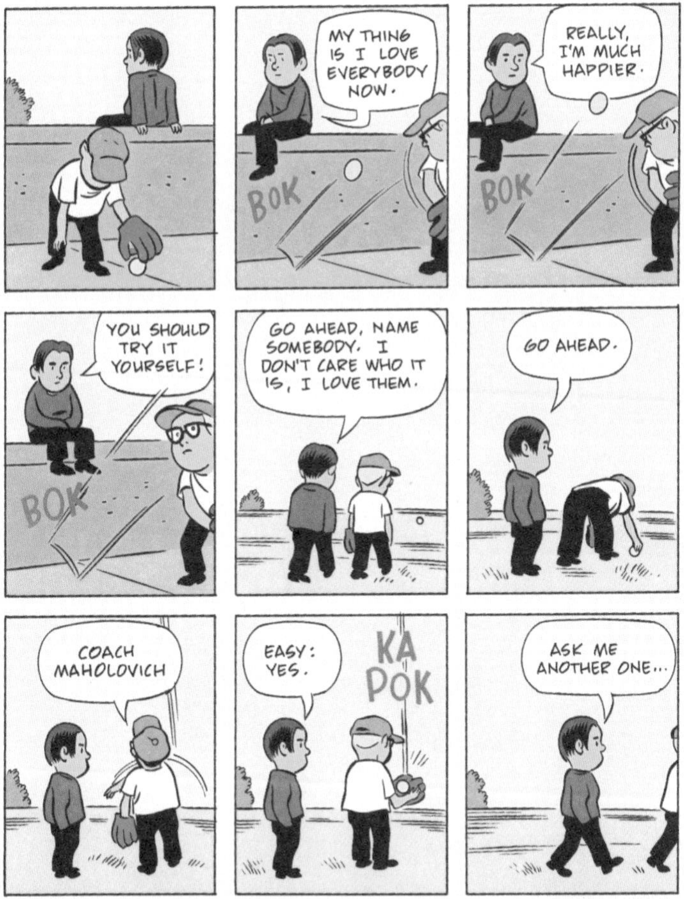
MY THING IS I LOVE EVERYBODY NOW.
BOK
REALLY, I'M MUCH HAPPIER.
BOK
YOU SHOULD TRY IT YOURSELF!
BOK
GO AHEAD, NAME SOMEBODY. I DON'T CARE WHO IT IS, I LOVE THEM.
GO AHEAD.
COACH MAHOLOVICH
EASY: YES.
KA POK
ASK ME ANOTHER ONE...

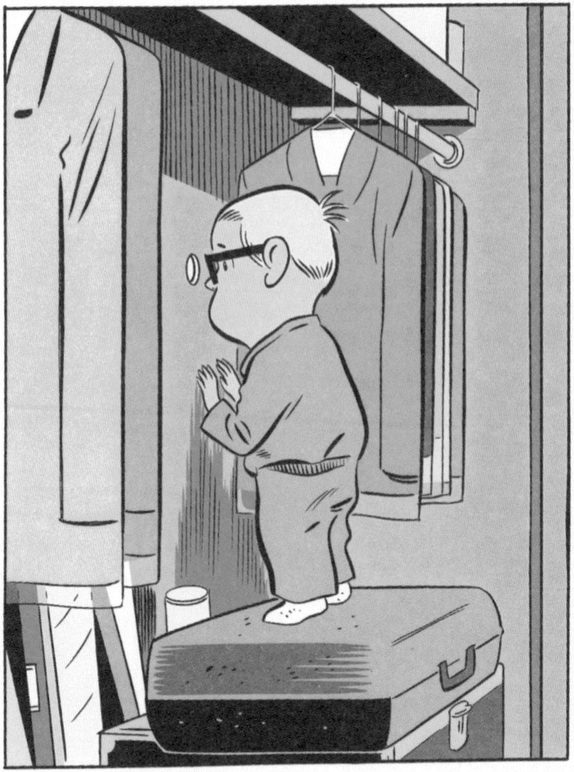

"VIOLET DARLING, I WANT YOU TO KNOW THAT I LOVE YOU, AND WILL ALWAYS LOVE YOU. NO MATTER WHERE YOU ARE, I WILL BE THINKING OF YOU EVERY MINUTE. I WILL WAIT FOREVER. MY DARLING."

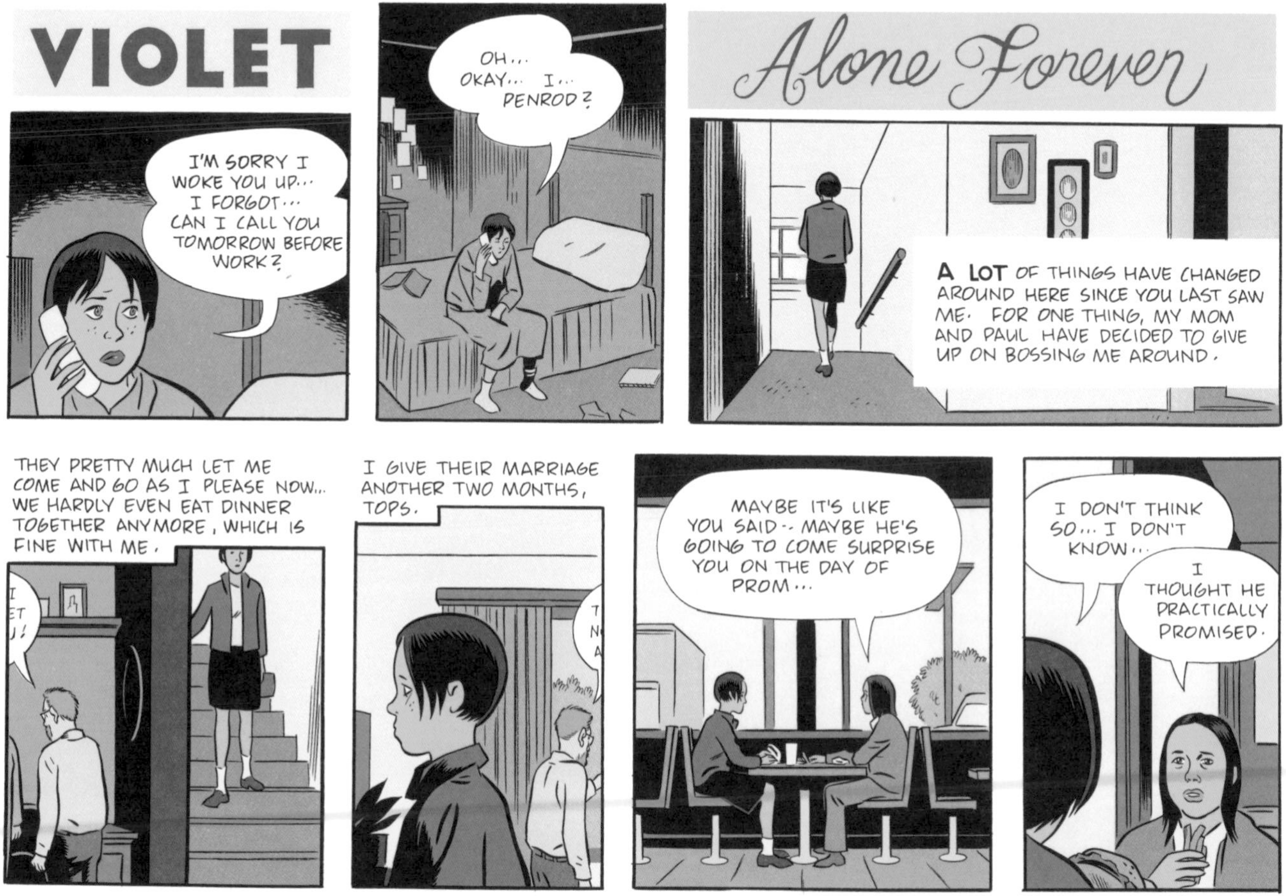
VIOLET
I'M SORRY I WOKE YOU UP... I FORGOT... CAN I CALL YOU TOMORROW BEFORE WORK?
OH... OKAY... I... PENROD?
Alone Forever
A LOT OF THINGS HAVE CHANGED AROUND HERE SINCE YOU LAST SAW ME. FOR ONE THING, MY MOM AND PAUL HAVE DECIDED TO GIVE UP ON BOSSING ME AROUND.
THEY PRETTY MUCH LET ME COME AND GO AS I PLEASE NOW... WE HARDLY EVEN EAT DINNER TOGETHER ANYMORE, WHICH IS FINE WITH ME.
I GIVE THEIR MARRIAGE ANOTHER TWO MONTHS, TOPS.
MAYBE IT'S LIKE YOU SAID -- MAYBE HE'S GOING TO COME SURPRISE YOU ON THE DAY OF PROM...
I DON'T THINK SO... I DON'T KNOW...
I THOUGHT HE PRACTICALLY PROMISED.

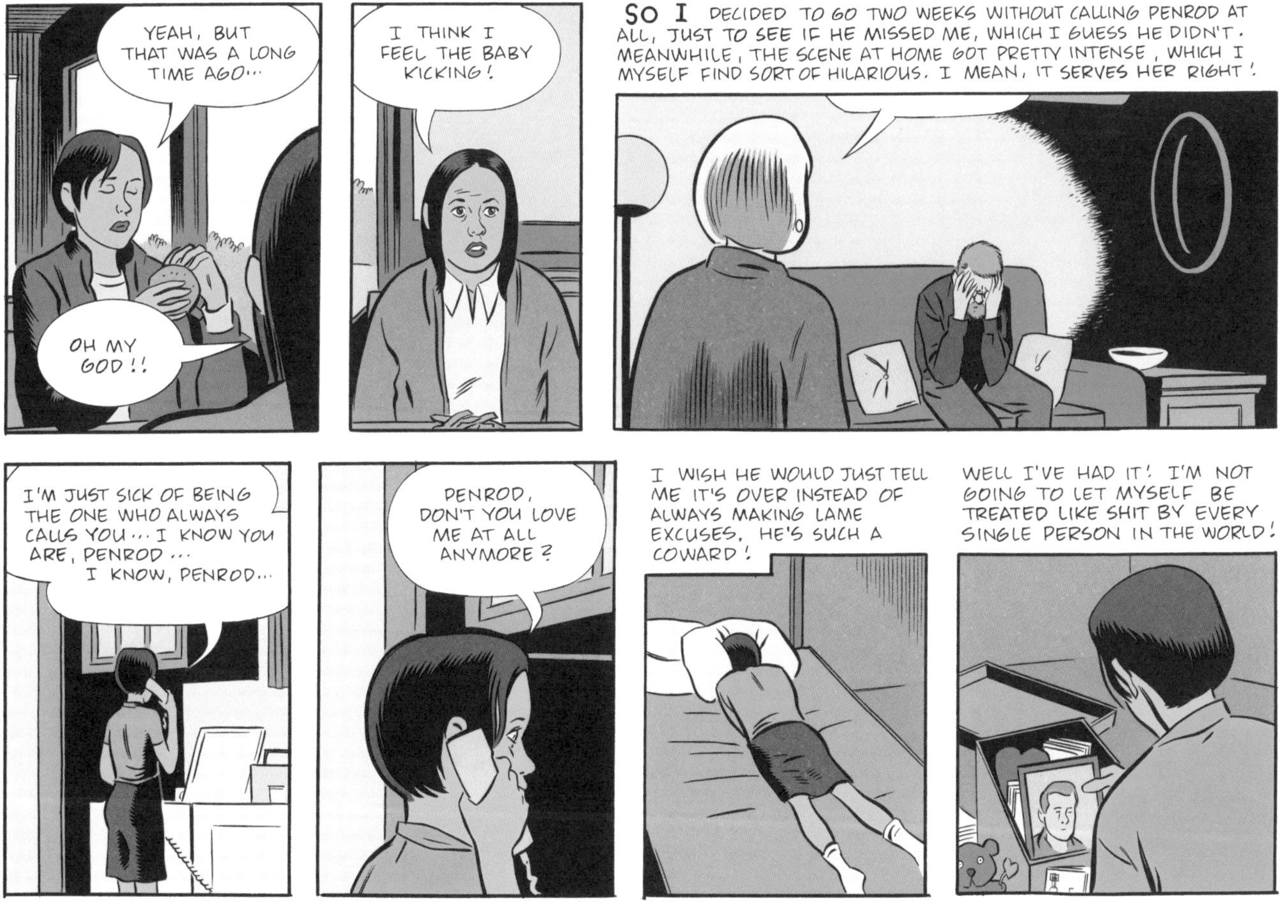
YEAH, BUT THAT WAS A LONG TIME AGO...
OH MY GOD!!
I THINK I FEEL THE BABY KICKING!
SO I DECIDED TO GO TWO WEEKS WITHOUT CALLING PENROD AT ALL, JUST TO SEE IF HE MISSED ME, WHICH I GUESS HE DIDN'T. MEANWHILE, THE SCENE AT HOME GOT PRETTY INTENSE, WHICH I MYSELF FIND SORT OF HILARIOUS. I MEAN, IT SERVES HER RIGHT!
I'M JUST SICK OF BEING THE ONE WHO ALWAYS CALLS YOU... I KNOW YOU ARE, PENROD... I KNOW, PENROD...
PENROD, DON'T YOU LOVE ME AT ALL ANYMORE?
I WISH HE WOULD JUST TELL ME IT'S OVER INSTEAD OF ALWAYS MAKING LAME EXCUSES. HE'S SUCH A COWARD!
WELL I'VE HAD IT! I'M NOT GOING TO LET MYSELF BE TREATED LIKE SHIT BY EVERY SINGLE PERSON IN THE WORLD!

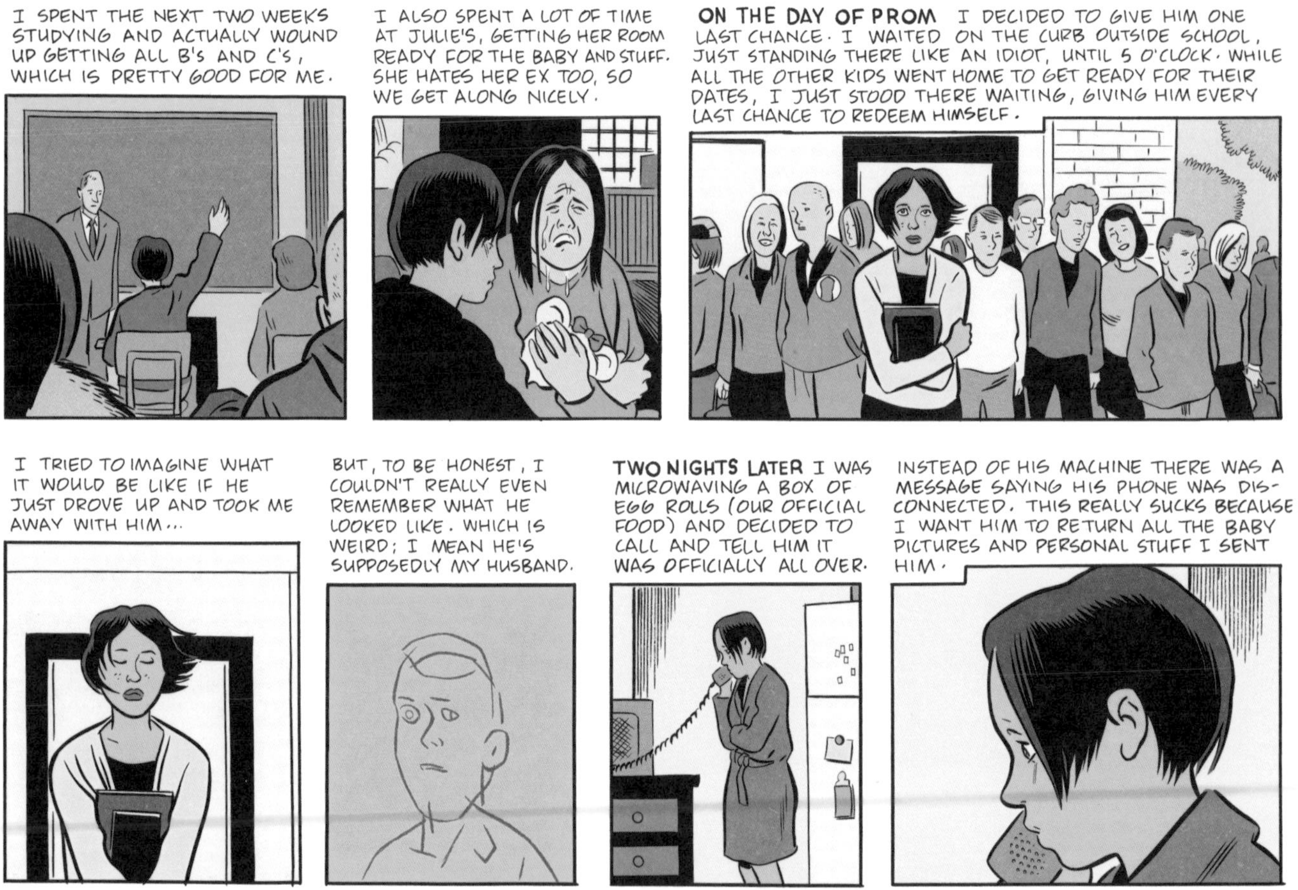
I SPENT THE NEXT TWO WEEKS STUDYING AND ACTUALLY WOUND UP GETTING ALL B'S AND C'S, WHICH IS PRETTY GOOD FOR ME.
I ALSO SPENT A LOT OF TIME AT JULIE'S, GETTING HER ROOM READY FOR THE BABY AND STUFF. SHE HATES HER EX TOO, SO WE GET ALONG NICELY.
ON THE DAY OF PROM I DECIDED TO GIVE HIM ONE LAST CHANCE. I WAITED ON THE CURB OUTSIDE SCHOOL, JUST STANDING THERE LIKE AN IDIOT, UNTIL 5 O'CLOCK. WHILE ALL THE OTHER KIDS WENT HOME TO GET READY FOR THEIR DATES, I JUST STOOD THERE WAITING, GIVING HIM EVERY LAST CHANCE TO REDEEM HIMSELF.
I TRIED TO IMAGINE WHAT IT WOULD BE LIKE IF HE JUST DROVE UP AND TOOK ME AWAY WITH HIM...
BUT, TO BE HONEST, I COULDN'T REALLY EVEN REMEMBER WHAT HE LOOKED LIKE. WHICH IS WEIRD; I MEAN HE'S SUPPOSEDLY MY HUSBAND.
TWO NIGHTS LATER I WAS MICROWAVING A BOX OF EGG ROLLS (OUR OFFICIAL FOOD) AND DECIDED TO CALL AND TELL HIM IT WAS OFFICIALLY ALL OVER.
INSTEAD OF HIS MACHINE THERE WAS A MESSAGE SAYING HIS PHONE WAS DISCONNECTED. THIS REALLY SUCKS BECAUSE I WANT HIM TO RETURN ALL THE BABY PICTURES AND PERSONAL STUFF I SENT HIM.

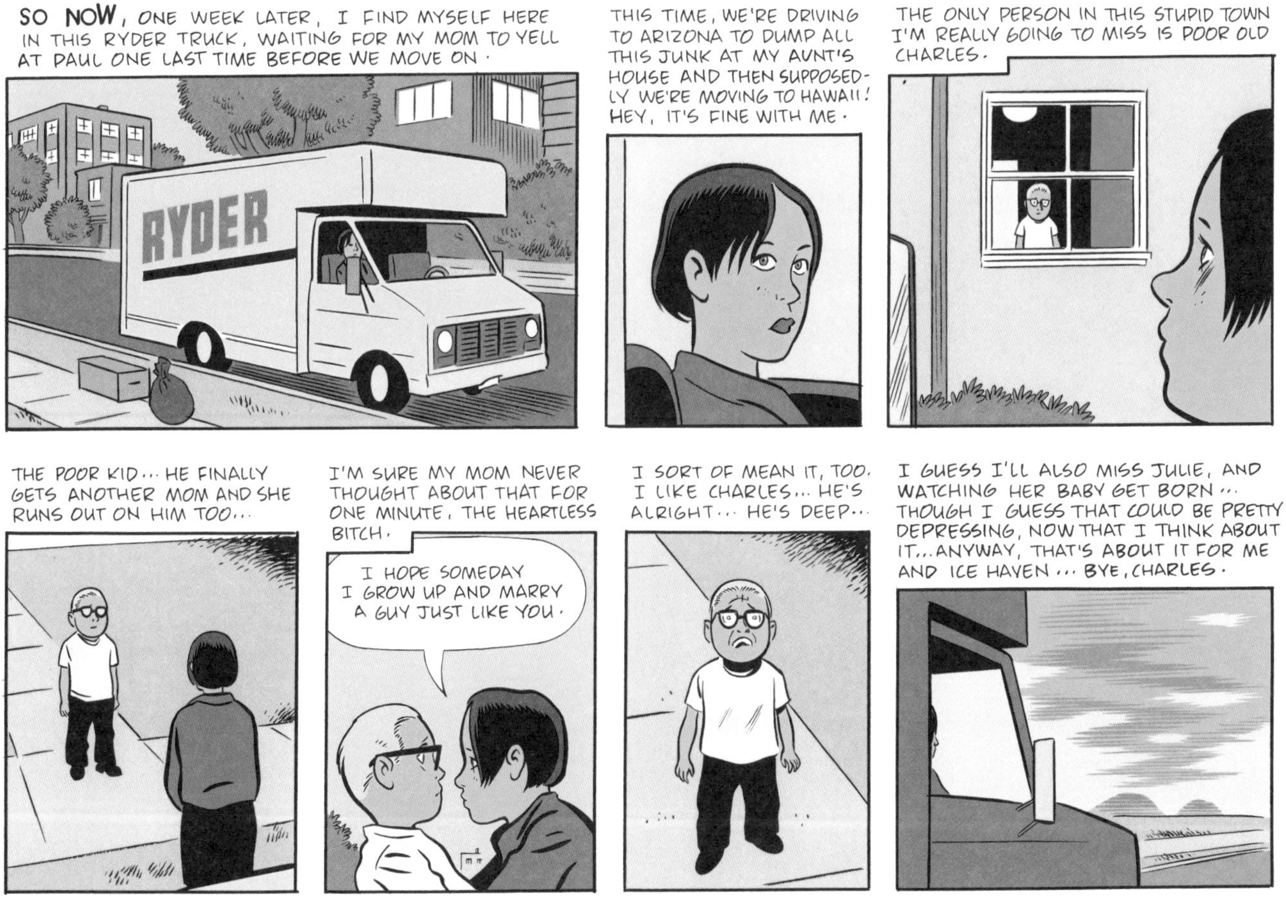
SO NOW, ONE WEEK LATER, I FIND MYSELF HERE IN THIS RYDER TRUCK, WAITING FOR MY MOM TO YELL AT PAUL ONE LAST TIME BEFORE WE MOVE ON.
RYDER
THIS TIME, WE'RE DRIVING TO ARIZONA TO DUMP ALL THIS JUNK AT MY AUNT'S HOUSE AND THEN SUPPOSEDLY WE'RE MOVING TO HAWAII! HEY, IT'S FINE WITH ME.
THE ONLY PERSON IN THIS STUPID TOWN I'M REALLY GOING TO MISS IS POOR OLD CHARLES.
THE POOR KID... HE FINALLY GETS ANOTHER MOM AND SHE RUNS OUT ON HIM TOO...
I'M SURE MY MOM NEVER THOUGHT ABOUT THAT FOR ONE MINUTE, THE HEARTLESS BITCH.
I HOPE SOMEDAY I GROW UP AND MARRY A GUY JUST LIKE YOU.
I SORT OF MEAN IT, TOO. I LIKE CHARLES... HE'S ALRIGHT... HE'S DEEP...
I GUESS I'LL ALSO MISS JULIE, AND WATCHING HER BABY GET BORN... THOUGH I GUESS THAT COULD BE PRETTY DEPRESSING, NOW THAT I THINK ABOUT IT... ANYWAY, THAT'S ABOUT IT FOR ME AND ICE HAVEN... BYE, CHARLES.

VIDA GOES TO HOLLYWOOD

And so, dear reader, I have a very important announcement to make: I am suspending publication of The Weekly. In fact, I don't even intend to publish the words you are now reading.

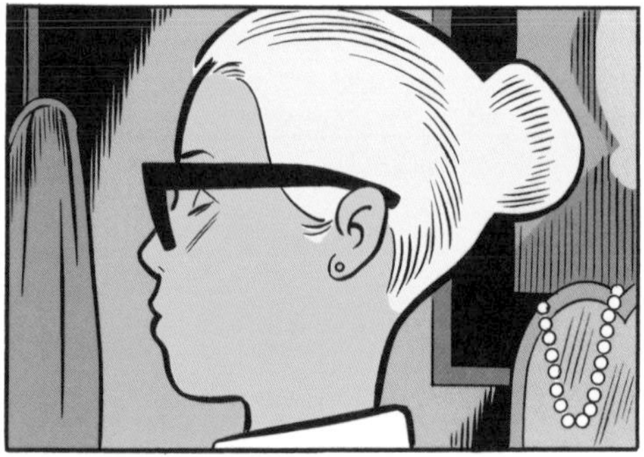

So how are you reading this, anyway? That's a good question. Are you my future biographer? Are you sitting in the Library of Congress right now, going through my papers? How exciting!

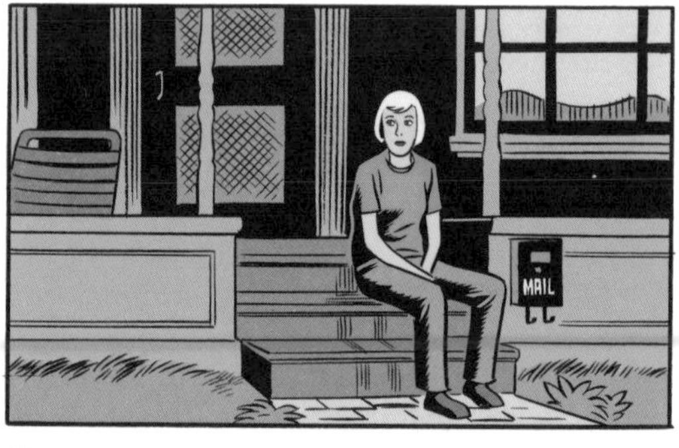
MAIL

Anyway, I never sold a single copy of the magazine (in fact, Pete Jr. of Pete's books asked me to take back my consignment copies because they were "taking up too much space"!), nor did I get any reviews, nor did any of my so-called heroes write to me.

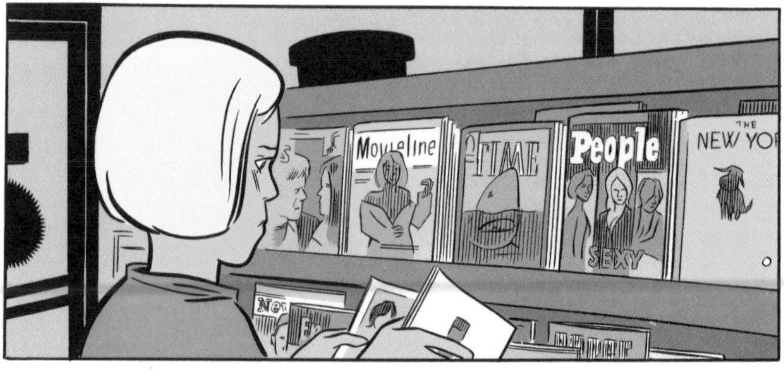
TIME
People
SEXY
THE
NEW YOR

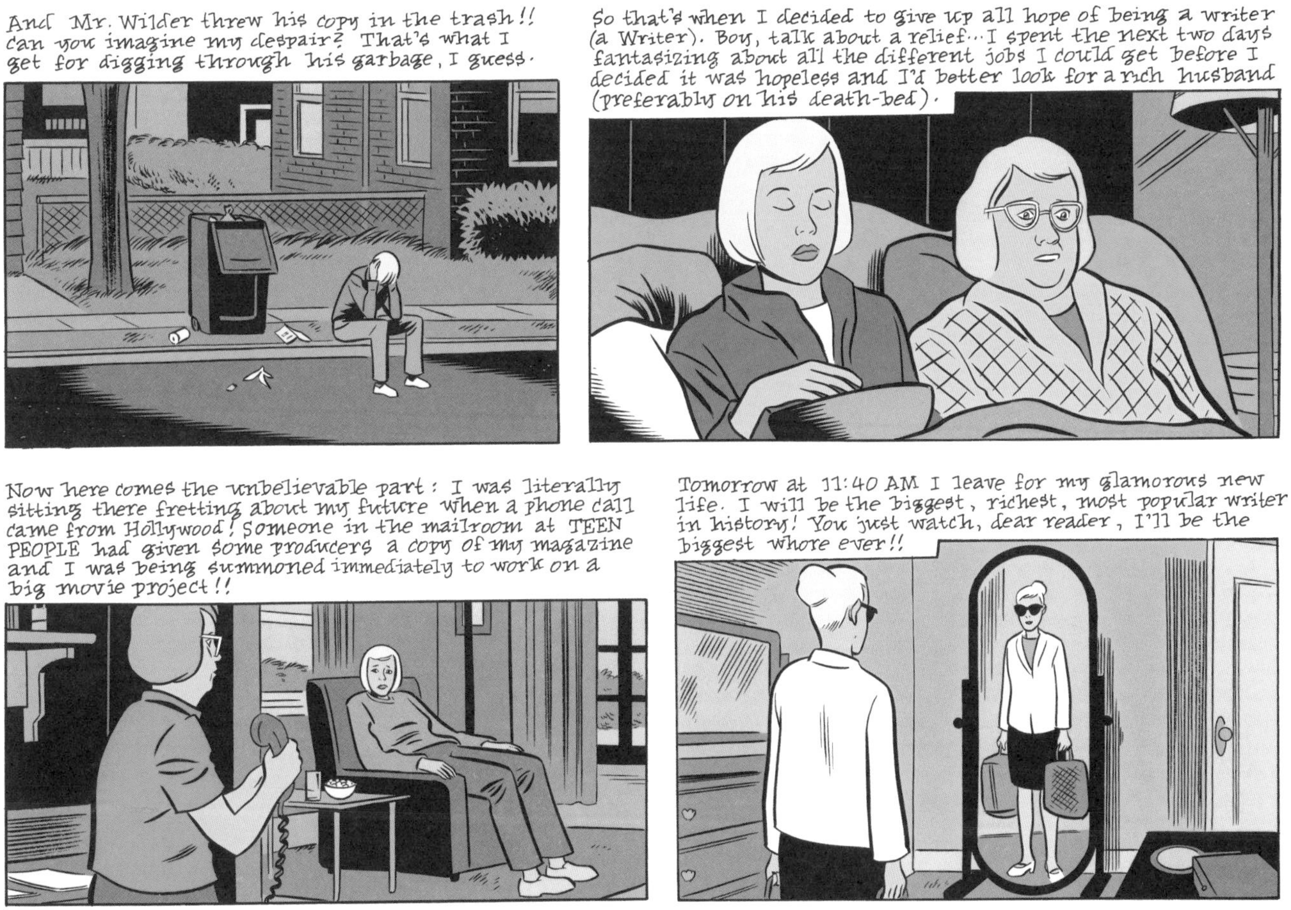
And Mr. Wilder threw his copy in the trash!! Can you imagine my despair? That's what I get for digging through his garbage, I guess.
So that's when I decided to give up all hope of being a writer (a Writer). Boy, talk about a relief... I spent the next two days fantasizing about all the different jobs I could get before I decided it was hopeless and I'd better look for a rich husband (preferably on his death-bed).
Now here comes the unbelievable part: I was literally sitting there fretting about my future when a phone call came from Hollywood! Someone in the mailroom at TEEN PEOPLE had given some producers a copy of my magazine and I was being summoned immediately to work on a big movie project!!
Tomorrow at 11:40 AM I leave for my glamorous new life. I will be the biggest, richest, most popular writer in history! You just watch, dear reader, I'll be the biggest whore ever!!

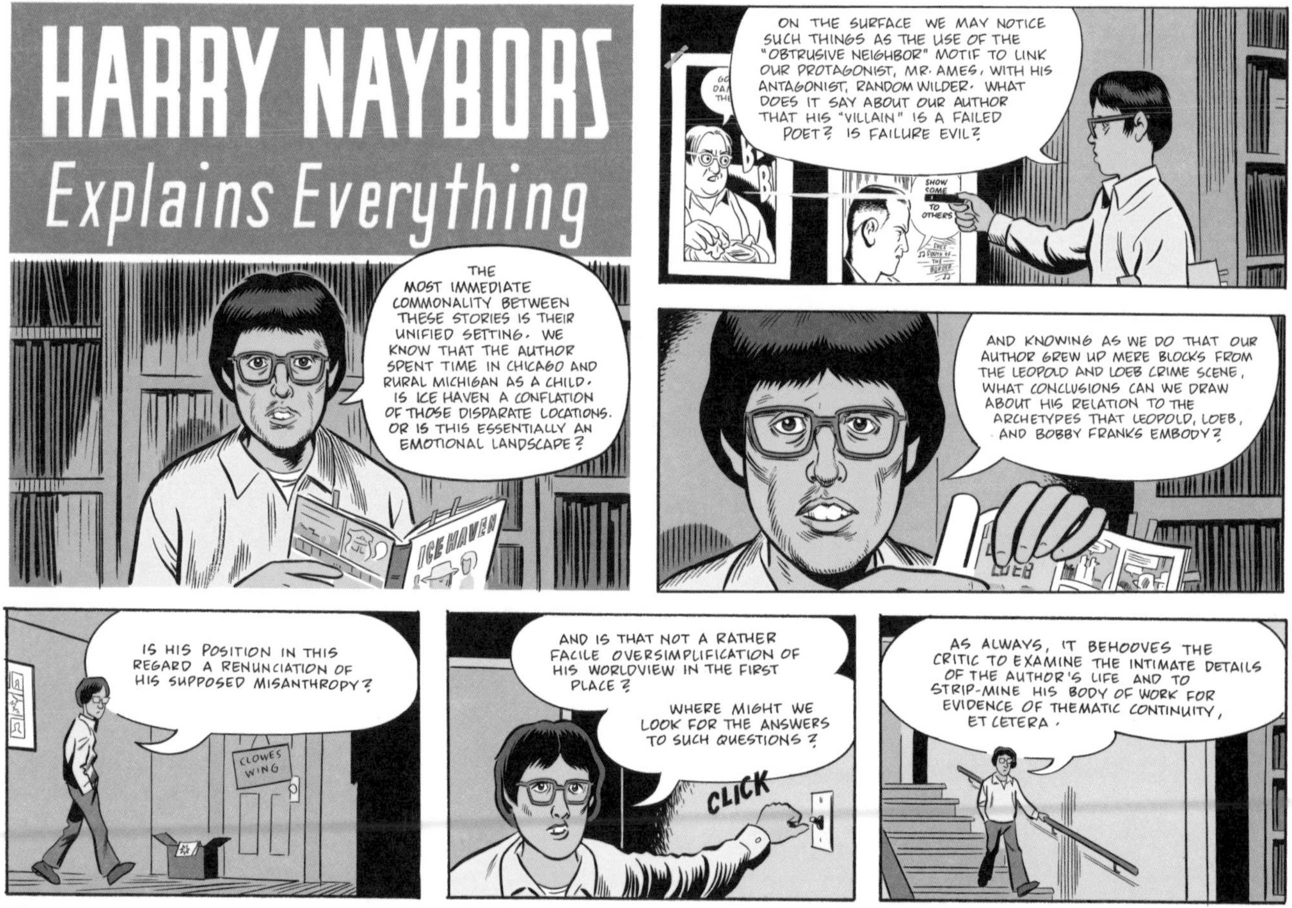
HARRY NAYBORS
Explains Everything
THE MOST IMMEDIATE COMMONALITY BETWEEN THESE STORIES IS THEIR UNIFIED SETTING. WE KNOW THAT THE AUTHOR SPENT TIME IN CHICAGO AND RURAL MICHIGAN AS A CHILD. IS ICE HAVEN A CONFLATION OF THOSE DISPARATE LOCATIONS. OR IS THIS ESSENTIALLY AN EMOTIONAL LANDSCAPE?
ICE HAVEN
ON THE SURFACE WE MAY NOTICE SUCH THINGS AS THE USE OF THE "OBTRUSIVE NEIGHBOR" MOTIF TO LINK OUR PROTAGONIST, MR. AMES, WITH HIS ANTAGONIST, RANDOM WILDER. WHAT DOES IT SAY ABOUT OUR AUTHOR THAT HIS "VILLAIN" IS A FAILED POET? IS FAILURE EVIL?
AND KNOWING AS WE DO THAT OUR AUTHOR GREW UP MERE BLOCKS FROM THE LEOPOLD AND LOEB CRIME SCENE, WHAT CONCLUSIONS CAN WE DRAW ABOUT HIS RELATION TO THE ARCHETYPES THAT LEOPOLD, LOEB, AND BOBBY FRANKS EMBODY?
IS HIS POSITION IN THIS REGARD A RENUNCIATION OF HIS SUPPOSED MISANTHROPY?
CLOWES WING
AND IS THAT NOT A RATHER FACILE OVERSIMPLIFICATION OF HIS WORLDVIEW IN THE FIRST PLACE?
WHERE MIGHT WE LOOK FOR THE ANSWERS TO SUCH QUESTIONS?
CLICK
AS ALWAYS, IT BEHOOVES THE CRITIC TO EXAMINE THE INTIMATE DETAILS OF THE AUTHOR'S LIFE AND TO STRIP-MINE HIS BODY OF WORK FOR EVIDENCE OF THEMATIC CONTINUITY, ET CETERA.

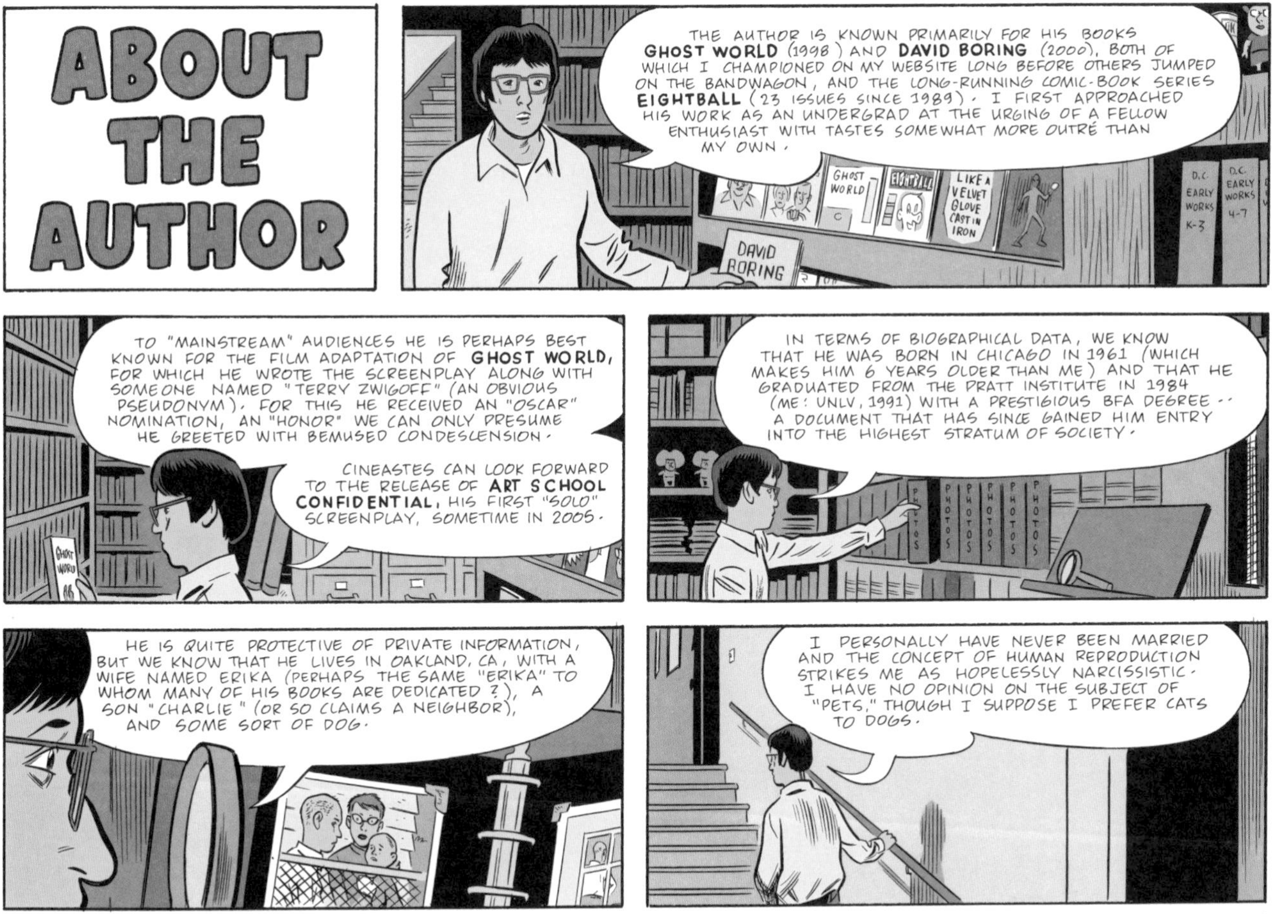

ABOUT THE AUTHOR
THE AUTHOR IS KNOWN PRIMARILY FOR HIS BOOKS **GHOST WORLD** (1998) AND **DAVID BORING** (2000), BOTH OF WHICH I CHAMPIONED ON MY WEBSITE LONG BEFORE OTHERS JUMPED ON THE BANDWAGON, AND THE LONG-RUNNING COMIC-BOOK SERIES **EIGHTBALL** (23 ISSUES SINCE 1989). I FIRST APPROACHED HIS WORK AS AN UNDERGRAD AT THE URGING OF A FELLOW ENTHUSIAST WITH TASTES SOMEWHAT MORE OUTRÉ THAN MY OWN.
GHOST WORLD
LIKE A VELVET GLOVE CAST IN IRON
DAVID BORING
D.C. EARLY WORKS K-3
D.C. EARLY WORKS 4-7
TO "MAINSTREAM" AUDIENCES HE IS PERHAPS BEST KNOWN FOR THE FILM ADAPTATION OF **GHOST WORLD**, FOR WHICH HE WROTE THE SCREENPLAY ALONG WITH SOMEONE NAMED "TERRY ZWIGOFF" (AN OBVIOUS PSEUDONYM). FOR THIS HE RECEIVED AN "OSCAR" NOMINATION, AN "HONOR" WE CAN ONLY PRESUME HE GREETED WITH BEMUSED CONDESCENSION.
CINEASTES CAN LOOK FORWARD TO THE RELEASE OF **ART SCHOOL CONFIDENTIAL**, HIS FIRST "SOLO" SCREENPLAY, SOMETIME IN 2005.
GHOST WORLD
IN TERMS OF BIOGRAPHICAL DATA, WE KNOW THAT HE WAS BORN IN CHICAGO IN 1961 (WHICH MAKES HIM 6 YEARS OLDER THAN ME) AND THAT HE GRADUATED FROM THE PRATT INSTITUTE IN 1984 (ME: UNLV, 1991) WITH A PRESTIGIOUS BFA DEGREE -- A DOCUMENT THAT HAS SINCE GAINED HIM ENTRY INTO THE HIGHEST STRATUM OF SOCIETY.
PHOTOS
PHOTOS
PHOTOS
PHOTOS
PHOTOS
PHOTOS
HE IS QUITE PROTECTIVE OF PRIVATE INFORMATION, BUT WE KNOW THAT HE LIVES IN OAKLAND, CA, WITH A WIFE NAMED ERIKA (PERHAPS THE SAME "ERIKA" TO WHOM MANY OF HIS BOOKS ARE DEDICATED?), A SON "CHARLIE" (OR SO CLAIMS A NEIGHBOR), AND SOME SORT OF DOG.
I PERSONALLY HAVE NEVER BEEN MARRIED AND THE CONCEPT OF HUMAN REPRODUCTION STRIKES ME AS HOPELESSLY NARCISSISTIC. I HAVE NO OPINION ON THE SUBJECT OF "PETS," THOUGH I SUPPOSE I PREFER CATS TO DOGS.

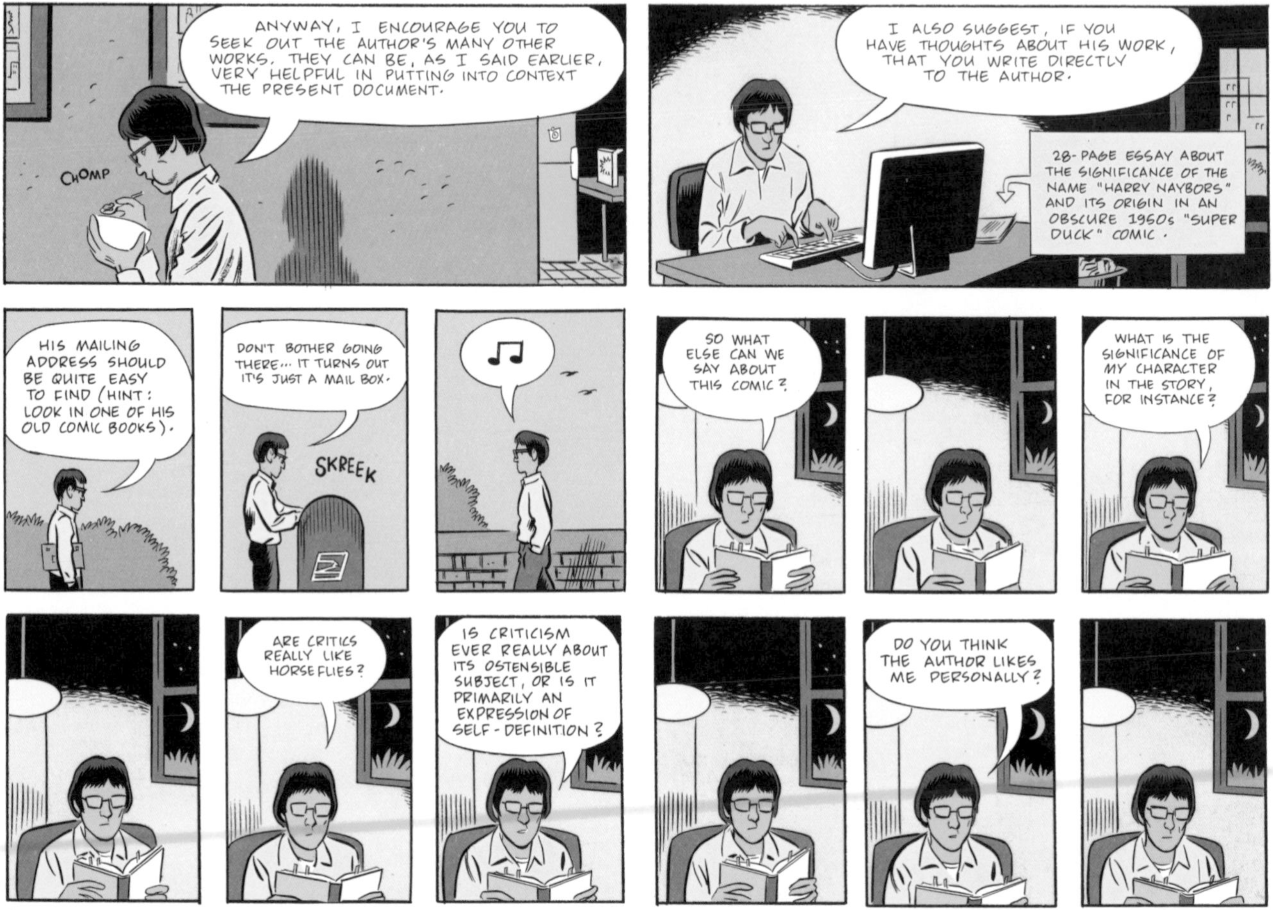
ANYWAY, I ENCOURAGE YOU TO SEEK OUT THE AUTHOR'S MANY OTHER WORKS. THEY CAN BE, AS I SAID EARLIER, VERY HELPFUL IN PUTTING INTO CONTEXT THE PRESENT DOCUMENT.
CHOMP
I ALSO SUGGEST, IF YOU HAVE THOUGHTS ABOUT HIS WORK, THAT YOU WRITE DIRECTLY TO THE AUTHOR.
28-PAGE ESSAY ABOUT THE SIGNIFICANCE OF THE NAME "HARRY NAYBORS" AND ITS ORIGIN IN AN OBSCURE 1950s "SUPER DUCK" COMIC.
HIS MAILING ADDRESS SHOULD BE QUITE EASY TO FIND (HINT: LOOK IN ONE OF HIS OLD COMIC BOOKS).
DON'T BOTHER GOING THERE... IT TURNS OUT IT'S JUST A MAIL BOX.
SKREEK
SO WHAT ELSE CAN WE SAY ABOUT THIS COMIC?
WHAT IS THE SIGNIFICANCE OF MY CHARACTER IN THE STORY, FOR INSTANCE?
ARE CRITICS REALLY LIKE HORSEFLIES?
IS CRITICISM EVER REALLY ABOUT ITS OSTENSIBLE SUBJECT, OR IS IT PRIMARILY AN EXPRESSION OF SELF-DEFINITION?
DO YOU THINK THE AUTHOR LIKES ME PERSONALLY?

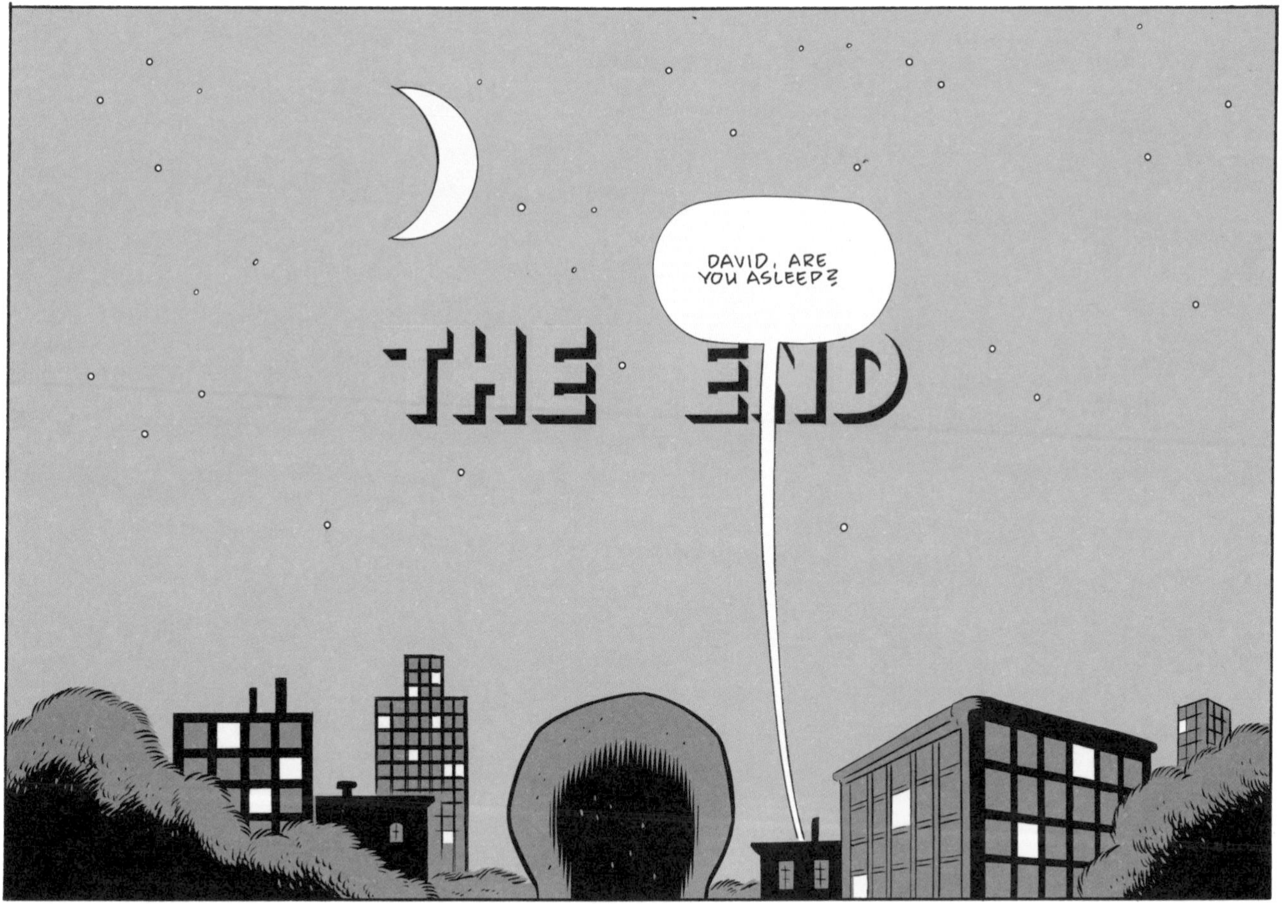
DAVID, ARE YOU ASLEEP?
THE END

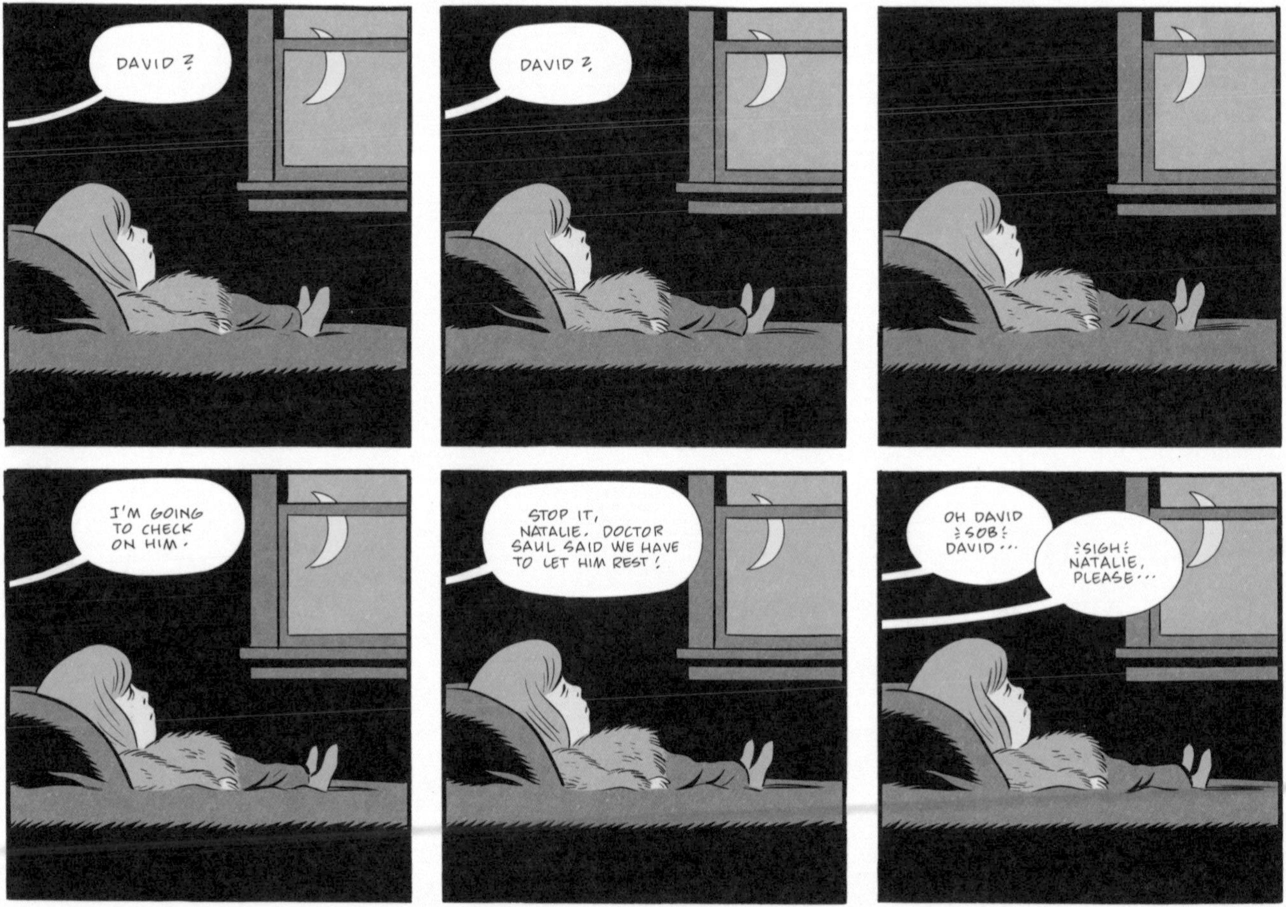
DAVID?
DAVID?
I'M GOING TO CHECK ON HIM.
STOP IT, NATALIE. DOCTOR SAUL SAID WE HAVE TO LET HIM REST!
OH DAVID :SOB: DAVID...
:SIGH: NATALIE, PLEASE...

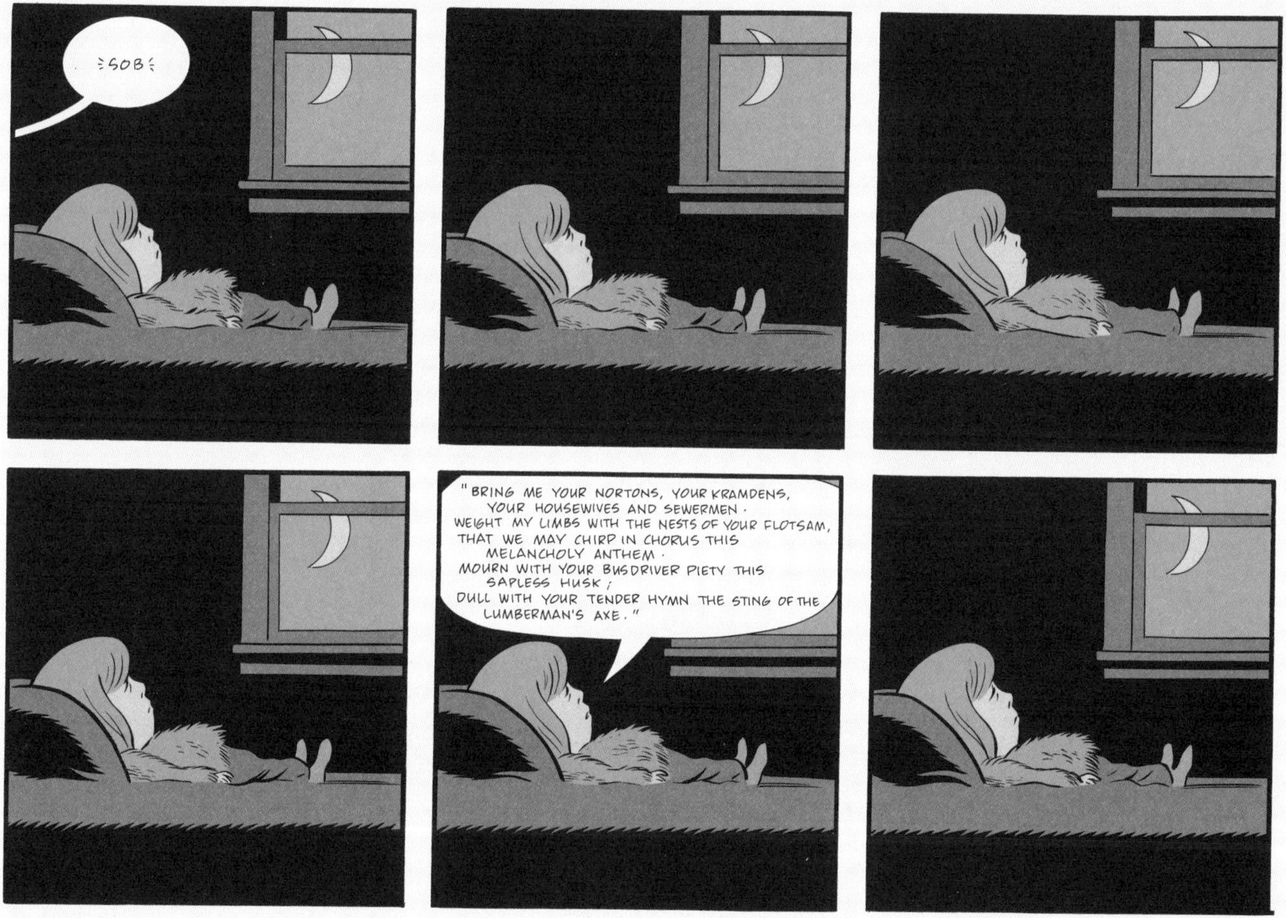
SOB
"BRING ME YOUR NORTONS, YOUR KRAMDENS, YOUR HOUSEWIVES AND SEWERMEN. WEIGHT MY LIMBS WITH THE NESTS OF YOUR FLOTSAM, THAT WE MAY CHIRP IN CHORUS THIS MELANCHOLY ANTHEM. MOURN WITH YOUR BUSDRIVER PIETY THIS SAPLESS HUSK; DULL WITH YOUR TENDER HYMN THE STING OF THE LUMBERMAN'S AXE."

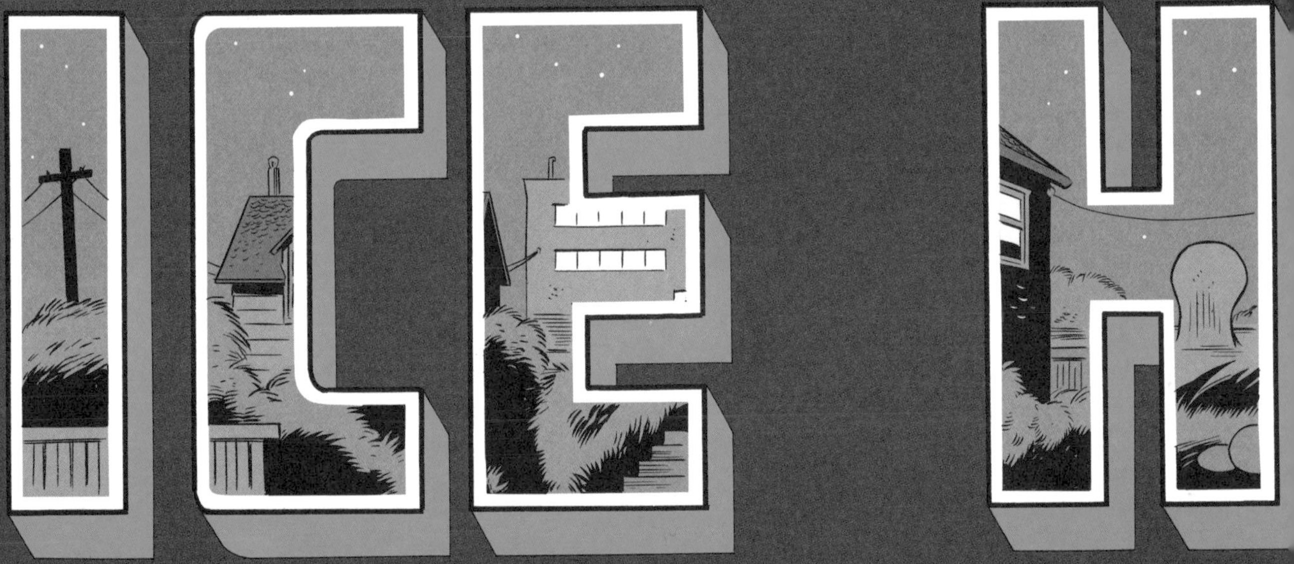
ICE H